SAMIR HUSNI'S GUIDE TO
NEW CONSUMER
MAGAZINES

1995 EDITION

SAMIR HUSNI'S GUIDE TO
NEW CONSUMER
MAGAZINES

Hearst Magazines Enterprises • New York

Editor
Samir A. Husni

Managing Editor
Steven C. Russell

Senior Editors
Elaine R. Abadie, Nirmala Bhat

Assistant Editors
Shu-Ling Ko, Takehiko Nomura

Photographers
Shana Langston, Steward K. Bain, Harry Briscoe

Assistant to the Editor
Judy Baker

HEARST MAGAZINES ENTERPRISES

President and Publisher
John Mack Carter

SVP & General Manager
Thomas W. Wolf

Senior Editor
Thomas O'Neil

Editors
Gary Hoenig, Suzy Parker, Shelley Youngblut, Chris Raymond,
Maisie Todd, Doris Alvarez-Ramirez, Merry Clark

Art Director
Mike Medina

Associate Art Directors
Anthony D'Elia, Matt Schwenk, Stephen Galluccio

To order individual copies, telephone 1-800-288-2131

ISBN: 0-688-14451-9

Printed in the United States of America
First edition
1 2 3 4 5 6 7 8 9 10

SAMIR HUSNI'S GUIDE TO
NEW CONSUMER MAGAZINES

NEW 1994 MAGAZINES BY CATEGORY

Whoever coined the phrase "There are no new ideas" was not only wrong, lacking in all imagination and probably a dunderhead — he or she was clearly not in the magazine business. Every year when University of Mississippi Professor Samir Husni comes out with his comprehensive

A NEW START FOR THE BIBLE ON NEW MAGAZINES

report on the newest titles dawning in the magazine world, I'm awed by the scope of the bright new ideas out there and the ingenuity used by publishers to bring them to print. There are always curious new trends to ponder (*Chicago Bride* and *Cincinnati Wedding* suggest that the recent boom in wedding titles has gone, if not loco, at least amazingly local) and mysteries we may never solve (what's behind those eight new magazines all about tattoos?). Only a few of the infant ventures will survive, of course, and indeed some are already dead as of this writing (*Over the Edge*, *Pure*). But that's not always the point. To many publishers, the payoff is sometimes just the thrill of bringing these new titles to life and, in publishing's maternity ward, it is Samir Husni who has established himself as the watchdog nurse on duty, our record keeper of birth certificates.

"This should be a book!" I exclaimed 10 years ago. Now we're publishing it.

I first met Samir in 1982 when I arrived on the campus of the University of Missouri for a journalism conference and encountered a young grad student so exceptional that, in 1978, his professors back in his native Lebanon shipped him off to the U.S. to study "for four or five years, till the civil war cools down," he says today, wryly. That hiatus was just about up when we met and he had to be thinking of his future while bombs continued to fall back home and faraway cousins dodged sniper's fire as they zigzagged their way home through Beirut streets. The newspaper headlines must have grown too much for this journalism student to bear because he turned his attention to magazines — more specifically to new ones. He did his doctorate dissertation on start-ups and, knowing that I share his odd passion for them, showed me the finished manuscript. "This should be a book!" I exclaimed when I saw how information-packed it was. He soon found a publisher and new editions have come out every year since.

Not surprisingly, Samir has a personality trait common to all smart publishers who attempt to launch new titles: he can spot a gap in a market and fill it. Back in the mid-1980s, academia had a need for an expert on start-ups, so soon after he got his Ph.D. this young man moved to Ole Miss and set himself up as the university world's equivalent to what I was doing out of corporate offices in New York and we continued to be great friends. We worked together often, serving jointly on industry panels, lecturing to each other's groups (me to his students at Ole Miss and him to my staff in New York and to the members of the American Society of Magazine Editors when I was its president) or just sharing wild ideas over breakfast when he happened to be passing through New York.

Being experienced in start-ups, I recently launched this new division at Hearst Magazines and made acquiring the publishing rights to Samir's book one of my first tasks. We are now officially in cahoots with each other and have marked the occasion by overhauling this book for its milestone 10th anniversary edition. We've added hard covers, expanded the editorial content to include "The 50 Most Notable Launches," given it a new graphic design and introduced color photos. My hope is that it continues to serve not only as the bible of our business but as an inspiration and invaluable resource to the publishing faithful whose new, daring ideas are poised to appear in our 11th, 12th and other future editions.

John Mack Carter
President
Hearst Magazines Enterprises

Three important characteristics define the status of the new-magazine industry: diversity, specialty and growth. In 1994, diversity was shown in a wide variety of new titles aimed at different segments of society. There were magazines for every age group (including audiences that can't even read

YEAR IN REVIEW: SPORTS NOW #1

yet) every race, and every lifestyle. Preschoolers got *Baby Bug*, meant to be read to them by their literate elders. The African-American man got his *Image* and the Hispanic woman got her *Que Linda! Urban Fitness* told city-dwelling gays and lesbians how to stay in shape, while *Fabio's Healthy Bodies* seemed to cater to female readers keenly interested in Fabio's lifestyle.

Magazines are becoming more specialized and narrowly focused all the time. Consider these titles: *U.S. Immigrant, Whitetail Slug Hunter, Angel Times, Favorite Cakes* and *Fiddler.*

Printed magazines are still the real information superhighway.

Every year the growth in the industry is reflected in the ever-increasing number of new magazines. In 1994, the total jumped to 832, an increase of 43 titles over 1993 and almost four times the number launched a decade ago (234 in 1985). Even the number of magazines published with an intended frequency of four times or more increased significantly, from 393 in 1993 to 414 in 1994.

Judging by the vital statistics of 1994's new magazines, and the early signs for 1995, the industry seems to be more vibrant than ever. With the exception of the sex and sports categories, most other areas have witnessed increases or at least maintained the status quo. Here are some observations on the 1994 crop compared to that of 1993.

• The story of the year: sex is no longer on top. After a five-year ride at number one, the number of new sex titles has dropped by more than half to a mere 44, compared to 95 in 1993. The total represents the fewest introductions in this category since 1987.

• Sports ended up tackling the top spot with 67 new magazines, although it did decline by 17 titles from the previous year.

• The two service categories of Epicurean and crafts, games & hobbies carved out the second and third places with sharp increases.

• For entrepreneurs who wanted to launch new magazines, the coastal states of New York and California continued to be the favorite spots. The comparative numbers were close, but New York would have steamed ahead if the start-ups from the nearby metro areas in New Jersey and Connecticut were added in. Over all, the Eastern states held sway.

• The leading frequency choice was bimonthly, followed by quarterly and monthly. It's curious to note that 44 new magazines declared no intended frequency in their first issue.

• The average cover price climbed above the $4 mark for the first time ever, reaching $4.15.

• The total number of pages in new magazines declined slightly; so did the tally of advertising pages.

• A record number of magazines offered subscriptions in 1994 — 361 compared to 275 the previous year. The average sub price increased $3.08 to $22.22, compared to $19.14 in 1993. The average discounted price that was offered by 119 magazines was $18.32, up $1.18 from 1993.

• The number of annuals dropped to 73 from a record 100 in 1993, but was still almost double the number published in 1992.

• Special issues and one-shots reached a record number of 289, which represents 30 more titles than in 1993.

Lastly, I'd like to add my voice to that of the Council for Periodical Distributors and Associations (CPDA), which has recently announced its opinion that magazines are making things happen. In fact, I think magazines prove that the real information super highway was, is and will always be found on their pages. So please sit back, relax, and enjoy this reading trip.

Samir Husni

Samir A. Husni, Ph.D.
Director, Magazine Service Journalism Program
The University of Mississippi

P.S.: Every effort was made to include all the new consumer magazines launched and distributed on the nation's newsstands or through the mail. If we have failed to include your magazine, please send us a copy of your premiere issue and we'll include it in next year's addendum section. The author assumes sole responsibility for the inclusions of the magazines in the guide.

Editorial Address:
Samir Husni's Guide to New Magazines
P.O. Box 2906
University, MS 38677
Telephone: (601) 232-7147
Fax: (601) 232-7765

Federal Express/UPS Mail:
Department of Journalism
University of Mississippi
331 Farley Hall
University, MS 38677

Total Number of New Magazines:	832
Number of Categories:	43
Total Number of Magazines with a Cover Price:	820
Total Number of Magazines with a Subscription Price:	361
Total Number of Magazines Offering a Discounted Subscription Price:	119
Total Number of Magazines Carrying a Least One Page of Advertising:	761
Total Number of Magazines Published with the Intent of a Frequency of Four Times or More:	414
Quarterly:	133
Bimonthly:	174
Monthly:	101
Other:	6
Magazines with No Frequency Declared:	44
Semi-annuals:	13
Annuals:	73
Specials and One Time Only:	289
Average Cover Price of a New 1994 Magazine:	$4.15
Average Subscription Price:	$22.22
Average Discount Subscription:	$18.32
Average Number of Pages:	91.54
Average Number of Ad Pages:	17.66

CATEGORY CHANGE INDICATORS 1993-1994

UP	DOWN	NO CHANGE
Military & Naval +16	Sex −51	Puzzles
Epicurean +15	Sports −17	Lifestyle & Service
Health +13	Home Service −10	Music
Crafts, Games & Hobbies +11	Travel −6	Metropolitan, Regional & State
Computer +10	Motorcycle −5	Children's
Automotive +9	Literary −5	Women's Fashion & Beauty

1994 TOP 20 CATEGORIES BY RANK

1. Sports	67	8. Automotive	33	15. Dressmaking & Needlework	23
2. Epicurean	45	9. Health	31	16. Arts & Antiques	19
3. Crafts, Games & Hobbies	44	10. Lifestyle & Serive	29	17. Business & Finance	18
3. Music	44	10. Media Personalities	29	17. Women's Fashion & Beauty	18
3. Sex	44	12. Video, Television & Movies	27	19. Metropolitan, Regional & State	17
6. Computers	41	13. Collectibles	24	20. Children's	15
7. Home Service	35	13. Military & Naval	24	20. Gay & Lesbian	15

TOP 10 STATES IN MAGAZINE LAUNCHES

1. New York	219	4. Illinois	36	9. Pennsylvania	18
2. California	186	6. Iowa	28	10. Alabama	16
3. New Jersey	56	7. Connecticut	19		
4. Florida	36	7. Indiana	19		

NEW MAGAZINES 1988–1994

	1988	1989	1990	1991	1992	1993	1994
Art & Antiques	5	1	5	6	9	13	19
Astrology	0	0	3	1	0	0	2
Automotive	29	26	22	19	17	24	33
Aviation	4	0	1	2	4	8	10
Boating & Yachting	7	0	5	1	2	4	4
Brides & Bridal	5	0	1	3	8	7	4
Business & Finance	12	8	11	5	3	13	18
Children's	11	5	12	7	15	17	15
Collectibles	0	3	13	11	11	18	25
Comics	6	7	5	14	21	17	13
Computers	25	22	9	17	18	31	41
Crafts, Games & Hobbies	15	24	21	32	35	33	44
Dogs & Pets	4	3	0	1	5	4	10
Dressmaking & Needlework	15	30	17	17	12	17	23
Electronics	6	8	8	7	7	4	3
Epicurean	9	22	15	14	23	30	45
Fishing & Hunting	14	12	8	18	15	10	12
Gardening	3	4	3	4	4	9	7
Gay & Lesbian	14	11	10	22	17	11	15
Health	11	12	24	7	15	18	31
Home Service	24	32	28	19	20	45	35
Humor	0	0	0	0	0	4	4
Lifestyle & Service	40	55	56	40	60	34	29
Literary	8	4	6	7	14	18	13
Media Personalities	10	4	41	34	33	22	30
Men's	0	0	4	0	4	7	8
Metropolitan, Regional & State	31	58	27	26	26	18	17
Military & Naval	10	23	18	26	12	8	24
Motorcycle	4	7	3	0	7	16	11
Music	23	29	21	19	32	41	44
Mystery & Adventure	6	2	4	5	16	13	15
Photography	4	2	3	3	1	1	1
Political	5	0	1	2	4	8	7
Puzzles	4	19	12	19	15	14	14
Religion	5	2	3	2	3	2	7
Science & Technology	2	0	2	2	2	5	10
Sex	46	73	62	66	97	95	44
Sports	43	36	42	41	40	84	67
Travel	6	11	8	7	10	20	14
Video & Movies	10	14	5	8	12	20	26
Women's	4	9	6	3	8	3	9
Women's Fashion & Beauty	18	14	13	9	4	15	17
Youth	12	6	5	5	12	9	12
Total Number of New Magazines	509	608	557	553	679	789	832

	1988	1989	1990	1991	1992	1993	1994
Average Cover Price	$3.47	$3.51	$3.61	$3.91	$3.89	$3.98	$4.14
Average Subscription Price	$23.00	$18.62	$18.50	$20.28	$19.78	$19.14	$22.22
Average Discounted Sub. Price	$15.25	$15.35	$13.10	$16.28	$16.95	$17.14	$18.30
Average Total Number of Pages	89	87	91	90	87	94	91.5
Average Total Number of Ad Pages	14	14	18	18	19	20	17.6

ARTS & ANTIQUES

Total Number: 19	Cover Price	Subscription Price	Discount Subscription Price	Pages	Ad Pages
Average	$4.85	$18.73	$20.00	81.59	16
Median	$4.99	$19.95	$20.00	84	18
Mode	$4.99	$19.95	$20.00	100	18
Minimum	$3.00	$3.75	$20.00	30	4
Maximum	$7.00	$29.95	$20.00	180	27
Valid Cases	19	11	1	19	15

ASTROLOGY

Total Number: 2	Cover Price	Subscription Price	Discount Subscription Price	Pages	Ad Pages
Average	$2.23	$8.36	$0	70	6
Median	$2.23	$8.36	$0	70	6
Mode	$2.23	$8.36	$0	70	6
Minimum	$1.95	$8.36	$0	64	4
Maximum	$2.50	$8.36	$0	76	8
Valid Cases	2	1	0	2	2

AUTOMOTIVE

Total Number: 33	Cover Price	Subscription Price	Discount Subscription Price	Pages	Ad Pages
Average	$4.09	$13.78	$10.77	92.73	15.66
Median	$3.95	$13.95	$11.95	96	14
Mode	$3.95	$13.95	$11.95	100	8
Minimum	$2.75	$5.00	$5.00	32	3
Maximum	$6.95	$32.00	$15.00	150	54
Valid Cases	33	10	5	33	31

AVIATION

Total Number: 10	Cover Price	Subscription Price	Discount Subscription Price	Pages	Ad Pages
Average	$5.75	$19.95	$0	90.8	8.2
Median	$5.95	$19.95	$0	96	7
Mode	$5.95	$19.95	$0	96	6
Minimum	$3.95	$19.95	$0	68	4
Maximum	$5.95	$19.95	$0	96	20
Valid Cases	10	1	0	10	10

BOATING & YACHTING

Total Number: 4	Cover Price	Subscription Price	Discount Subscription Price	Pages	Ad Pages
Average	$4.71	$22.49	$7.48	110.5	25.75
Median	$4.95	$22.49	$7.48	100	26.5
Mode	$2.95	$9.97	$7.48	74	18
Minimum	$2.95	$9.97	$7.48	74	18
Maximum	$6.00	$35.00	$7.48	168	32
Valid Cases	4	2	1	4	4

BRIDES & BRIDAL

Total Number: 4	Cover Price	Subscription Price	Discount Subscription Price	Pages	Ad Pages
Average	$3.59	$12.98	$12.50	113.5	52.3
Median	$3.95	$12.98	$12.50	112	35.5
Mode	$3.95	$11.95	$12.50	84	31
Minimum	$1.95	$11.95	$12.50	84	31
Maximum	$4.50	$14.00	$12.50	146	107
Valid Cases	4	2	1	4	4

BUSINESS & FINANCE

Total Number: 18	Cover Price	Subscription Price	Discount Subscription Price	Pages	Ad Pages
Average	$3.91	$37.88	$22.88	82.7	26.4
Median	$3.95	$30.50	$21.22	82	19.5
Mode	$4.95	$9.95	$9.95	24	1
Minimum	$1.95	$9.95	$9.95	24	1
Maximum	$5.95	$99.00	$47.95	156	88
Valid Cases	17	14	6	18	18

CHILDREN'S

Total Number: 15	Cover Price	Subscription Price	Discount Subscription Price	Pages	Ad Pages
Average	$2.75	$18.03	$16.46	43.1	6.3
Median	$2.95	$17.95	$16.46	44	6
Mode	$2.95	$29.97	$14.97	36	3
Minimum	$1.49	$9.97	$14.97	12	1
Maximum	$5.00	$29.97	$17.95	84	13
Valid Cases	15	9	2	15	8

COLLECTIBLES

Total Number: 25	Cover Price	Subscription Price	Discount Subscription Price	Pages	Ad Pages
Average	$4.21	$21.05	$14.98	77.75	18.8
Median	$3.95	$19.00	$14.98	81	17
Mode	$3.95	$18.00	$12.00	84	6
Minimum	$.75	$12.00	$12.00	24	3
Maximum	$6.00	$32.00	$17.95	160	42
Valid Cases	25	17	2	24	25

COMICS

Total Number: 13	Cover Price	Subscription Price	Discount Subscription Price	Pages	Ad Pages
Average	$4.71	$21.70	$96.43	96.4	10
Median	$3.95	$21.70	$100.00	100	7.5
Mode	$3.95	$20.00	$100.00	100	5
Minimum	$1.95	$20.00	$36.00	36	4
Maximum	$12.95	$23.40	$290.00	290	23
Valid Cases	13	2	13	14	13

COMPUTERS

Total Number: 41	Cover Price	Subscription Price	Discount Subscription Price	Pages	Ad Pages
Average	$4.44	$28.54	$22.05	109.3	33.5
Median	$4.95	$24.97	$19.97	100	22.5
Mode	$4.95	$9.95	$19.97	100	8
Minimum	$.95	$9.95	$9.95	24	6
Maximum	$9.00	$60.00	$38.00	356	124
Valid Cases	40	27	15	41	41

CRAFTS, GAMES & HOBBIES

Total Number: 44	Cover Price	Subscription Price	Discount Subscription Price	Pages	Ad Pages
Average	$4.73	$23.52	$20.71	83.1	17
Median	$4.95	$19.95	$18.98	80	9.5
Mode	$4.95	$19.95	$19.95	68	2
Minimum	$1.49	$9.88	$9.88	16	1
Maximum	$9.95	$89.95	$47.95	180	92
Valid Cases	41	20	8	44	42

DOGS & PETS

Total Number: 10	Cover Price	Subscription Price	Discount Subscription Price	Pages	Ad Pages
Average	$4.31	$20.87	$18.00	64.8	25.7
Median	$3.95	$20.00	$18.00	56	16
Mode	$2.95	$20.00	$18.00	32	9
Minimum	$2.95	$10.00	$18.00	32.	9
Maximum	$7.00	$29.97	$18.00	132	63
Valid Cases	9	8	1	10	9

DRESSMAKING & NEEDLEWORK

Total Number: 23	Cover Price	Subscription Price	Discount Subscription Price	Pages	Ad Pages
Average	$4.04	$19.14	$14.97	71.1	8
Median	$3.95	$19.97	$15.00	68	6
Mode	$3.95	$19.97	$9.95	68	2
Minimum	$2.95	$9.95	$9.95	32	2
Maximum	$4.95	$29.97	$19.97	148	24
Valid Cases	23	6	3	23	22

ELECTRONICS

Total Number: 3	Cover Price	Subscription Price	Discount Subscription Price	Pages	Ad Pages
Average	$3.98	$16.45	$0	92	23
Median	$3.50	$16.45	$0	92	24
Mode	$3.50	$12.95	$0	84	13
Minimum	$3.50	$12.95	$0	84	13
Maximum	$4.95	$19.95	$0	100	32
Valid Cases	3	2	0	3	3

EPICUREAN

Total Number: 45	Cover Price	Subscription Price	Discount Subscription Price	Pages	Ad Pages
Average	$2.93	$29.67	$25.00	90.4	9.8
Median	$2.95	$28.00	$24.00	96	4
Mode	$2.95	$26.00	$21.00	68	2
Minimum	$1.95	$26.00	$21.00	60	1
Maximum	$5.50	$35.00	$30.00	132	43
Valid Cases	45	3	3	45	37

FISHING & HUNTING

Total Number: 12	Cover Price	Subscription Price	Discount Subscription Price	Pages	Ad Pages
Average	$3.69	$12.28	$11.95	97.7	18.5
Median	$3.45	$12.95	$11.95	84	18.5
Mode	$2.95	$12.95	$10.95	100	28
Minimum	$2.25	$10.95	$10.95	44	2
Maximum	$6.95	$12.95	$12.95	260	33
Valid Cases	12	3	2	12	12

GARDENING

Total Number: 7	Cover Price	Subscription Price	Discount Subscription Price	Pages	Ad Pages
Average	$3.81	$28.00	$24.00	94.3	15.8
Median	$3.95	$28.00	$24.00	84	10
Mode	$3.95	$28.00	$24.00	84	2
Minimum	$2.95	$28.00	$24.00	84	2
Maximum	$5.00	$28.00	$24.00	140	53
Valid Cases	7	1	1	7	7

GAY & LESBIAN

Total Number: 15	Cover Price	Subscription Price	Discount Subscription Price	Pages	Ad Pages
Average	$5.13	$31.55	$0	112	17.9
Median	$4.95	$24.00	$0	132	22
Mode	$4.95	$24.00	$0	132	3
Minimum	$3.95	$16.00	$0	48.	3
Maximum	$5.99	$75.00	$0	180	32
Valid Cases	15	7	0	15	15

HEALTH

Total Number: 31	Cover Price	Subscription Price	Discount Subscription Price	Pages	Ad Pages
Average	$3.39	$20.10	$18.64	87.5	16.7
Median	$2.95	$18.00	$17.95	84	13
Mode	$2.95	$18.00	$9.97	68	2
Minimum	$1.95	$7.50	$9.97	36	2
Maximum	$9.95	$59.00	$28.00	188	65
Valid Cases	31	14	3	31	24

HOME SERVICE

Total Number: 35	Cover Price	Subscription Price	Discount Subscription Price	Pages	Ad Pages
Average	$4.21	$17.55	$14.79	129.4	14.6
Median	$3.95	$17.00	$15.95	132	10
Mode	$3.95	$19.95	$8.48	132	10
Minimum	$.46	$6.65	$8.48	12	1
Maximum	$8.95	$30.00	$19.95	324	50
Valid Cases	34	9	3	35	35

HUMOR

Total Number: 4	Cover Price	Subscription Price	Discount Subscription Price	Pages	Ad Pages
Average	$4.70	$24.43	$23.40	97	10.7
Median	$3.95	$26.40	$23.40	100	10
Mode	$2.95	$19.95	$23.40	100	2
Minimum	$2.95	$19.95	$23.40	40	2
Maximum	$7.95	$26.95	$23.40	148	20
Valid Cases	4	3	1	4	3

LIFESTYLE & SERVICE

Total Number: 29	Cover Price	Subscription Price	Discount Subscription Price	Pages	Ad Pages
Average	$3.63	$19.73	$13.19	86.5	21.7
Median	$3.00	$18.00	$13.75	86	16.5
Mode	$2.95	$18.00	$9.75	100	9
Minimum	$.99	$9.75	$9.75	24	1
Maximum	$9.95	$65.76	15.99	196	60
Valid Cases	29	18	6	29	26

LITERARY

Total Number: 13	Cover Price	Subscription Price	Discount Subscription Price	Pages	Ad Pages
Average	$5.40	$21.01	$14.36	82.9	8.3
Median	$4.00	$18.00	$14.36	68	5.5
Mode	$3.95	$14.00	$13.75	52	5
Minimum	$2.75	$12.00	$13.75	48	1
Maximum	$15.00	$35.00	$14.97	154	36
Valid Cases	13	11	2	13	12

MEDIA PERSONALITIES

Total Number: 30	Cover Price	Subscription Price	Discount Subscription Price	Pages	Ad Pages
Average	$3.69	$21.42	$14.85	80.8	10.8
Median	$3.50	$19.99	$14.85	78	7
Mode	$3.95	$16.00	$14.85	68	6
Minimum	$2.25	$16.00	$14.85	44	1
Maximum	$11.95	$29.70	$14.85	132	40
Valid Cases	30	4	1	38	25

MEN'S

Total Number: 8	Cover Price	Subscription Price	Discount Subscription Price	Pages	Ad Pages
Average	$4.52	$24.71	$18.90	113.8	28.7
Median	$4.95	$21.95	$15.95	108	26
Mode	$2.95	$15.00	$14.80	64	8
Minimum	$2.95	$15.00	$14.80	64	8
Maximum	$5.95	$39.95	$25.95	184	68
Valid Cases	8	4	3	8	7

METROPOLITAN, REGIONAL & STATE

Total Number: 17	Cover Price	Subscription Price	Discount Subscription Price	Pages	Ad Pages
Average	$5.04	$16.43	$13.49	86.6	25.8
Median	$4.95	$16.50	$13.49	68	19
Mode	$5.95	$9.00	$9.00	68	14
Minimum	$2.95	$9.00	$9.00	28	8
Maximum	$9.95	$24.00	$18.00	170	72
Valid Cases	13	6	4	17	16

MILITARY & NAVAL

Total Number: 24	Cover Price	Subscription Price	Discount Subscription Price	Pages	Ad Pages
Average	$5.06	$26.99	$0	92.2	8.6
Median	$4.95	$29.70	$0	96	7.5
Mode	$5.95	$29.70	$0	96	5
Minimum	$2.95	$12.95	$0	64	2
Maximum	$6.00	$39.95	$0	132	21
Valid Cases	24	7	0	24	24

MOTORCYCLES

Total Number: 11	Cover Price	Subscription Price	Discount Subscription Price	Pages	Ad Pages
Average	$4.55	$16.68	$10.97	95.1	20.6
Median	$4.95	$14.00	$10.97	100	22
Mode	$4.95	$13.95	$9.98	100	2
Minimum	$2.95	$13.95	$9.98	36	2
Maximum	$5.95	$25.00	$11.95	124	40
Valid Cases	11	5	2	11	11

MUSIC

Total Number: 44	Cover Price	Subscription Price	Discount Subscription Price	Pages	Ad Pages
Average	$4.25	$20.76	$17.90	72.2	12.7
Median	$3.95	$17.50	$17.74	72	12
Mode	$4.95	$10.00	$10.00	68	12
Minimum	$1.49	$10.00	$10.00	24	1
Maximum	$15.00	$46.50	$29.95	116	48
Valid Cases	44	17	6	44	38

MYSTERY & ADVENTURE

Total Number: 15	Cover Price	Subscription Price	Discount Subscription Price	Pages	Ad Pages
Average	$3.63	$17.59	$15.36	86.7	17.9
Median	$3.50	$15.60	$15.49	84	14
Mode	$2.95	$14.95	$8.95	84	14
Minimum	$1.95	$8.95	$8.95	44	1
Maximum	$5.95	$29.95	$21.50	164	69
Valid Cases	15	9	4	15	15

PHOTOGRAPHY

Total Number: 1	Cover Price	Subscription Price	Discount Subscription Price	Pages	Ad Pages
Average	$9.95	$49.90	$0	100	0
Median	$9.95	$49.90	$0	100	0
Mode	$9.95	$49.90	$0	100	0
Minimum	$9.95	$49.90	$0	100	0
Maximum	$9.95	$49.90	$0	100	0
Valid Cases	1	1	0	1	0

POLITICAL

Total Number: 7	Cover Price	Subscription Price	Discount Subscription Price	Pages	Ad Pages
Average	$4.33	$30.17	$24.32	52	7
Median	$3.95	$24.00	$19.95	48	6
Mode	$3.95	$18.00	$18.00	20	1
Minimum	$3.00	$17.00	$18.00	20	1
Maximum	$5.95	$49.00	$35.00	100	18
Valid Cases	7	6	3	7	5

PUZZLES

Total Number: 14	Cover Price	Subscription Price	Discount Subscription Price	Pages	Ad Pages
Average	$1.99	$11.13	$15.73	100.6	5.3
Median	$1.39	$8.80	$17.50	84	5
Mode	$.99	$7.37	$11.75	68	4
Minimum	$.99	$5.88	$11.75	68	2
Maximum	$4.95	$17.95	$17.95	196	9
Valid Cases	14	10	3	14	14

RELIGION

Total Number: 7	Cover Price	Subscription Price	Discount Subscription Price	Pages	Ad Pages
Average	$3.88	$19.24	$12.49	58.6	10.6
Median	$3.50	$21.49	$12.49	60	12
Mode	$1.95	$24.00	$10.00	68	1
Minimum	$1.95	$10.00	$10.00	32	1
Maximum	$6.00	$24.00	$14.97	84	17
Valid Cases	5	4	2	7	7

SCIENCE & TECHNOLOGY

Total Number: 10	Cover Price	Subscription Price	Discount Subscription Price	Pages	Ad Pages
Average	$6.30	$38.20	$98.00	65.8	10.9
Median	$4.95	$30.00	$98.00	64	7
Mode	$4.95	$8.85	$98.00	84	1
Minimum	$2.95	$8.85	$98.00	24	1
Maximum	$10.00	$98.00	$98.00	100	32
Valid Cases	10	9	1	10	9

SEX

Total Number: 44	Cover Price	Subscription Price	Discount Subscription Price	Pages	Ad Pages
Average	$4.96	$31.28	$14.95	114.4	22
Median	$4.99	$25.99	$14.95	100	24
Mode	$4.99	$25.97	$14.95	100	24
Minimum	$3.50	$17.95	$14.95	76	8
Maximum	$6.95	$75.00	$14.95	292	49
Valid Cases	44	10	1	44	43

SPORTS

Total Number: 67	Cover Price	Subscription Price	Discount Subscription Price	Pages	Ad Pages
Average	$4.26	$19.08	$15.72	104.7	18.9
Median	$3.95	$18.88	$11.99	100	19
Mode	$4.95	$14.95	$11.95	116	19
Minimum	$2.00	$5.95	$9.97	16	1
Maximum	$12.95	$39.50	$35.00	228	46
Valid Cases	66	24	12	67	62

TRAVEL

Total Number: 14	Cover Price	Subscription Price	Discount Subscription Price	Pages	Ad Pages
Average	$3.75	$21.05	$15.63	99.3	30.6
Median	$3.95	$18.99	$14.95	96	20
Mode	$3.95	$12.00	$12.00	134	14
Minimum	$2.50	$12.00	$12.00	44	10
Maximum	$5.95	$36.00	$19.95	180	91
Valid Cases	14	8	3	14	14

VIDEO, TELEVISION & MOVIES

Total Number: 26	Cover Price	Subscription Price	Discount Subscription Price	Pages	Ad Pages
Average	$4.40	$23.55	$25.33	95.1	20.3
Median	$3.95	$18.97	$19.95	76	13
Mode	$3.95	$15.00	$15.00	68	13
Minimum	$1.50	$13.97	$15.00	36	1
Maximum	$9.95	$52.00	$52.00	252	52
Valid Cases	26	14	5	26	25

WOMEN'S

Total Number: 9	Cover Price	Subscription Price	Discount Subscription Price	Pages	Ad Pages
Average	$3.74	$18.13	$16.00	95.8	22.1
Median	$3.95	$19.89	$16.00	100	20
Mode	$2.95	$24.00	$16.00	84	20
Minimum	$2.50	$5.99	$16.00	48	1
Maximum	$4.95	$24.00	$16.00	124	65
Valid Cases	9	6	1	9	9

WOMEN'S FASHION & BEAUTY

Total Number: 17	Cover Price	Subscription Price	Discount Subscription Price	Pages	Ad Pages
Average	$3.22	$16.09	$7.97	87.9	20.8
Median	$2.99	$14.99	$7.97	82.	11.5
Mode	$2.95	$15.00	$7.97	68	12
Minimum	$1.99	$9.95	$7.97	24	3
Maximum	$3.95	$30.00	$7.97	268	128
Valid Cases	17	8	1	17	14

YOUTH

Total Number: 12	Cover Price	Subscription Price	Discount Subscription Price	Pages	Ad Pages
Average	$2.97	$14.72	$12.00	92.5	22.8
Median	$2.95	$15.00	$12.00	100	25
Mode	$2.95	$15.00	$12.00	108	10
Minimum	$1.95	$7.80	$12.00	40	9
Maximum	$4.00	$20.00	$12.00	138	40
Valid Cases	12	8	1	11	11

THE 50 MOST NOTABLE LAUNCHES

Note: The information in this section was the latest available at press time.

One of the many strengths of new magazines is the role that they play as reflectors of society. Among the 1994 crop, some even captured the spirit of the country — or at least their publishers' vision of that spirit.

The process of selecting the 50 most notable magazine launches from a total of 832 was not easy. There was no litmus test to determine if a magazine made the cut or not. That's also true for trying to devise the

WHAT IS "NOTABLE"?

formula for a launch. "Magazines are creative work," Merrill Panitt, the longtime editorial director of *TV Guide* under its Walter H. Annenberg ownership, once told me. "You can't put a scale or a measure to what or how a magazine is created. It is all in the creative world of its editors and publishers."

While trying to pick the 50 most notable launches of 1994, the one thing my staff and I were sure about was that being "notable" was not about being good. It was about impact, innovation and even a little bit like *Time* picking "Man of the Year." In selecting the Ayatollah Khomeni and Adolph Hitler, *Time* did not necessarily approve or agree with those men's actions. The magazine was merely hailing them as the outstanding figures of their times. Thus the methodology for picking our top 50 boiled down to weighing responses to the following questions:

1.) How much publicity did the magazine generate? We scanned the media and gathered all the information we could find about each launch. Some new magazines had more articles written about them than all the articles that appeared in the premiere issue of the magazine itself. *Swing* is a good example.

2.) How relevant was the magazine to the leading issues of the time? No one argues that the changes in the political climate, the emphasis on family values, the impact of the so-called Generation X, and the continuous boom in the computer market via the internet have topped the media coverage of 1994. Various aspects of those influences can be found in such notable start-ups as *Might, Home PC* and *Aspire.*

3.) Was the magazine notably diverse and specialized? Aiming at a specific segment of society within a larger segment is what *Yolk* tried to do. It targeted the Asian American twentysomething set rather than try to reach the entire Asian-American population. *Realms of Fantasy* and *Louis L'Amour Western Magazine* went after those core American subcultures that love a good science fiction page-turner or a John Wayne film celebrating the adventurous spirit of our nation's prairie past.

4.) How innovative were the magazines? New titles usually fit into one of three categories: the ground-

breakers that help create a new forum or agenda; the copy cats that imitate the ground-breakers and sometimes overpower them; and the cheap imitators that are willing to take the chance of making it based on the
success, or seeming success, of the other titles already in the field. This past year's ground-breakers included *Saveur*, a food and cooking magazine that elegantly defied the trend toward lean-and-light cuisine. *Fine
Cooking*, on the other hand, delivered a step-by-step guide to cooking — and nothing else but cooking —
in the crowded field of Epicurean titles.

5.) Was the magazine so bizarre it had to be included? If the answer was "yes," we included it.
Mouth2Mouth, with its tag line proclaiming "Voted World's Best Magazine," automatically made our
list. *Pure* clearly did, too, just by calling itself "Erotic entertainment by women for men."

Using letters delivered by Federal Express, we notified publishers of their inclusion on our list and
asked for the most recent and relevant information about their titles. If the urgency of our request did not
produce results, we made follow-up telephone calls, but we weren't always successful in getting complete
information. Several publications failed to respond at all, including the two Time Inc. test magazines
Makeover and *Mouth2Mouth*. Others like *Pure* said they ceased publication and had thrown all perti-
nent information away. Some publishers told us that their magazines are in hibernation and are awaiting
the "light" to be awakened, such as *Family Computing* and *Clarity*.

Aspire

Published by:
Royal Magazine Group
404 BNA Drive, Suite 400,
Building 200
Nashville TN 37217
Phone Number: 800-348-5080
Launch Date: August/
September 1994
Publisher: Timothy L. Gilmour
Editor: Mary E. Hopkins
Frequency: Bimonthly
Cover Price: $2.95
Subscription Price: $21.00
**Number of issues published
since launch:** 4
Circulation: 190,000
Ad Rates: Four-Color Page -
$2,040 / B&W Page - $1,795

Publication Profile: "To aspire to a healthier body, a stronger self-image, and a closer relationship with God." Formerly *Today's Better Life*, the magazine for Christian readers plans to target 500 commercial news racks and stands and 500 test markets. Since its launch, *Aspire* reduced its cover price from $3.95 to $2.95 and changed its tagline from "for a healthy body, mind and spirit" to "a Christian lifestyle magazine." It acquired the subscription list of *Clarity* (which folded in November), also among this year's top 50 notable magazines.

"Religion magazines aren't known for their sense of humor, but *Aspire* knows the way to readers' minds is through the funny bone." —*USA Today*

Readership Profile: 89 percent of *Aspire's* readers are female. 41.7 percent of its subscribers are 35 to 44 years old. 75.3 percent are married, and 76.2 percent of these have children. 8 out of 10 readers (79.2 percent) own their own homes and half of the readers are either professionals (23.2 percent) or homemakers (24.8 percent). Nearly half of *Aspire's* readers (49.5 percent) have incomes of $45,000+, while 32.2 percent make between $45,000 and $74,999.

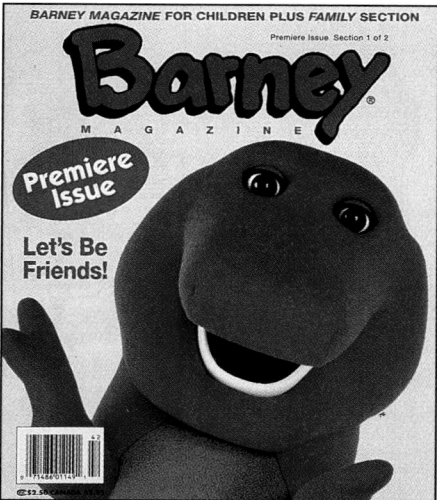

Barney Magazine

Published by:
Welsh Publishing Group Inc.
300 Madison Ave.
New York NY 10017
Phone Number: 212-687-0680
Launch Date: Summer 1994
Publisher: Donald E. Welsh
Editor: Kathy Henderson
Frequency: 5/year
Cover Price: $2.50
Subscription Price: $12.50
**Number of issues published
since launch:** 3
Circulation: 500,000
Ad Rates: Four-Color Page -
$16,500 / B&W Page - $13,200

Publication Profile: A two-part magazine designed to help children develop and to offer practical advice to parents, *Barney Magazine* for children and *Barney Magazine Family* for parents were created with the same focus as the PBS children's television program, "Barney & Friends."

Readership Profile: n/a

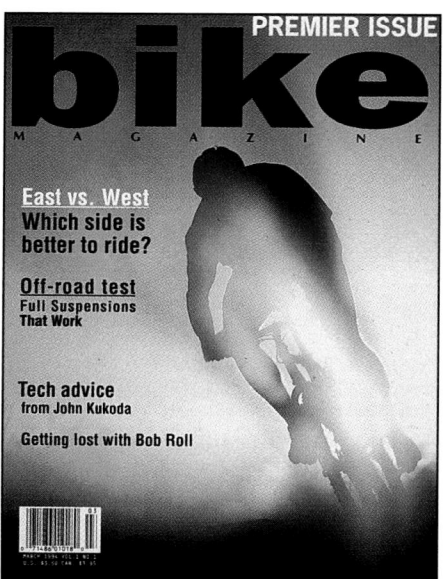

Bike Magazine

Published by:
Surfer Publications Inc.
33046 Calle Aviador
San Juan Capistrano CA 92675
Phone Number: 714-496-5922
Launch Date: March 1994
Publisher: Brent Diamond
Editor: Steve Casimiro
Frequency: 9/year
Cover Price: $3.50
Subscription Price: $12.95
**Number of issues published
since launch:** 6
Circulation: 16,000
Ad Rates: Four-Color Page -
$4,900 / B&W Page - $3,185

Publication Profile: "Compelling words and mind-blowing photos for the dedicated mountain bike rider." *Bike Magazine* brings the reader "as close as possible to the hard-core riding experience as you can get without riding."

Beginning with the March 1995 issue, *Bike Magazine* increased annual publication from six issues to nine. It also added new columns and redesigned some sections.

Readership Profile: The average age of *Bike Magazine* readers is 28. 93 percent of its subscribers are male. 61.9 percent are single. 47.5 percent own their own home. 31.7 percent are professionals. 76.7 percent attended college. Average household income is $50,000 to $75,000.

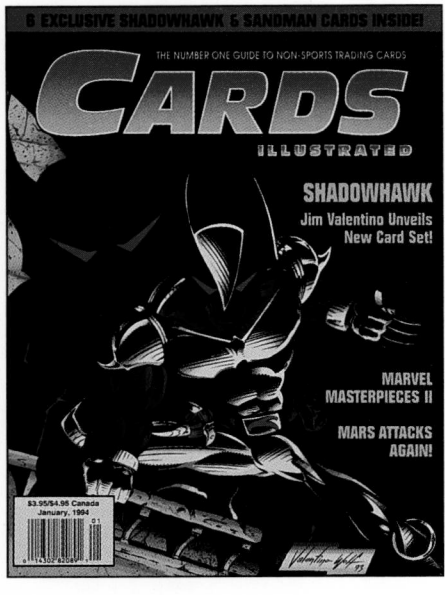

Cards Illustrated

Published by:
Warrior Publications Inc.
1920 Highland Ave., Suite 222
Lombard IL 60148
Phone Number: 708-916-7222
Launch Date: January 1994
Publisher: Steve Harris
Editor: Don Butler
Frequency: Monthly
Cover Price: $3.99
Subscription Price: $29.95
Number of issues published since launch: 15
Circulation: 100,000
Ad Rates: Four-Color Page - $2,400 / B&W Page - $2,000

Publication Profile: "The number one guide to non-sports trading cards features information about the latest cards and the artists who design them."

The price increased with the November 1994 issue from $3.95 to $3.99.

Readership Profile: n/a

Civilization

Published by:
L.O.C. Associates L.P.
475 Park Ave., 7th Floor
New York NY 10016
Phone Number: 212-532-6400
Launch Date: November/December 1994
Publisher: Raymond J. Sachs
Editor: Stephen G. Smith
Frequency: Bimonthly
Cover Price: $4.50
Subscription Price: $20.00
Number of issues published since launch: 3
Circulation: 200,000
Ad Rates: Four-Color Page - $16,100 / B&W Page - $12,800

Publication Profile: "A glossy magazine affiliated with the Library of Congress that covers literature and the arts." *Civilization* is "not afraid to be old-fashioned."

Readership Profile: 64.7 percent of readers are male. The average age of the readers is 53.3 years. 64.7 percent have a household income of $50,000+. 72.1 percent graduated college. 81.6 percent own their home. 69.4 percent regularly participate in athletic, cultural and civic activities.

Clarity

Published by:
The Navigators/Nav Press
7899 Lexington Drive
Colorado Springs CO 80920
Phone Number: 719-548-7442
Launch Date: n/a
Publisher: Kent R. Wilson
Editor: Judith Corchman
Frequency: Bimonthly
Cover Price: $3.50
Subscription Price: $18.97
Number of issues published since launch: 3
Circulation: 65,000
Ad Rates: Four-Color Page - $2,215 / B&W Page - $2,045

Publication Profile: "A healthy mind and body magazine for Christian women," *Clarity* has been in hibernation since Guideposts Associates Inc. acquired it in the summer of 1994. They will not produce the next issue until sometime in late 1995 after studying a new marketing strategy. No significant changes are anticipated in the product itself.

After delivering issue number three, subscribers' money was refunded or an alternate magazine, *Aspire*, was delivered to fulfill remaining liability.

Readership Profile: The magazine is designed for women who are college-educated, and who want to keep learning, exploring, and make a difference. Although directed at Christians, it should appeal to a broader audience — women seeking knowledge.

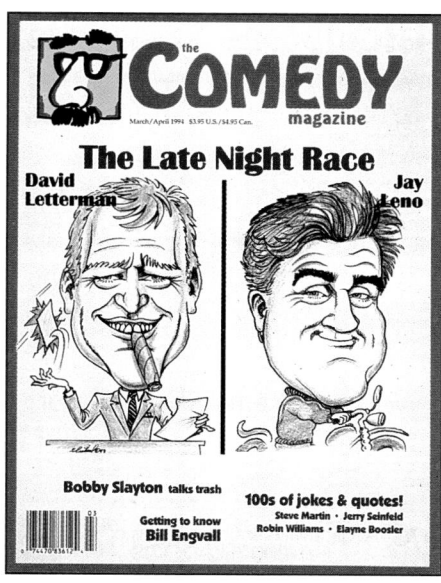

The Comedy Magazine

Published by:
Quality Services Co.
5290 Overpass Road
Santa Barbara CA 93111
Phone Number: 805-904-7841
Launch Date: May 1994
Publisher: Walter Jurek
Editor: Walter Jurek
Frequency: Bimonthly
Cover Price: $3.95
Subscription Price: $19.95
Number of issues published since launch: 6
Circulation: 15,000
Ad Rates: Four-Color Page - $2,700 / B&W Page - $1,600

Publication Profile: "In the 1990s, what the country needs is some good humor. This magazine won't solve the budget deficit or solve the problems of the world...but it will put a smile on your face." *The Comedy Magazine* covers comedy-related entertainment found on TV, in clubs, and in feature films.

Readership Profile: "An audience of upscale men and women who have a bright and humorous outlook on life. Its readers are men between 21 and 49 years old and women 18 to 34 years old, who have attended college and have an above-average income."

Computer Life

Published by:
Ziff-Davis Publishing Company
135 Main St., 14th Floor
San Francisco CA 94105
Phone Number: 415-357-5200
Launch Date: October 1994
Publisher: J. Scott Briggs
Editor: Chris Shipley
Frequency: Monthly
Cover Price: $2.95
Subscription Price: $24.97
Number of issues published since launch: 5
Circulation: 350,000
Ad Rates: Four-Color Page - $16,995 / B&W Page - $13,075

Publication Profile: A slick monthly aimed at the home personal computer market for "sophisticated consumers. Writers and editors take you along on their personal journeys through the rapidly unfolding world of new things to do with computers." With plenty of fun information, too, including how to e-mail the Rolling Stones or where to order Grateful Dead wrist rests, *Computer Life* is clearly going for a younger market, a *Details* for techies.
    Computer Life increased its cover price from $1.95 to $2.95 with the January 1995 issue. Its paid circulation jumped by 50,000 to 350,000 since its launch.
    "[It] conveys one main message: Computing is hot."
—*Advertising Age*

Readership Profile: Geared towards adults in their 20s through their 50s.

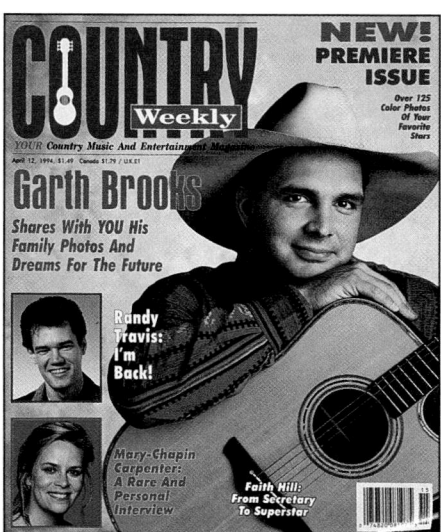

Country Weekly

Published by:
Country Weekly Inc.
600 S.E. Coast Ave.
Lantana FL 33462
Phone Number: 407-540-1005
Launch Date: April 12, 1994
Publisher: Country Weekly, Inc.
Editor: Roger Capettini
Frequency: Weekly
Cover Price: $1.49
Subscription Price: $46.50
Number of issues published since launch: 46
Circulation: 75,000
Ad Rates: Four-Color Page - $9,000 / B&W Page - n/a

Publication Profile: A country music and entertainment magazine that offers "an inside look into the lives and lifestyles of hundreds of artists that country music fans love." Iain Calder, president of the parent publication, *National Enquirer*, told *Media Week* that *Country Weekly*, "...won't be in any way gossipy and probing into big, dark secrets."

Readership Profile: n/a

Eco Traveler

Published by:

Skies America Publishing Company

2230 S.W. Mohawk St.

Tualatin OR 97062

Phone Number: 503-520-1955

Launch Date: March/April 1994

Publisher: Lisa Tabb

Editor: Suzanne K. Eggleston

Frequency: Bimonthly

Cover Price: $2.95

Subscription Price: $18

Number of issues published since launch: 7

Circulation: 100,000

Ad Rates: Four-Color Page - $6,140 / B&W Page - $4,610

Publication Profile: "A travel magazine for people who are socially responsible, *Eco Traveler* is for people who want to see the world and protect its environmental integrity." It contains travel tips, great getaways, and stories about innovative ways and places to travel.

Suzanne K. Eggleston replaced Perry Garfinkel as editor of premiere issue, which was sent free to 150,000 readers (the newsstand price was lowered by a dollar from $3.95). The format has been redesigned since its launch.

Readership Profile: n/a

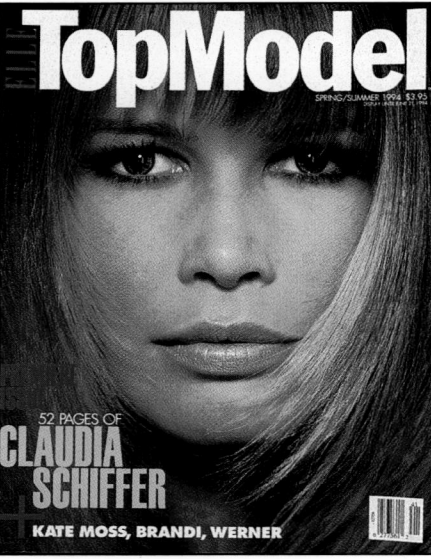

Elle TopModel

Published by:

Elle Publishing L.P.

1633 Broadway

New York NY 10019

Phone Number: 212-767-6000

Launch Date: Spring/Summer 1994

Publisher: Philippe Guelton

Editor: Martine Sicard

Frequency: Quarterly

Cover Price: $3.95

Subscription Price: n/a

Number of issues published since launch: 3

Circulation: 125,000

Ad Rates: Four-Color Page - $10,000 / B&W Page - n/a

Publication Profile: This *Elle* spinoff focuses on one supermodel each issue, enabling readers to "share the secrets of these famed beauties and find out what the life of a model is really like." Hawking itself as the "magazine of living myths," it explores the public and private lives of top models and spotlights tomorrow's fashion-world celebrities.

As of the third issue the magazine dropped Elle from its name.

"Perhaps the most overt attempt to capitalize on the interest in models." — *The Wall Street Journal*

Readership Profile: Average age is 22.2 years old, 84 percent are female, 63 percent are college-educated, and 85 percent are single. 62 percent are employed full-time or part-time, with an average income of $12,151. 59 percent of the readers want to be a model or are considering being one.

Escape

Published by:

ESCAPE Magazine Inc.

2525 Beverly

Santa Monica CA 90405

Phone Number: 310-392-5235

Launch Date: Winter 1994

Publisher: Joe Robinson

Editor: Joe Robinson

Frequency: Quarterly

Cover Price: $3.95

Subscription Price: $18.00

Number of issues published since launch: 5

Circulation: 70,000

Ad Rates: Four-Color Page - $3,300 / B&W Page - $2,400

Publication Profile: "For active, adventurous, global travelers. It celebrates travel, not as a holiday but as a way of life." According to the *Utne Reader, Escape* is to other travel magazines what the *Lonely Planet* travel guides are to *Fodor's* guides.

Book size increased from 100 to 108 pages, and advertising pages more than doubled to an average of 30.

Readership Profile: Aimed at adventure travelers who make up 20 percent of the entire travel market. *Escape* readers work hard and play hard. 40 percent are male. Average household income is $55,000.

Family Computing

Published by:
Scholastic Inc.
555 Broadway
New York NY 10022
Phone Number: 212-505-4220
Launch Date: October 1994
Publisher: Scholastic Inc.
Editor: Nick Sullivan
Frequency: Special
Cover Price: Free
Subscription Price: n/a
**Number of issues published
since launch:** 1
Circulation: 1,000,000
Ad Rates: Four-Color Page -
$35,000 / B&W Page - n/a

Publication Profile: "A resource guide for families looking to make computers an integral part of their children's learning and growth," *Family Computing* was polybagged with *Home Office Computing* and *Family & Child*.

"Returning to a market where it flopped a decade ago, Scholastic Inc. is dusting off the *Family Computing* to re-enter the now booming home computer market."—*Advertising Age*

Readership Profile: n/a

FamilyPC

Published by:
Disney Computer Magazines, Inc. &
Ziff Communications Company
114 5th Avenue
New York NY 10011
Phone Number: 212-633-3620
Launch Date: September/
October 1994
Publisher: Jake Winebaum
Editor: Jake Winebaum
Frequency: 10/year
Cover Price: $2.95
Subscription Price: $9.95
**Number of issues published
since launch:** 4
Circulation: 200,000
(+ bonus 50,000)
Ad Rates: Four-Color Page -
$9,900 / B&W Page - $7,425

Publication Profile: A consumer-oriented magazine aimed at families with children between three and 12 to "help you and your kids discover new ways to use your computer."

After a special introductory price of 95 cents per issue for the first two issues, *FamilyPC* raised its cover price to $2.95, then discounted the price to $1.95 at the newsstands. The first issue was also polybagged with the Disney-owned *Family Fun* and Ziff-Davis Publishing's *PC Computing* and *MacUser*. After the first four bimonthly issues, the magazine started publishing 10 times a year.

"More visually inviting."—*The Wall Street Journal*

Readership Profile: Predominantly male (60 percent), well-educated (80 percent attended college), upscale (median household income of $65,400). The average age is 37 years old, with 2.5 children between three and 12 (93 percent).

Fine Cooking

Published by:
The Taunton Press Inc.
63 S. Main St.
Newton CT 06470-5506
Phone Number: 800-283-7252
Launch Date: February/March 1994
Publisher: Paul Roman
Editor: Martha Holmberg
Frequency: Bimonthly
Cover Price: $4.95
Subscription Price: $26
**Number of issues published
since launch:** 7
Circulation: 120,000
Ad Rates: Four-Color Page -
$4,050 / B&W Page - $3,000

Publication Profile: *Fine Cooking* is "all about life in the kitchen. It provides expert, unbiased information on food, food preparation, and the principles of good cooking." Even the advertising adheres to this mandate.

Circulation jumped from 85,000 to 120,000 since its launch.

Readership Profile: "People seeking out new cooking techniques, new approaches to meals, and new information on equipment supplies and goods that will improve their cooking abilities."

FLUX

Published by:
Harris Publications Inc.
1115 Broadway
New York NY 10010
Phone Number: 212-807-7100
Launch Date: June 1994
Publisher: Dennis S. Page
Editorial Director: Brad Tolinski
Frequency: Quarterly
Cover Price: $3.95
Subscription Price: $9.97
Number of issues published since launch: 3
Circulation: 120,000
Ad Rates: Four-Color Page - $3,660 / B&W Page - $2,345

Publication Profile: "One of the year's more graphically challenging new magazines, *FLUX* covers video games, music, and comic books with a slacker slant." From its fourth issue onwards, *FLUX* will also be available in the direct comic book market, in a comic-sized format with a different cover than the newsstand edition.

"It's every adolescent's dream and every mother's nightmare." —*Focus*

Readership Profile: Predominantly male (93.7 percent), young (52.8 percent under 16 years old, 20.7 percent between 16 and 17), and white (82.3 percent). Over half of the readers work full-time or part-time, with an annual average family income of $47,895.

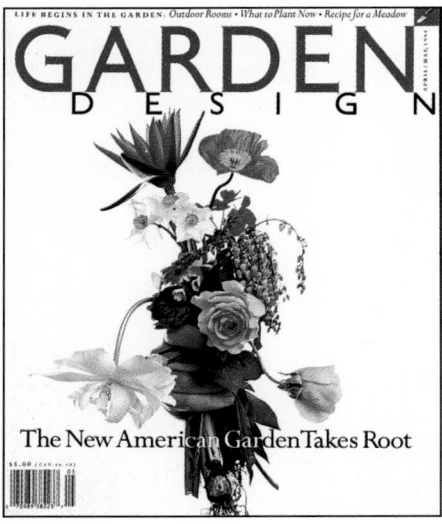

Garden Design

Published by:
Meigher Communications, L.P.
100 Avenue of the Americas
New York NY 10013
Phone Number: 800-234-5118
Launch Date: May/June 1994
Publisher: Joe Armstrong
Editor: Dorothy Kalins
Frequency: Bimonthly
Cover Price: $5.00
Subscription Price: $24/year, $42.95/2 years
Number of issues published since launch: 7
Circulation: 150,000
Ad Rates: Four-Color Page - $9,000 / B&W Page - $6,600

Publication Profile: "To celebrate the gardener as artist and writer, philosopher and photographer, horticulturist and nurturer." The relaunch of *Garden Design* has been treated as a completely new launch by Meigher Communications.

The subscription price was reduced from $28 for the first issue (May/June 1994) to $24.

"It's like a stroll through a Japanese garden—minimalist and relaxing."—*USA Today*

"A luxurious magazine for affluent people who garden."—*The New York Times*

Readership Profile: 38 percent of readers are male, 62 percent female. Their average age is 43 years old. 71 percent are college graduates and 43 percent attended graduate school. The household income for 63 percent is $60,000+. 54 percent are professionals. 42 percent spent $5,000+ decorating and furnishing their homes over the past 2 years. 80 percent entertain in the garden or exterior of the home. Average value of primary home $250,400

German Life

Published by:
Zeitgeist Publishing
1 Corporate Drive
Grantsville MD 21536
Phone Number: 301-895-3859
Launch Date: June/July 1994
Publisher: Lisa A. Fitzpatrick
Editor: Michael Koch
Frequency: Bimonthly
Cover Price: $3.95
Subscription Price: $19.95
Number of issues published since launch: 5
Circulation: 30,662
Ad Rates: Four-Color Page - $3,150 / B&W Page - $2,205

Publication Profile: A magazine for Americans of German descent that relays "all sides—the colors, and flavors, people and events that shape German culture today."

Readership Profile: The typical *German Life* reader is mature (52.2 years old), married (62 percent), male (60 percent), affluent ($63,600 annual income), with a college education. 87 percent of those employed hold executive, professional or managerial positions. 77 percent have friends or relatives in Germany.

Girls' Life

Published by:
Monarch Avalon Inc.
4517 Harford Road
Baltimore MD 21214
Phone Number: 410-254-9200
Launch Date: August/
September 1994
Publisher: Karen Bokram
Editor: Karen Bokram
Frequency: Bimonthly
Cover Price: $2.95
Subscription Price: $17.95
**Number of issues published
since launch:** 4
Circulation: 75,000
Ad Rates: Four-Color Page -
$5,000 / B&W Page - $4,500

Publication Profile: "Treats girls like smart, unique, opinionated and valuable people" with articles about fashion, sports, reading, horses, the environment, friends, and family. A junior version of *Seventeen, Girls' Life* focuses on some of the "more innocent concerns of youth," taking girls in "the tweens market" seriously.

Rate base is set at 100,000 for August/September 1995 and 150,000 for December/January 1996.

"It reinforces the idea that girls count."—*Folio*

Readership Profile: Girls 7 to 14 years old, with disposable incomes of up to $20 per week, who are thought to be more brand conscious than the older teen market. Parents are the secondary market.

The Golfer

Published by:
Briar & Wood Inc.
42 W. 38th St.
New York NY 10018
Phone Number: 212-768-8360
Launch Date: March 1994
Publisher: H.K. Pickens
Editor: H.K. Pickens
Frequency: 6/year
Cover Price: $4.00
Subscription Price: $24.00
**Number of issues published
since launch:** 3
Circulation: 250,000
(paid subscribers 51,500)
Ad Rates: Four-Color Page -
$10,875 / B&W Page - $10,875

Publication Profile: "Capturing the essence of golf in words and pictures, *The Golfer*...covers the great courses, best equipment, leading personalities and talks to golfers like no other magazine. Going beyond instruction...it celebrates the lifestyle of the game."

Readership Profile: Attempting to reach an upscale diverse audience, such as the private club member, in a similar fashion to its 14-year-old sister publication, *The Racquet.*

HomePC

Published by:
CMP Publications Inc.
600 Community Drive
Manhasset NY 11030
Phone Number: 516-562-7673
Launch Date: June 1994
Publisher: Dan Schwartz
Editor: Ellen Pearlman
Frequency: Monthly
Cover Price: $2.95
Subscription Price: $21.97
**Number of issues published
since launch:** 7
Circulation: 350,000
Ad Rates: Four-Color Page -
$11,850 / B&W Page - $9,000

Publication Profile: Aimed at computer users of all ages, *HomePC* covers computer "entertainment, education, and productivity." Product-oriented, it contains articles on kids' software and also software on investment, art, and wine.

The newsstand price was slashed to 95 cents from $2.95 for the first two issues in order to woo subscribers.

"More gender-neutral...with an article on more software specifically for girls." —*The Wall Street Journal*

Readership Profile: High income (yearly average $57,800), well-educated (89 percent attended college). The average reader is male (66 percent), 45 years of age, with children (76 percent), and a computer user who has used PCs for an average of five years (at work and at home).

Home Theater Technology

Published by:
CurtCo Publishing
20700 Ventura Blvd., Suite 100
Woodland Hills CA 91364
Phone Number: 818-598-0800
Launch Date: October 1994
Publisher: Megean Roberts
Editor: Lawrence E. Ullman
Frequency: Monthly
Cover Price: $3.95
Subscription Price: $23.95
Number of issues published since launch: 5
Circulation: 60,000
Ad Rates: Four-Color Page - $12,880 / B&W Page - $9,660

Publication Profile: Subtitled "the media system authority," the magazine features product reviews, comprehensive buyer's guides to equipment, and technical tips to set up your own home theater, or get the most of an existing one.

Focuses on new audio/video products, systems and technologies in the home electronic entertainment market.

Readership Profile: n/a

In Style

Published by:
Time Inc.
Time & Life Building
Rockefeller Center
New York NY 10020
Phone Number: 212-891-0410
Launch Date: June 1994
Publisher: Ann W. Jackson
Editor: Martha Nelson
Frequency: Monthly
Cover Price: $2.95
Subscription Price: $19.97
Number of issues published since launch: 9
Circulation: 550,000
Ad Rates: Four-Color Page - $24,500 / B&W Page - $?

Publication Profile: "Celebrities at home, sometimes in the shower or tub," are featured in *In Style*, a new spinoff from *People*. It offers "an intimate look at celebrity lifestyles in vivid pictures and inside stories that will move you, amuse you, and inform you."

The launch circulation 500,000 was increased to 550,000 in January 1995, and the cover price increased from $2.49 to $2.95 with the December 1994 issue.

"This is pure escapism, fabulously laid out."—*USA Today*

Readership Profile: 47 percent college graduates, affluent ($49,900 median household income), 56 percent professional/managerial, with a median age of 34.9 years old. And—surprise, surprise—91 percent female.

Inter@ctive Week

Published by:
Inter@ctive Enterprises
100 Quentin Roosevelt Blvd.,
Suite 508
Garden City NY 11530
Phone Number: 516-229-3700
Launch Date: October 10, 1994
Publisher: Beth Haggerty
Editor: Susan Older
Frequency: Biweekly
Cover Price: $6.00
Subscription Price: $60.00
Number of issues published since launch: 5
Circulation: 60,000
Ad Rates: Four-Color Page - $10,550 / B&W Page - $8,350

Publication Profile: Billed as the first publication devoted solely to the interactive market, *Inter@ctive Week* covers the information superhighway, that convergence of the telecommunications, computer, cable, and other digital technology markets. It covers news, features and trends that are "going to have a profound impact on society."

The publication was launched as a monthly, and later shifted to a biweekly publishing schedule.

Readership Profile: Personnel in corporate management, communication/network/PS management, engineering/technical management, product development management and marketing management.

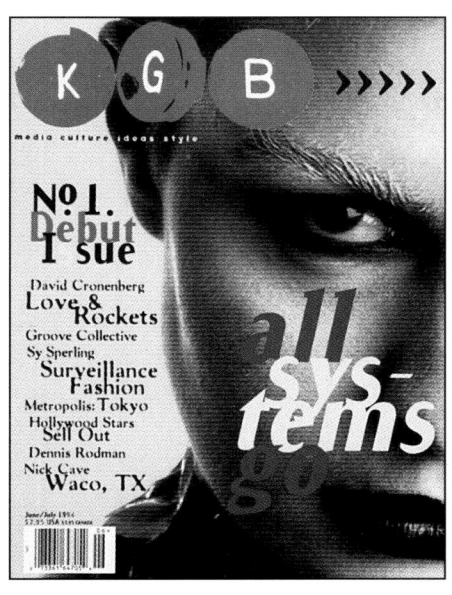

KGB

Published by:
KGB Media Inc.
133 Bowery
New York NY 10002
Phone Number: 212-343-1512
Launch Date: June/July 1994
Publisher: Lukas Barr and
Sean Gullette
Editor: Lukas Barr and Sean Gullette
Frequency: Bimonthly
Cover Price: $2.95
Subscription Price: $15.00
**Number of issues published
since launch:** 2
Circulation: 20,000
Ad Rates: Four-Color Page -
$4,000 / B&W Page - $3,000

Publication Profile: A "reality-based counter-media" publication for the twentysomething crowd, *KGB* focuses on underground culture, media, ideas and style—apt for a magazine that has appropriated the acronym of a totalitarian police agency for its name. *KGB* began as *Blast* in 1989 at Harvard University, where the editors were undergraduates.

"Reading *KGB* is akin to watching MTV...there is a relentless attention paid to appearing cool...[and] anything that conveys a jaunty disregard for everything." —*Dallas Morning News*

The writing is not only reasonably legible but sharp, and the magazine practices an offbeat kind of democratism." —*San Diego Union-Tribune.*

Readership Profile: Generation X, the 40 million people between 18 and 30 years old, who spend $125 billion a year on goods and services.

Latin Style

Published by:
Latin Style Magazine
P.O. Box 2969
Venice CA 90294-2969
Phone Number: 310-452-8452
Launch Date: August 1994
Publisher: Walter Martinez
Editor: Walter Martinez
Frequency: Monthly
Cover Price: $2.50
Subscription Price: $20.00
**Number of issues published
since launch:** 4
Circulation: 90,000
Ad Rates: Four-Color Page -
$3,300 / B&W Page - $2,310

Publication Profile: Entertainment and celebrities for the Latin-American community—a magazine that talks culture, art, music, and fashion with a mix of profiles, interviews, and articles.

Readership Profile: n/a

Louis L'Amour Western Magazine

Published by:
Dell Magazines
1540 Broadway
New York NY 10036
Phone Number: 212-782-8532
Launch Date: March 1994
Publisher: Christopher Haas-Heye
Editor: Elana Lore
Frequency: Bimonthly
Cover Price: $2.95
Subscription Price: $17.70,
Discounted $15.97
**Number of issues published
since launch:** 7
Circulation: 160,000
Ad Rates: Four-Color Page -
$2,240 / B&W Page - $1,280

Publication Profile: A "selection of the finest western fiction being written today" that illuminates the American-West — its rough-hewn history, traditions and people. Named after one of the most prolific writers of Western fiction, the magazine showcases new writers of traditional and not-so-traditional western fiction, and nonfiction travel articles, profiles, historical pieces, and interviews with authors.

"The wild west makes a comeback in a new Dell magazine."
—*The New York Times*

Readership Profile: Western fiction fans, "the man who loves the frontier and wild west period of American history." The audience is 70 percent male, 36 to 64 years old, largely non-urban, with a household income of $35,000+, in predominantly the southern, western, southwestern and northwestern United States.

Makeover

Published by:
Time Inc.
Rockefeller Center
New York NY 10020-1393
Phone Number: 212-522-4117
Launch Date: Summer 1994
Publisher: Time Inc.
Editor: Susan Toepfer
Frequency: Monthly
Cover Price: $1.49
Subscription Price: $12.00
Number of issues published since launch: 1
Circulation: 75,000
Ad Rates: Four-Color Page - n/a / B&W Page - n/a

Publication Profile: A *People* spinoff, subtitled "Easy ways to change your look and life." It focuses on personal appearance makeovers (diet, makeup, fitness, and attire), home makeovers (how to redesign a kitchen) and personality makeovers (how to overcome shyness) to help in "making the best of what you've got."

Readership Profile: n/a

Marie Claire

Published by:
Hearst Corporation and Comary Inc.
250 West 55th St., 5th Floor
New York NY 10019
Phone Number: 212-649-4450
Launch Date: September/October 1994
Publisher: Peg Farrell
Editor: Bonnie Fuller
Frequency: Bimonthly
Cover Price: $2.95
Subscription Price: $14.97
Number of issues published since launch: 3
Circulation: 350,000
Ad Rates: Four-Color Page - $20,300 / B&W Page - $11,700

Publication Profile: This U.S. edition of the French women's fashion magazine, *Marie Claire* is a joint venture between Hearst Magazines and Comary, Inc., a U.S. subsidiary of Marie Claire Album S.A. It features "fashion and beauty trends, information, and advice" and includes profiles, first-person stories, social commentaries, and stories on culture, travel, and politics.

The rate base increased by 100,000 since its launch and will increase to 400,000 in the second half of 1995.

Readership Profile: A magazine for women, *Marie Claire's* readers are between 25 and 44 years old, with a median individual earned income of $33,000 and household income of $47,000. Mostly unmarried (52 percent), highly educated (65 percent attended/graduated college), and employed (72 percent), of which 34 percent are in the professional/managerial capacity.

Might

Published by:
Gigantic Publishing Company
150 Fourth St., Suite 650A
San Francisco CA 94103
Phone Number: 415-896-1528
Launch Date: February 1994
Publisher: David Eggers
Editor: David Eggers
Frequency: Bimonthly
Cover Price: $4.00
Subscription Price: $20.00
Number of issues published since launch: 5
Circulation: 30,000
Ad Rates: Four-Color Page - $4,740 / B&W Page - $2,400

Publication Profile: "A goddamn brain picnic for the young and restless," *Might*, the new *Spy*-like magazine started by San Francisco-based college grads, is smart, satirical, and for young people, "but there are no beauty tips, no dating hints or articles about partying. It's about careers, politics, pop culture and random other stuff. *Might* doesn't take itself or its 'generation' too seriously."

In July, the quarterly *Might* went bimonthly, hiked its cover price by fifty cents to $4.00 and added 10 more pages.

"A hip, witty, and outspoken magazine for the twentysomethings."—*San Francisco Chronicle*

"The most promising recent example...Generation X has started taking the media into its own hands."—*Elle*

Readership Profile: "*Might* readers are college-educated, motivated and influential. They move. They shake." 34 percent are between 18 and 24 years old, 40 percent are between 25 and 29 years old. They are largely male (53 percent), educated (53 percent finished college), and work full-time (58 percent).

Mouth2Mouth

Published by:
Time Inc. Ventures
270 North Canon Drive, #2038
Beverly Hills CA 90210
Phone Number: n/a
Launch Date: Spring 1994
Publisher: Carol A. Smith
Editor: Angela Janklow Harrington
Frequency: Bimonthly
Cover Price: $2.50
Subscription Price: $15.00
Number of issues published since launch: 2
Circulation: n/a
Ad Rates: Four-Color Page - n/a / B&W Page - n/a

Publication Profile: A super-hip look at celebrities, fashion, and trends, targeted at teenagers of both sexes. Time Inc. Ventures invested over $1 million in the magazine edited by Harrington, daughter of high-powered literary agent Mort Janklow (whose clients include novelists Jackie Collins and Sidney Sheldon). "The idea is to boldly go where no magazine has gone before," and it did go—"on hiatus," while Harrington takes maternity leave (or at least that is the official line).

But a post-Christmas letter to subscribers from its fulfillment office promised them a return for the full amount of the subscription "because we can't guarantee that you will receive the future issues you have requested."

Readership Profile: n/a

NetGuide

Published by:
CMP Publications Inc.
600 Community Dr.
Manhasset NY 11030
Phone Number: 516-562-7392
Launch Date: December 1994
Publisher: Donald F. Tydeman
Editor: Patrice Adcroft
Frequency: Monthly
Cover Price: $2.95
Subscription Price: $22.97
Number of issues published since launch: 4
Circulation: 200,000
Ad Rates: Four-Color Page - $12,500 / B&W Page - $9,500

Publication Profile: The guide to online services and the Internet for the 25 million people "hooked on surfing cyberspace." The major focus is topical listings of what is available on online services, BBSs, and the Internet, and includes news, hardware and software reviews, how-to articles, and other features.

NetGuide was launched at a special price of $1.95.

"Jump on this one right away."—*Phoenix Gazette*

"Experienced cybersurfers or wet-behind-the-ears newbies can enjoy...*NetGuide*."—*Atlanta Journal-Constitution*

Readership Profile: An affluent audience, representing the cream of the purchasing market.

New Rave

Published by:
AmLon Publishing Group Inc.
7060 Hollywood Blvd., Suite 805
Hollywood CA 90028
Phone Number: 213-463-2211
Launch Date: August 1994
Publisher: Hank Londoner
Editor: Larry Wiichman
Frequency: Monthly
Cover Price: $4.99
Subscription Price: $39.95
Number of issues published since launch: 8
Circulation: 100,000
Ad Rates: Four-Color Page - $3,750 / B&W Page - $2,900

Publication Profile: "The MTV of men's magazines: sex, fun, and rock'n'roll." Raunchier than *Playboy* and younger than *Penthouse*, it's a "ride through a wonderland of high-tech electronics, erotica, sports, humor, and other male-oriented diversions."

Readership Profile: Male, single (70 percent), 18 to 35 years old, with an average annual income of $27,000, and a high-school education.

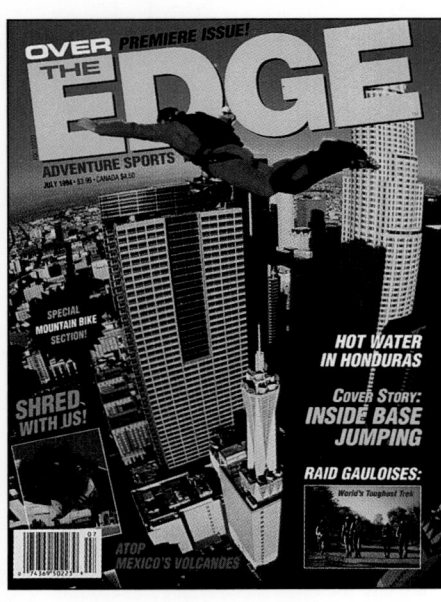

Over The Edge

Published by:
HG Publications Inc.
9171 Wilshire Blvd., Suite 300
Beverly Hills CA 90210
Phone Number: 303-939-8422
Launch Date: July 1994
Publisher: Larry Flynt
Editor: Michael Bane
Frequency: Bimonthly
Cover Price: $3.99
Subscription Price: $19.95
**Number of issues published
since launch:** 3
Circulation: 200,000
Ad Rates: Four-Color Page -
n/a / B&W Page - n/a

Publication Profile: Features adventure sports, adventure travel, how-tos, training and gear. Editor Michael Bane said that, despite exceeding expectations, *Over The Edge* folded with the November issue. Publisher Larry Flynt pulled the plug, disappointed with newsstand sales of its premiere issue.

Readership Profile: n/a

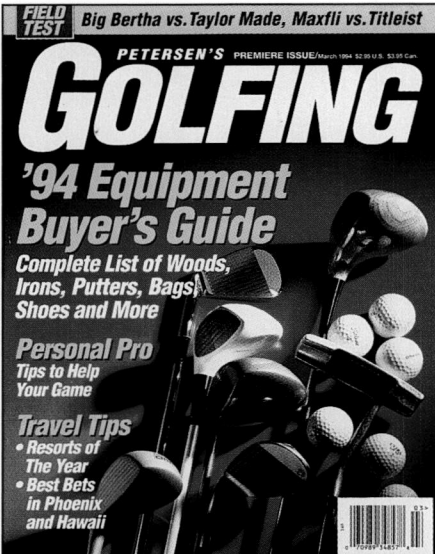

Petersen's Golfing

Published by:
Petersen Publishing Company
6420 Wilshire Blvd.
Los Angeles CA 90048-5515
Phone Number: 213-782-2800
Launch Date: March 1994
Publisher: Richard Holcomb
Editor: Ken Ven Kampen
Frequency: Monthly
Cover Price: $2.95
Subscription Price: $19.94
**Number of issues published
since launch:** 13
Circulation: 175,000
Ad Rates: Four-Color Page -
$12,675 / B&W Page - $8,450

Publication Profile: A golf review magazine that "will give you all the truth and substance you can handle when it comes to your game and your money." *Petersen's Golfing* provides "the golf enthusiast with service-driven information on equipment, instruction, and travel."

Ken Ven Kampen replaced Michael Corcoran as editor and the publication changed from saddle stitching to perfect bound. The circulation rate base jumped 75 percent to 175,000 since its launch.

Readership Profile: Golfing enthusiasts who are well-educated, well-established, and well above the national average in key demographic areas. *Petersen's Golfing* readers are big buyers and during the last year, 79.5 percent made a major equipment purchase, 66.2 percent replaced the grips on their clubs, 62.3 percent took a golf vacation.

POZ

Published by:
Strubco Inc.
349 West 12th St.
New York NY 10014
Phone Number: 212-242-2163
Launch Date: April 1994
Publisher: Sean O'Brien Strub
Editor: Richard Perez-Feria
Frequency: Bimonthly
Cover Price: $3.95
Subscription Price: n/a
**Number of issues published
since launch:** 6
Circulation: 100,000
Ad Rates: Four-Color Page -
$8,500 / B&W Page - $5,950

Publication Profile: "*POZ* takes a literary approach with *Vanity Fair*-style profiles and highly personal commentary" to inform, provoke, entertain and reflect the reality of AIDS-infected lives. "Being positive isn't negative" is its message.

Since its launch, *POZ* increased its size from 60 to 88 pages and upped its cover price from $3.50 to $3.95. A number of copies were distributed free to AIDS-involved households, physicians with HIV-related practices, and treatment centers.

"*POZ* is an extraordinarily well-written, meticulously crafted periodical...[and] would like to become a vital community bulletin board for a growing number of HIV-positive Americans."
—*Utne Reader*

Readership Profile: Those infected and affected by AIDS, including friends, caregivers, and relatives. The target audience is highly affluent—more than 50 percent of the estimated 14.3 million gay Americans have a household income over $50,000, and nearly half have a college or post-graduate education.

Pure

Published by:
HG Publications Inc.
9171 Wilshire Blvd., Suite 300
Beverly Hills CA 90210
Phone Number: 800-714-0499
Launch Date: August 1994
Publisher: Larry Flynt
Editor: Scott Schalin
Frequency: Bimonthly
Cover Price: $4.99
Subscription Price: $19.95
**Number of issues published
since launch:** 5
Circulation: 100,000
Ad Rates: Four-Color Page -
n/a / B&W Page - n/a

Publication Profile: Explicit pictorials of sexy women and articles on sexual techniques, from "the seedy to the sublime."

The magazine folded after the fifth issue and no information was available—"everything's been thrown out."

Readership Profile: n/a

Realms Of Fantasy

Published by:
Sovereign Company Inc.
457 Carlisle Drive
Herndon VA 22070
Phone Number: 703-471-1556
Launch Date: October 1994
Publisher: Mark Hintz
Editor: Shawna McCarthy
Frequency: Bimonthly
Cover Price: $3.50
Subscription Price: $14.95
**Number of issues published
since launch:** 3
Circulation: 55,000
Ad Rates: Four-Color Page -
$1,950 / B&W Page - $1,200

Publication Profile: Short fiction about dragons, fairies, magic kingdoms, etc. *Realms Of Fantasy* covers everything from "the latest Arthurian sagas to new heroic quests, from ancient to contemporary fantasy, and everything in-between. There are also fantasy book reviews, art, illustrations, games, and interviews with writers and artists.

Readership Profile: Readers are well-educated (82 percent attended college), upscale (average household income is $53,730) adults (37.1 years average age). Mostly male (55 percent), they purchase an average of $527.92 of merchandise a year through mail order and spend 3.06 hours a day reading.

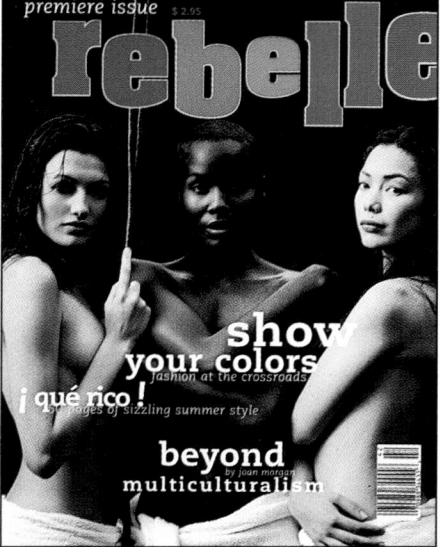

Rebelle

Published by:
Cerlin Inc.
c/o Rebelle
130 Prince St.
New York NY 10012
Phone Number: 212-343-5802
Launch Date: Summer 1994
Publisher: Karen Rogala
Editor: Randall Koral
Frequency: 10/year
Cover Price: $2.95
Subscription Price: $15.00
**Number of issues published
since launch:** 1
Circulation: 100,000
Ad Rates: Four-Color Page -
$6,500 / B&W Page - $4,000

Publication Profile: Multiculturalism hits the magazine world. *Rebelle*, launched by two Haitian-born fashion photographers, is "about rebelling against the fashion establishment, about seeing images you would not see in other magazines (*Vogue* and *Elle* are virtually all white, *Essence* is all black)." It aims "to provide a sophisticated cultural resource, a forum wide enough to welcome every kind of reader." Besides fashion, beauty, and fitness, it covers art, music, food, and aspects of pop culture influenced by ethnic communities. "*Rebelle* is a celebration of American diversity."

"*Rebelle's* on the front lines of a brave new world of color, where multiculturalism means everyone and visibility for all." —*Detroit Free Press*

Readership Profile: A largely female readership, between 18 and 35 years old, with a median household income of $36,303.

The Sandwich Generation

Published by:
Carol Abaya Associates
P.O. Box 132
Wickatunk NJ 07765-0132
Phone Number: 908-536-6215
Launch Date: Summer 1994
Publisher: Carol Abaya
Editor: Carol Abaya
Frequency: n/a
Cover Price: $2.95
Subscription Price: $14.00
**Number of issues published
since launch:** 4
Circulation: 40,000
Ad Rates: Four-Color Page -
$1,800 / B&W Page - $1,400

Publication Profile: Addresses the problems faced by adults caring for aging parents, those people caught in what has been termed "the Sandwich Generation." It attempts to answer the troubling questions of role reversal and parent caregiving and to better prepare the Sandwich Generation for a new role that society has not prepared anyone to play.

Readership Profile: n/a

Saveur

Published by:
Meigher Communications L.P.
100 Avenue of the Americas
New York NY 10013-1605
Phone Number: 212-334-1212
Launch Date: July 1994
Publisher: Joe Armstrong
Editor: Dorothy Kalins
Frequency: Bimonthly
Cover Price: $5.00
Subscription Price: $24.00
**Number of issues published
since launch:** 4
Circulation: 100,000
Ad Rates: Four-Color Page -
$6,000 / B&W Page - $4,400

Publication Profile: "A lush new magazine for people with sophisticated tastes in food," *Saveur*, the U.S. edition of a popular European food magazine, "tells the life story of food - visiting the places it comes from, meeting the people who created it." Features travel pieces, a calendar of world food events, restaurant advice, and authentic recipes from around the world for "true-blue foodies, hobby cooks and travellers." "Not about convenience or low-fat" food.
"Stunning food photographs." —*Chicago Tribune*
"A *Gourmet* for the '90s." —*New York*

Readership Profile: "Appeals to an upscale exclusive baby boomer crowd": women (73 percent), between 35 and 54 years old (49 percent), well-educated (94 percent attended/graduated college), extremely affluent (51 percent have a an average household income of $75,000+, and 28 percent a have a HHI of $100,000+)

Sci-Fi Entertainment

Published by:
Sovereign Media Company Inc.
457 Carlisle Drive
Herndon VA 22070
Phone Number: 703-471-1556
Launch Date: June 1994
Publisher: Mark Hintz
Editor: Edward Flixman
Frequency: Bimonthly
Cover Price: $3.50
Subscription Price: $14.95/Year
**Number of issues published
since launch:** 5
Circulation: 110,000
Ad Rates: Four-Color Page -
$1,420 / B&W Page - $890

Publication Profile: The official magazine of the Sci-Fi Channel, *Sci-Fi Entertainment* is a media-oriented magazine featuring all science fiction entertainment: from movies and TV, to online services, video games, SF art, books, and more. "Written by and for knowledgeable science fiction buffs."

Readership Profile: Mostly male (62 percent), upscale (average household income of $53,202), with an average age of 39 years old. 60 percent of the subscribers own home computers and purchase an average of 34 books and $452 of merchandise through mail order each year.

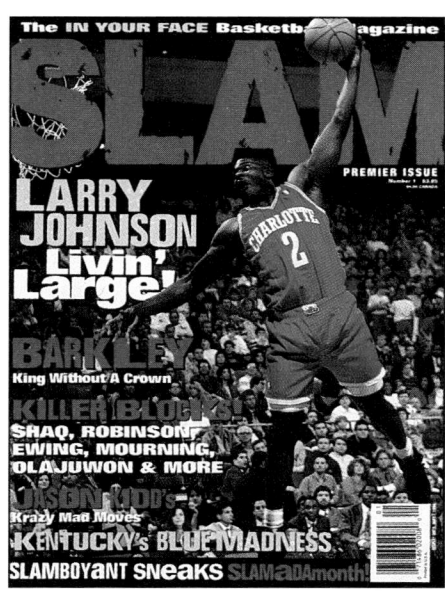

Slam

Published by:
Harris Publications Inc.
115 Broadway
New York NY 10010
Phone Number: 212-807-7100
Launch Date: September 1994
Publisher: Dennis S. Page
Editor: Tony Gervino
Frequency: Bimonthly
Cover Price: $3.95
Subscription Price: $9.97
Number of issues published since launch: 4
Circulation: 125,000
Ad Rates: Four-Color Page - $4,900 / B&W Page - $3,700

Publication Profile: This basketball magazine features the larger-than-life players who have made the NBA so popular.

Since its launch, the magazine went from quarterly to bimonthly and Tony Gervino replaced Corey Johnson as editor.

Readership Profile: Predominantly white (77.5 percent) and male (88.5 percent), almost half of *Slam's* readers (45.4 percent) are under 16 years of age and in high school. 42.5 percent of the readers are on their school basketball team and 47.7 percent are on an organized basketball team outside of school.

Spec

Published by:
24th St. Publishing Inc.
P.O. Box 4028
San Francisco CA 94140
Phone Number: 415-282-939
Launch Date: November 1994
Publisher: Matthew Jaffe
Editor: Matthew Jaffe
Frequency: Bimonthly
Cover Price: $2.95
Subscription Price: $19.00
Number of issues published since launch: 2
Circulation: 25,000
Ad Rates: Four-Color Page - $1,750 / B&W Page - $1,250

Publication Profile: A theme-oriented mix of fanzine and general interest magazine for Generation X. "The idea is neither to give lip-service to celebrities, nor to be voice-of-a-generation, but rather to be a part of the times."

The cover price dropped from $4.00 to $2.95.

Readership Profile: Most of *Spec's* readers are young, between 21 and 29 years old, well-paid, with an average income of $33,124, and highly educated (77 percent college graduates, 15 percent attend college). 55 percent of readers are male.

Spider

Published by:
Carus Publishing Company
The Cricket Magazine Group
315 Fifth St.
Peru IL 61354
Phone Number: 815-224-6656
Launch Date: January 1994
Publisher: Robert W. Harper
Editor: Christine Walske
Frequency: Monthly
Cover Price: $3.95
Subscription Price: $29.97
Number of issues published since launch: 14
Circulation: 78,000
Ad Rates: Four-Color Page - n/a / B&W Page - n/a

Publication Profile: "Specially written for children who have reached that amazing age when they first get excited about reading on their own." This is an ad-free magazine published by the same folks who publish *Cricket* and *Ladybug* for older and younger children respectively.

Christine Walske replaced Lynn Gutknecht as the editor-in-chief.

Readership Profile: Spider weaves a web of wonder for kids six to nine years old.

Swing

Published by:
The Swing Corporation
342 Madison Ave.
New York NY 10017
Phone Number: 212-935-8519
Launch Date: November 1994
Publisher: David Lauren
Editor: David Lauren
Frequency: 10/year
Cover Price $2.50
Subscription Price: $16.00
**Number of issues published
since launch:** 4
Circulation: 100,000
Ad Rates: Four-Color Page -
$5,000 / B&W Page - $4,125

Publication Profile: A sober magazine by and for twenty somethings, who "swing" politics, pop culture and society in their general direction. With its youthful takes on politics and society, *Swing* strives to appeal to a dual audience. "We are not going after slackers," says founder and editor David Lauren, son of Ralph.

Distributed on college campuses, newsstands, thrift shops, cafes, computer, and record stores, the cover price increased from $2.00 to $2.50 in March 1995.

"*Swing* could be *The New Yorker* disguised in Generation X drag." —*Fort Worth Star-Telegram*

Readership Profile: n/a

Troika

Published by:
Lone Tout Publications Inc.
P.O. Box 1006
Weston CT 06883
Phone Number: 203-227-5377
Launch Date: Spring 1994
Publisher: Eric S. Meadow
Editor: Celia R. Meadow
Frequency: Quarterly
Cover Price: $3.00
Subscription Price: $10.00
**Number of issues published
since launch:** 4
Circulation: 100,000
Ad Rates: Four-Color Page -
$8,000 / B&W Page - $6,000

Publication Profile: A general interest magazine about "wit, wisdom and wherewithal," *Troika* is "aimed at 'reformed Yuppies'... young urban professionals who simply got old." *Troika*, meaning triumverate, covers lifestyle, culture, ethics, science, leisure, and more. Since its launch, book size has increased from 84 to 100 pages.

"*Troika*...is in many ways reminiscent of the late *Wigwag*, which in turn was a generation removed from, but spiritually related to, *The New Yorker*."—*Advertising Age*

Readership Profile: Geared to a highly educated, upscale readership in the 30s to 50s age bracket.

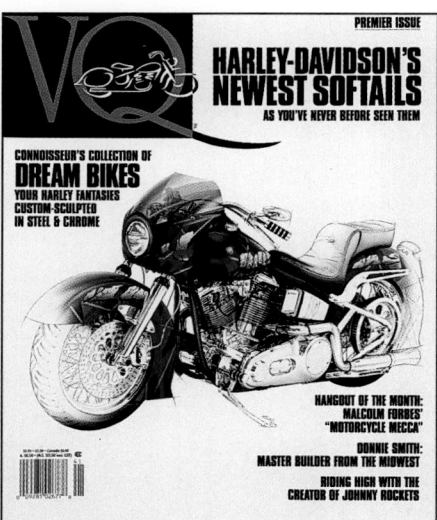

VQ

Published by:
Paisano Publications Inc.
28210 Dorothy Drive
Agoura Hills, CA 91301-2693
Phone Number: 818-889-8740
Launch Date: January 1994
Publisher: Joe Teresi
Editor: Dick Teresi
Frequency: Quarterly
Cover Price: $5.95
Subscription Price: $19.95
**Number of issues published
since launch:** 5
Circulation: n/a
Ad Rates: Four-Color Page -
$2,000 / B&W Page - $2,320

Publication Profile: "Dedicated to the upwardly mobile Harley rider with places to go and people to meet," *VQ* features high-quality pictures and articles about customized motorcycles."

Readership Profile: At an average age of 31 years old, *VQ's* readers are predominantly male (93.3 percent) with an average annual household income of $59,000. 53.7 percent are married and 49.2 percent have finished junior college up to post-graduate. 72.9 percent own at least one motorcycle and 63.6 percent have been riding them for more than 10 years.

Women's Self Defense

Published by:

Creative Arts Inc.

Spectrum Building

4901 N.W. 17th Way, Suite 600

Fort Lauderdale FL 33309

Phone Number: 305-772-2788

Launch Date: March 1994

Publisher: David Harvard

Editor: Kathy S. Bentley

Frequency: 9/year

Cover Price: $3.95

Subscription Price: $24.00

Number of issues published since launch: 3

Circulation: n/a

Ad Rates: Four-Color Page - n/a / B&W Page - n/a

Publication Profile: Addresses ways women can protect themselves, not only physically but in other areas such as law and medicine. Focuses on information about experts, organizations, associations, and a host of specialized products designed for self-protection.

The magazine has ceased publication.

Readership Profile: n/a

Yolk

Published by:

InformAsian Media Inc.

P.O. Box 862130

Los Angeles, CA 90086-2130

Phone Number: 310-917-7252

Launch Date: October 1994

Publisher: InformAsian Media Inc.

Editor: Larry J. Tazuma

Frequency: Quarterly

Cover Price: $3.95

Subscription Price: $18/6 issues

Number of issues published since launch: 2

Circulation: 25,000

Ad Rates: Four-Color Page - n/a / B&W Page - n/a

Publication Profile: A magazine with an attitude that targets Generation X, *Yolk* looks at American pop culture with a distinctly Asian-American perspective. "If you have the balls to be original, we have the space to print it," says editor Larry Tazuma. "*Yolk* simply stands for the color of our skin—it symbolizes the 'Yellow is Beautiful' movement."

Tazuma replaced Philip W. Chung after first issue.

"*Yolk's* pages hold everything from celebrity interviews, to social issues like Asians with HIV, to exploding the myth that Asians have small penises." —*L.A. Downtown News*

Readership Profile: n/a

NEW CONSUMER MAGAZINES

OF 1994

Note: The information in this section pertains only to the premiere issue of each title.

47

Art Revue

Published by:

Innovative Artists Agency

302 W. 13th St.

Loveland CO 80537

Date: Winter 1994

(first newsstand issue)

Frequency: Quarterly

Cover Price: $3.00

Subscription Price: $20.00

Discount Subscription Price: $20.00

Total Number of Pages: 52

Total Number of Ad Pages: 24

Publisher: Paul McNutt

Editor: Jan McNutt

Editorial Concept: An art magazine focusing on traditional painting and sculpture.

Blur

Published by:

Ride Design

417 N. Second St.

Silverton OR 97381

Date: 1994

Frequency: Quarterly

Cover Price: $5.00

Subscription Price: n/a

Discount Subscription Price: n/a

Total Number of Pages: 32

Total Number of Ad Pages: 5

Publisher: Scott Clum

Editor: Anne Telford

Editorial Concept: Progressive art and music for the ultra-hip crowd.

Civilization

Published by:

L.O.C. Associates L.P.

475 Park Ave., 7th Floor

New York NY 10016

Date: November/December 1994

Frequency: Bimonthly

Cover Price: $4.50

Subscription Price: $20.00

Discount Subscription Price: n/a

Total Number of Pages: 100

Total Number of Ad Pages: 18

Publisher: L.O.C. Associates L.P.

Editor: Stephen G. Smith

Editorial Concept: The magazine of the Library of Congress featuring literature, history, culture, and social issues.

The Echoes Report

Published by:

Deco Echoes Publications

P.O. Box 2321

Mashpee MA 02649

Date: Fall 1994 *(first newsstand issue)*

Frequency: Quarterly

Cover Price: $3.50

Subscription Price: $16.50

Discount Subscription Price: n/a

Total Number of Pages: 44

Total Number of Ad Pages: 8

Publisher: William Scott Cheverie

Editor: Suzanne Cheverie

Editorial Concept: "Focused on 20th Century style and design."

The Medieval & Renaissance Times

Published by:

Medieval & Renaissance Times Inc.

1205 Easton Ave.

Somerset NJ 08873

Date: Summer 1994

Frequency: Bimonthly

Cover Price: $6.00

Subscription Price: $29.95

Discount Subscription Price: n/a

Total Number of Pages: 84

Total Number of Ad Pages: 10

Publisher: John N. Lupin III

Editor: John N. Lupin III

Editorial Concept: "To promote Medieval and Renaissance studies."

The Sondheim Review

Published by:

The Sondheim Review

2230 E. Bradford Ave., Unit G

Milwaukee WI 53211-4059

Date: Summer 1994

Frequency: Quarterly

Cover Price: $5.95

Subscription Price: $19.95

Discount Subscription Price: n/a

Total Number of Pages: 32

Total Number of Ad Pages: 0

Publisher: The Sondheim Review

Editor: Paul Salsini

Editorial Concept: "Dedicated to the musical theater's foremost composer and lyricist."

Stage Directions

Published by:

SMW Communications Inc.

3020 Beacon Blvd.

West Sacramento CA

Date: January 1994

(first issue in new format)

Frequency: 10/year

Cover Price: $3.50

Subscription Price: $26.00

Discount Subscription Price: n/a

Total Number of Pages: 30

Total Number of Ad Pages: 10

Publisher: Susan M. Warshing

Editor: Stephen Peithman

Editorial Concept: "For and about regional, community, and academic theater."

Subliminal Tattoos

Published by:

Robert DuPree Writes Pictures

9604 SE 5th St.

Vancouver WA 98664

Date: 1994

Frequency: Quarterly

Cover Price: $3.95

Subscription Price: $15.00

Discount Subscription Price: n/a

Total Number of Pages: 96

Total Number of Ad Pages: 8

Publisher: Robert DuPree

Editor: Robert DuPree

Editorial Concept: An alternative arts magazine.

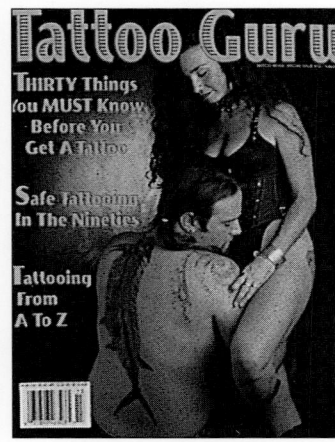

Tattoo Guru

Published by:

Outlaw Biker Enterprises Inc.

450 Seventh Ave., Suite 2305

New York NY 10123

Date: 1994

Frequency: Quarterly

Cover Price: $4.99

Subscription Price: n/a

Discount Subscription Price: n/a

Total Number of Pages: 68

Total Number of Ad Pages: 23

Publisher: Casey Exton

Editor: n/a

Editorial Concept: "The ultimate guide to getting a tattoo."

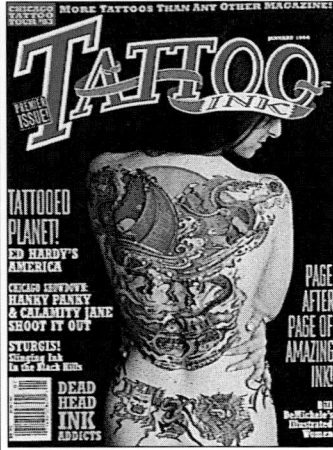

Tattoo Ink

Published by:

Harris Publications Inc.

1115 Broadway, 8th Floor

New York NY 10010

Date: January 1994

Frequency: Bimonthly

Cover Price: $4.95

Subscription Price: n/a

Discount Subscription Price: n/a

Total Number of Pages: 100

Total Number of Ad Pages: 4

Publisher: Stanley R. Harris

Editor: Jane Ryan Beck

Editorial Concept: "To celebrate the eclectic lifestyles of tattooed peoples."

Tattoo Savage

Published by:

Paisano Publications Inc.

28210 Dorothy Drive

Agoura Hills CA 91301

Date: 1994

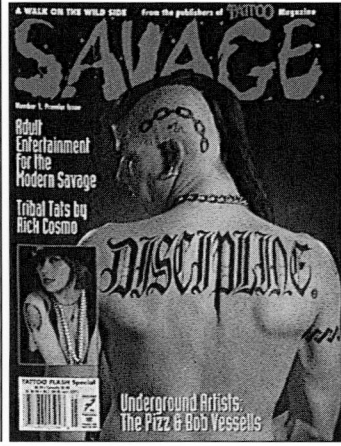

Frequency: Quarterly

Cover Price: $4.95

Subscription Price: $13.95

Discount Subscription Price: n/a

Total Number of Pages: 96

Total Number of Ad Pages: 15

Publisher: Joe Teriss

Editor: Phantom

Editorial Concept: "Radical tattoos and body piercing for those who walk on the wild side."

Tattoo World

Published by:

Butterfly Publications Ltd.

462 Broadway, 4th Floor

New York NY 10013

Date: 1994

Frequency: Quarterly

Cover Price: $5.99

Subscription Price: $19.95

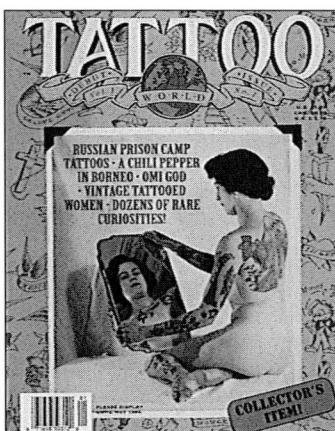

Discount Subscription Price: n/a

Total Number of Pages: 100

Total Number of Ad Pages: 0

Publisher: Jason Childs

Editor: P.J. Reshen

Editorial Concept: Intricate and unique tattoos from around the world.

3rd Word

Published by:

Third Word Publishing Inc.

25 E. Delaware, Suite 205

Chicago IL 60611

Date: 1994

Frequency: Bimonthly

Cover Price: $3.00

Subscription Price: $15.00

Discount Subscription Price: n/a

Total Number of Pages: 68

Total Number of Ad Pages: 18

Publisher: Penelope Larson-Hillman

Editor: Brendan Baber

Editorial Concept: "Arts in Chicago."

World Art

Published by:

G&B Arts International Ltd.

Two Gateway Center

Newark NJ 07102-0301

Date: November 1994

Frequency: Quarterly

Cover Price: $7.00

Subscription Price: $21.00

Discount Subscription Price: n/a

Total Number of Pages: 124

Total Number of Ad Pages: 25

Publisher: Ashley Crawford

Editor: Ray Edgar & Sarah Bayliss

Editorial Concept: "The magazine of contemporary visual arts."

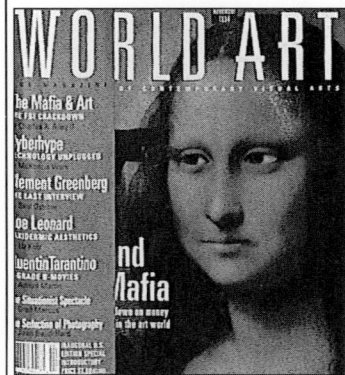

The Artist's Magazine Guide to Getting Started in Art

Published by:
F&W Publications Inc.
1507 Dana Ave.
Cincinnati OH 45207
Date: 1994
Frequency: Special
Cover Price: $3.95
Subscription Price: n/a
Discount Subscription Price: n/a
Total Number of Pages: 92
Total Number of Ad Pages: 18
Publisher: Jeffrey M. Lapin
Editor: Michael Ward

Editorial Concept: Ideas to help you unleash your own special creativity in drawing and painting.

Drawing Highlights

Published by:
BPI Communications
1515 Broadway
New York NY 10036
Date: 1994
Frequency: Special
Cover Price: $6.95
Subscription Price: n/a
Discount Subscription Price: n/a
Total Number of Pages: 180
Total Number of Ad Pages: 9

Publisher: Don Frost
Editor: M. Stephen Doherty
Editorial Concept: Techniques for drawing people, still-lifes, etc., in a variety of styles.

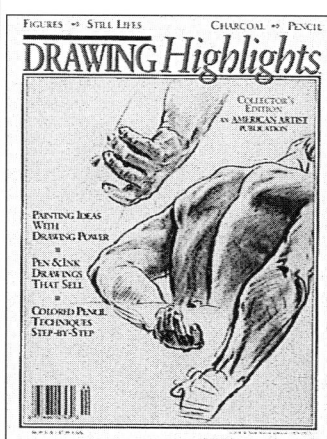

Sex Tattoos & Rock 'n' Roll

Published by:
Butterfly Publications Ltd.
462 Broadway, 4th Floor
New York NY 10013
Date: 1994
Frequency: n/a
Cover Price: $4.99
Subscription Price: n/a
Discount Subscription Price: n/a
Total Number of Pages: 100
Total Number of Ad Pages: 0
Publisher: Jason Childs
Editor: Chris Pfouts
Editorial Concept: "Two of the world's most expressive art mediums (rock and tattoos) together at last."

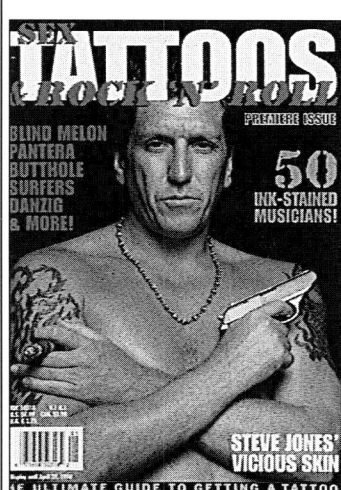

Skin Art Presents Tattoo World

Published by:
Outlaw Biker Enterprises Inc.
450 Seventh Ave., Suite 2305
New York NY 10123
Date: 1994
Frequency: Special
Cover Price: $4.99
Subscription Price: n/a
Discount Subscription Price: n/a
Total Number of Pages: 84
Total Number of Ad Pages: 27
Publisher: Casey Exton
Editor: n/a
Editorial Concept: "Greatest collection of international ink ever assembled."

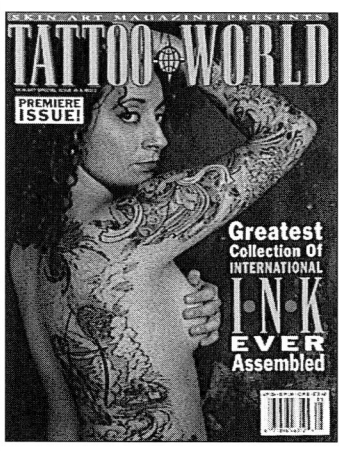

Tattoo Tour Philadelphia

Published by:
Outlaw Biker Enterprises Inc.
450 Seventh Ave., Suite 2305
New York NY 10123
Date: 1994
Frequency: Special
Cover Price: $4.99
Subscription Price: n/a
Discount Subscription Price: n/a
Total Number of Pages: 68
Total Number of Ad Pages: 22
Publisher: Casey Exton
Editor: Roy Sundance
Editorial Concept: "The only tattoo mag devoted totally to tour convention coverage."

Astro Signs Digest

Published by:

JMT Publications Inc.

350 Theodore Frend Ave.

Rye NY 10580

Date: April 1994

Frequency: Bimonthly

Cover Price: $1.95

Subscription Price: $8.36

Discount Subscription Price: n/a

Total Number of Pages: 64

Total Number of Ad Pages: 4

Publisher: Joshua Tabach

Editor: Rochelle Gordon

Editorial Concept: "Jam-packed with accurate horoscopes for two months in an easy-to-understand format."

Annual, Special or Frequency Unknown

Arlene Dahl's Spring Horoscope

Published by:

National Enquirer Inc.

Lantana FL 33464

Date: Spring 1994

Frequency: Special

Cover Price: $2.50

Subscription Price: n/a

Discount Subscription Price: n/a

Total Number of Pages: 76

Total Number of Ad Pages: 8

Publisher: National Enquirer Inc.

Editor: Mike Nevard

Editorial Concept: Horoscopes and Zodiac profiles, with a special emphasis on celebrities.

5.0 Mustang

Published by:

Petersen Publishing Company

6420 Wilshire Blvd.

Los Angeles CA 90048

Date: June 1994

Frequency: Bimonthly

Cover Price: $2.95

Subscription Price: $13.95

Discount Subscription Price: $11.95

Total Number of Pages: 100

Total Number of Ad Pages: 34

Publisher: John Dianna

Editor: Jerry Pitt

Editorial Concept: Technical tips on getting the most speed from your modern-era Mustang.

Black Streets Magazine

Published by:

Black Streets Magazine

P.O. Box 5593

Long Beach CA 90805

Date: Spring 1994

Frequency: Monthly

Cover Price: $3.50

Subscription Price: $32.00

Discount Subscription Price: n/a

Total Number of Pages: 40

Total Number of Ad Pages: 7

Publisher: Gregory Alan Pittman

Editor: Charles Dean

Editorial Concept: An automotive magazine geared toward fans of customized vehicles.

Custom & Classic Trucks

Published by:

Petersen Publishing Company

6420 Wilshire Blvd.

Los Angeles CA 90048

Date: April 1994

Frequency: Bimonthly

Cover Price: $3.95

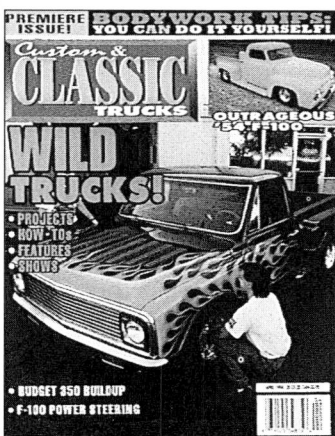

Subscription Price: $13.95

Discount Subscription Price: $11.95

Total Number of Pages: 80

Total Number of Ad Pages: 19

Publisher: John Dianna

Editor: Bob Carpenter

Editorial Concept: "Devoted to the fast-growing segment of the truck market that is interested in older, American-made pickups."

Drag Racing & Hi Performance Illustrated

Published by:

Rosecrans Corporation

8621 Wilshire Blvd., Suite 131

Beverly Hills CA 90211

Date: January/February 1994

Frequency: Bimonthly

Cover Price: $2.95

Subscription Price: $13.95

Discount Subscription Price: n/a

Total Number of Pages: 92

Total Number of Ad Pages: 15

Publisher: Rosecrans Corporation

Editor: James Preston Scroggs

Editorial Concept: The people and machines of pro drag racing.

Electric Car

Published by:

Argus Publishers Corporation

12100 Wilshire Blvd.

Los Angeles CA 90025

Date: Winter 1994

Frequency: Quarterly

Cover Price: $3.95

Subscription Price: $15.00

Discount Subscription Price: n/a

Total Number of Pages: 84

Total Number of Ad Pages: 0

Publisher: Martha Doyle

Editor: Greg N. Brown

Editorial Concept: "To bring you the continuing saga of this exciting technology."

Electrifying Times

Published by:

Electrifying Times

63600 Deschutes Market Road

Bend OR 97701

Date: Summer/Fall 1994

Frequency: 3/year

Cover Price: $2.75

Subscription Price: $8.00

Discount Subscription Price: n/a

Total Number of Pages: 32

Total Number of Ad Pages: 10

Publisher: Electrifying Times

Editor: n/a

Editorial Concept: "Nationwide coverage of solar and electric car racing, rally events, latest battery technology, and company profiles."

Eurosport Car

Published by:

McMullen and Yee Publishing Inc.

774 S. Placentia Ave.

Placentia CA 92670

Date: Winter 1994

Frequency: Quarterly

Cover Price: $3.25

Subscription Price: n/a

Discount Subscription Price: n/a

Total Number of Pages: 96

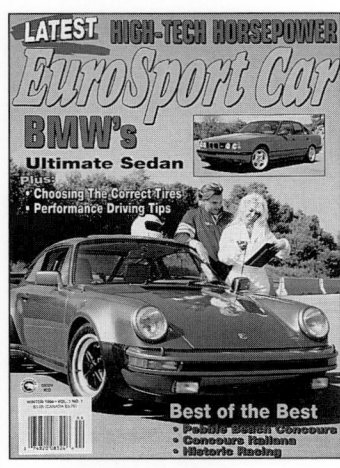

Total Number of Ad Pages: 13
Publisher: McMullen and Yee
Editor: Alan Paradise
Editorial Concept: "Articles that are easy to follow, informative, and entertaining."

Popular Mechanics CarSmart

Published by:
The Hearst Corporation
959 Eighth Ave.
New York NY 10019

Date: December 1994
Frequency: n/a
Cover Price: $2.95
Subscription Price: n/a
Discount Subscription Price: n/a
Total Number of Pages: 150
Total Number of Ad Pages: 27
Publisher: Robert B. Dillingham
Editor: Joe Oldham
Editorial Concept: "The information source for auto consumers."

Power Wagon & Sport Utes

Published by:
RHO Publications
1580 Hampton Road
Bensalem PA 19020-4610
Date: Spring/Summer 1994
Frequency: Semi-annually
Cover Price: $3.50
Subscription Price: $5.00
Discount Subscription Price: n/a
Total Number of Pages: 68
Total Number of Ad Pages: 17

Publisher: RHO Publications
Editor: Robert Oskiera
Editorial Concept: For the Dodge truck and jeep enthusiast.

Tex Smith's Hot Rod Mechanix

Published by:
CSK Publishing Company Inc.
299 Market St.
Saddle Brook NJ 07662
Date: May 1994
Frequency: Bimonthly
Cover Price: $3.25
Subscription Price: $15.95
Discount Subscription Price: n/a
Total Number of Pages: 84
Total Number of Ad Pages: 16
Publisher: Ralph Monti
Editor: Ron Ceridono
Editorial Concept: "Crammed with vital information for hard-core hot rodders."

V8 Power

Published by:
Speedco
9952 Hamilton Ave.
Huntington Beach CA 92646
Date: Spring 1994
Frequency: Quarterly
Cover Price: $3.95
Subscription Price: $9.99
Discount Subscription Price: n/a
Total Number of Pages: 116
Total Number of Ad Pages: 17
Publisher: Kipp Kington
Editor: Evan Griffey
Editorial Concept: Photos and stories about big-engine cars and trucks.

Annual, Special or Frequency Unknown

1994 Buyer's Guide to Electric Vehicles

Published by:
Spirit Publications

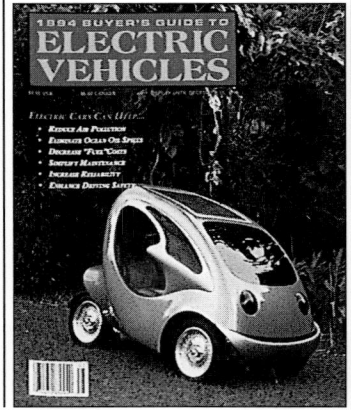

P.O. Box 7093
Kamuela HI 96743
Date: 1994
Frequency: Annual
Cover Price: $4.95
Subscription Price: n/a
Discount Subscription Price: n/a
Total Number of Pages: 36
Total Number of Ad Pages: 5
Publisher: Philip Terpstra
Editor: Gerard Terpstra
Editorial Concept: Provides up-to-date information on electric vehicles and related supplies.

30 Years of Mustang

Published by:
Petersen Publishing Company
6420 Wilshire Blvd.
Los Angeles CA 90048
Date: 1994
Frequency: Special

Cover Price: $3.95
Subscription Price: n/a
Discount Subscription Price: n/a
Total Number of Pages: 102
Total Number of Ad Pages: 8
Publisher: John Dianna
Editor: Jerry Pitt
Editorial Concept: The complete story of one of America's favorite sports cars.

4-Wheel Tech, Tips & How-Tos

Published by:
Petersen Publishing Company

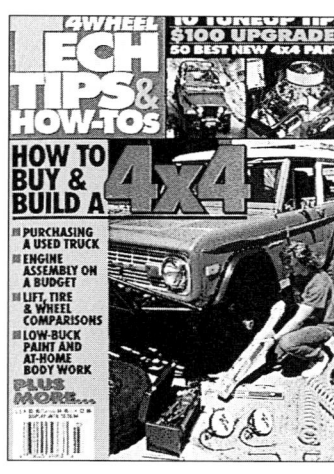

6420 Wilshire Blvd.

Los Angeles CA 90048

Date: 1994

Frequency: Special

Cover Price: $3.95

Subscription Price: n/a

Discount Subscription Price: n/a

Total Number of Pages: 100

Total Number of Ad Pages: 8

Publisher: John Dianna

Editor: Mathew Pearson

Editorial Concept: How to buy and build a 4x4.

Cars & Parts Corvette

Published by:

Amos Press Inc.

911 Vandemark Road

Sidney OH 45365

Date: Spring 1994

Frequency: n/a

Cover Price: $4.95

Subscription Price: n/a

Discount Subscription Price: n/a

Total Number of Pages: 116

Total Number of Ad Pages: 20

Publisher: Walter Reed

Editor: Robert J. Stevens

Editorial Concept: "Covering the entire Corvette scene."

Classic Chevy Builders' Guide

Published by:

Petersen Publishing Company

6420 Wilshire Blvd.

Los Angeles CA 90048

Date: 1994

Frequency: Special

Cover Price: $4.95

Subscription Price: n/a

Discount Subscription Price: n/a

Total Number of Pages: 148

Total Number of Ad Pages: 23

Publisher: John Dianna

Editor: Chuck Lombardo Sr.

Editorial Concept: How to build '55-'57 classic Chevys.

Corvette Classics

Published by:

Starlog Telecommunications Inc.

475 Park Ave. South

New York NY 10016

Date: 1994

Frequency: Special

Cover Price: $6.95

Subscription Price: n/a

Discount Subscription Price: n/a

Total Number of Pages: 84

Total Number of Ad Pages: 6

Publisher: Norman Jacobs

Editor: Michael Benson

Editorial Concept: "Corvette anniversary special. Five decades! Four fantastic foldouts! Eighty-two pages of great color photos!"

Hot Mustangs!

Published by:

CSK Publishing Company Inc.

299 Market St.

Saddle Brook NJ 07662

Date: 1994

Frequency: Annually

Cover Price: $4.50

Subscription Price: n/a

Discount Subscription Price: n/a

Total Number of Pages: 92

Total Number of Ad Pages: 54

Publisher: Ralph Monti

Editor: Jim Campisano

Editorial Concept: Customizing your Mustang for the most street and drag appeal.

Hot Rod Bodywork & Painting

Published by:

Petersen Publishing Company

6420 Wilshire Blvd.

Los Angeles CA 90048

Date: 1994

Frequency: Special

Cover Price: $3.95

Subscription Price: n/a

Discount Subscription Price: n/a

Total Number of Pages: 100

Total Number of Ad Pages: 9

Publisher: John Dianna

Editor: Tara Baukus

Editorial Concept: How to make your hot rod the best looking machine on the street.

Hot Rod Camaros

Published by:

Petersen Publishing Company

6420 Wilshire Blvd.

Los Angeles CA 90048

Date: 1994

Frequency: Special

Cover Price: $3.95

Subscription Price: n/a

Discount Subscription Price: n/a

Total Number of Pages: 100

Total Number of Ad Pages: 21

Publisher: John Dianna

Editor: David Freiburger

Editorial Concept: How to build the ultimate hot rod racing Camaro, both classic and late-model.

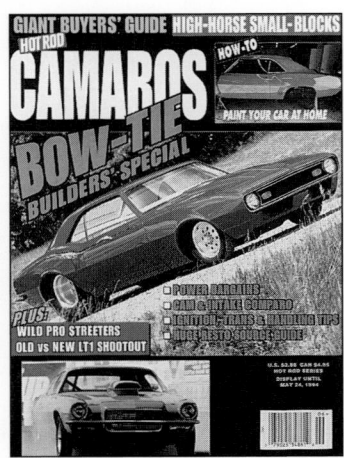

Hot Rod High Performance Buyer's Guide

Published by:

Petersen Publishing Company

6420 Wilshire Blvd.

Los Angeles CA 90048

Date: 1994

Frequency: Special

Cover Price: $3.95

Subscription Price: n/a

Discount Subscription Price: n/a

Total Number of Pages: 100

Total Number of Ad Pages: 11

Publisher: John Dianna

Editor: Karin Smith

Editorial Concept: Selecting, ordering, and using the right parts for your hot rod.

Hot Rod Hot Chevys

Published by:

Petersen Publishing Company

6420 Wilshire Blvd.

Los Angeles CA 90048-5515

Date: 1994

Frequency: Special

Cover Price: $3.95

Subscription Price: n/a

Discount Subscription Price: n/a

Total Number of Pages: 100

Total Number of Ad Pages: 14

Publisher: John Dianna

Editor: David Freiburger

Editorial Concept: Tips for purchasing a Chevy hot rod.

Hot Rod How-Tos

Published by:

Challenge Publications Inc.

7950 Deering Ave.

Canoga Park CA 91304

Date: 1994

Frequency: Special

Cover Price: $4.95

Subscription Price: n/a

Discount Subscription Price: n/a

Total Number of Pages: 96

Total Number of Ad Pages: 12

Publisher: Edwin A. Schnepf

Editor: Jon Gobetti

Editorial Concept: Tips on building a hot rod from the ground up.

Hot Rod Junior

Published by:

Petersen Publishing Company

6420 Wilshire Blvd.

Los Angeles CA 90048

Date: 1994

Frequency: Special

Cover Price: $2.95

Subscription Price: n/a

Discount Subscription Price: n/a

Total Number of Pages: 100

Total Number of Ad Pages: 8

Publisher: John Dianna

Editor: Randy Lorentzen

Editorial Concept: A magazine about hot rod cars, go-carts, and models designed to introduce younger readers to hot-rodding.

How to Build a 4x4

Published by:

Petersen Publishing Company

6420 Wilshire Blvd.

Los Angeles CA 90048

Date: 1994

Frequency: Special

Cover Price: $4.95

Subscription Price: n/a

Discount Subscription Price: n/a

Total Number of Pages: 148

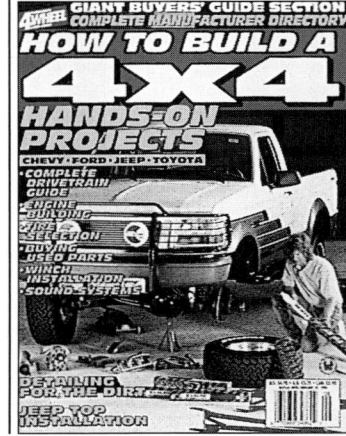

Total Number of Ad Pages: 23

Publisher: John Dianna

Editor: Tom Madigan

Editorial Concept: Tips, ideas, and parts to build a monster truck.

How to Build a Budget Street Machine

Published by:

Petersen Publishing Company

6420 Wilshire Blvd.

Los Angeles CA 90048

Date: 1994

Frequency: Special

Cover Price: $3.95

Subscription Price: n/a

Discount Subscription Price: n/a

Total Number of Pages: 100

Total Number of Ad Pages: 9

Publisher: John Dianna

Editor: Cole Quinnell

Editorial Concept: How to build a mean hot rod on the cheap.

How to Build Your First Race Car

Published by:

Petersen Publishing Company

6420 Wilshire Blvd.

Los Angeles CA 90048

Date: 1994

Frequency: Special

Cover Price: $3.95

Subscription Price: n/a

Discount Subscription Price: n/a

Total Number of Pages: 100

Total Number of Ad Pages: 16

Publisher: John Dianna

Editor: Bob Carpenter

Editorial Concept: Strategies, tools, and parts to make a speed demon suitable for the track.

Mopar Tech Special

Published by:

Harris Publications Inc.

1115 Broadway Inc.

New York NY 10010

Date: 1994

Frequency: Special

Cover Price: $3.50

Subscription Price: n/a

Discount Subscription Price: n/a

Total Number of Pages: 84

Total Number of Ad Pages: 26

Publisher: Stanley R. Harris

Editor: Richard Ehrenberg

Editorial Concept: "The best low-buck step-by-step how-tos and performance tips for racers, restorers, and enthusiasts."

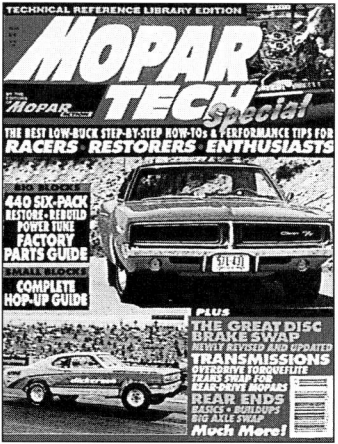

Mustang Milestones

Published by:

Trader Publishing Company

P.O. Box 9059

Clearwater FL 34618

Date: 1994

Frequency: Special

Cover Price: $3.95

Subscription Price: n/a

Discount Subscription Price: n/a

Total Number of Pages: 92

Total Number of Ad Pages: 19

Publisher: Trader Publishing

Editor: Jason Scott

Editorial Concept: "Thirty years with America's original pony car."

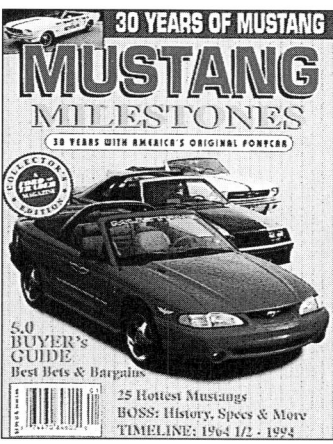

Road & Track Specials: Guide to the New 1994 Ford Mustang

Published by:

Hachette Filipacchi Magazines Inc.

1633 Broadway

New York NY 10019

Date: 1994

Frequency: Special

Cover Price: $5.95

Subscription Price: n/a

Discount Subscription Price: n/a

Total Number of Pages: 84

Total Number of Ad Pages: 3

Publisher: Daniel Filipacchi

Editor: Ron Sessions

Editorial Concept: Photos and technical info on the Ford sports car.

Sport-Utility Vehicles, Vans, and Pickups 1995 Buyer's Guide

Published by:

Sports Mirror Publications Inc.

6 W. 18th St.

New York NY 10011

Date: 1994

Frequency: Annually

Cover Price: $4.95

Subscription Price: n/a

Discount Subscription Price: n/a

Total Number of Pages: 100

Total Number of Ad Pages: 0

Publisher: Gerald Rothberg

Editor: Alan Paul

Editorial Concept: A complete guide to the sizzling new models.

Stock Car Spectacular Presents Nascar's Greatest Races

Published by:

Starlog Communications

475 Park Ave. South

New York NY 10016

Date: 1994

Frequency: Special

Cover Price: $5.95

Subscription Price: n/a

Discount Subscription Price: n/a

Total Number of Pages: 68

Total Number of Ad Pages: 7

Publisher: Norman Jacobs

Editor: Michael Benson

Editorial Concept: "Most exciting action in stock car history!"

Test Drive

Published by:

The Publications Company

422 W. Congress

Detroit MI 48226

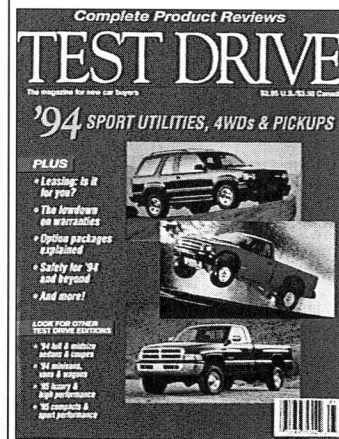

Date: 1994

Frequency: Special

Cover Price: $2.95

Subscription Price: n/a

Discount Subscription Price: n/a

Total Number of Pages: 68

Total Number of Ad Pages: 9

Publisher: John W. Tripp

Editor: Jane Ryan

Editorial Concept: Test reports on new vehicles and buying tips.

Airways

Published by:

Keokee Publishing

311 N. Second Ave.

Sandpoint ID 83864

Date: March/April 1994

Frequency: Bimonthly

Cover Price: $3.95

Subscription Price: $19.95

Discount Subscription Price: n/a

Total Number of Pages: 68

Total Number of Ad Pages: 20

Publisher: John Wegg

Editor: John Wegg

Editorial Concept: A global review of commercial flight.

Annual, Special or Frequency Unknown

Affordable Ultralights

Published by:

Challenge Publications Inc.

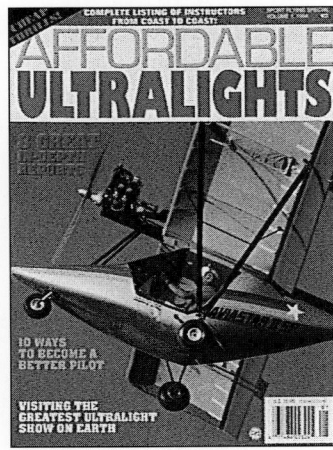

7950 Deering Ave.

Canoga Park CA 91304

Date: 1994

Frequency: Special

Cover Price: $5.95

Subscription Price: n/a

Discount Subscription Price: n/a

Total Number of Pages: 96

Total Number of Ad Pages: 8

Publisher: Edwin A. Schnepf

Editor: Norm Goyer

Editorial Concept: The thrill of flying low-cost personal aircraft.

Golden Age Biplanes

Published by:

Challenge Publications Inc.

7950 Deering Ave.

Canoga Park CA 91304

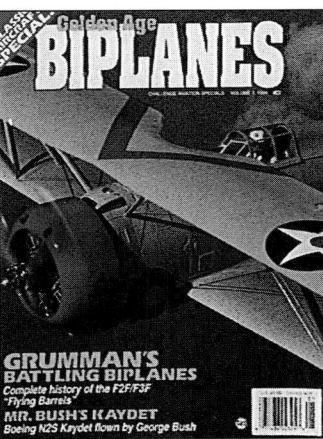

Date: 1994

Frequency: Special

Cover Price: $5.95

Subscription Price: n/a

Discount Subscription Price: n/a

Total Number of Pages: 96

Total Number of Ad Pages: 7

Publisher: Edwin A. Schnepf

Editor: Michael O'Leary

Editorial Concept: Stories and pictures of classic biplanes for the restoration or aviation enthusiast.

Lightning

Published by:

Challenge Publications Inc.

7950 Deering Ave.

Canoga Park CA 91304

Date: 1994

Frequency: Special

Cover Price: $5.95

Subscription Price: n/a

Discount Subscription Price: n/a

Total Number of Pages: 88

Total Number of Ad Pages: 7

Publisher: Edwin A. Schnepf

Editor: Michael O'Leary

Editorial Concept: The history and exploits of the Lockheed YP bomber.

Nose Art

Published by:

Challenge Publications Inc.

7950 Deering Ave.

Canoga Park CA 91304

Date: 1994

Frequency: Special

Cover Price: $5.95

Subscription Price: n/a

Discount Subscription Price: n/a

Total Number of Pages: 96

Total Number of Ad Pages: 9

Publisher: Edwin A. Schnepf

Editor: Michael O'Leary

Editorial Concept: Photos and stories about the pin-up art that adorned vintage fighter planes.

Sport Flying Special: Those Amazing Cub Clones

Published by:

Challenge Publications Inc.

7950 Deering Ave.

Canoga Park CA 91304

Date: 1994

Frequency: Special

Cover Price: $5.95

Subscription Price: n/a

Discount Subscription Price: n/a

Total Number of Pages: 96

Total Number of Ad Pages: 10

Publisher: Edwin A. Schnepf

Editor: Norm Goyer

Editorial Concept: Photos and articles on the Piper Cub.

Ten Best Affordable Aircraft

Published by:

Challenge Publications Inc.

7950 Deering Ave.

Canoga Park CA 91304

Date: 1994

Frequency: Special

Cover Price: $5.95

Subscription Price: n/a

Discount Subscription Price: n/a

Total Number of Pages: 96

Total Number of Ad Pages: 6

Publisher: Edwin A. Schnepf

Editor: Norm Goyer

Editorial Concept: Articles on small, affordable aircraft for the prospective buyer.

Warbirds '94

Published by:

Challenge Publications Inc.

7950 Deering Ave.

Canoga Park CA 91304

Date: 1994

Frequency: Special

Cover Price: $5.95

Subscription Price: n/a

Discount Subscription Price: n/a

Total Number of Pages: 96

Total Number of Ad Pages: 6

Publisher: Edwin A. Schnepf

Editor: Edwin A. Schnepf

Editorial Concept: Guide to more

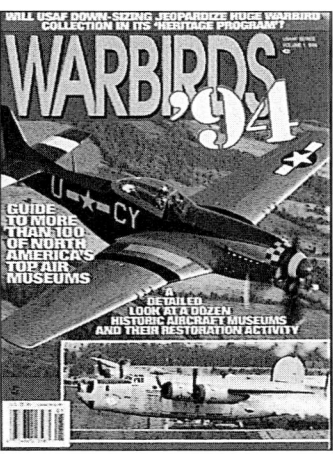

than 100 of North America's top air museums.

Warplanes of the Skunk Works

Published by:

Challenge Publications Inc.

7950 Deering Ave.

Canoga Park CA 91304

Date: 1994

Frequency: Special

Cover Price: $5.95

Subscription Price: n/a

Discount Subscription Price: n/a

Total Number of Pages: 88

Total Number of Ad Pages: 5

Publisher: Edwin A. Schnepf

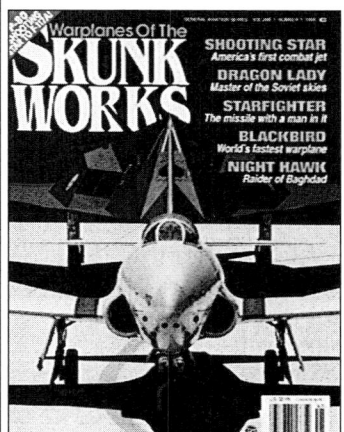

Editor: Michael O'Leary

Editorial Concept: The history and impact of cutting-edge aircraft produced by the famed Lockheed unit.

Wings That Won the War

Published by:

Challenge Publications Inc.

7950 Deering Ave.

Canoga Park CA 91304

Date: 1994

Frequency: Special

Cover Price: $5.95

Subscription Price: n/a

Discount Subscription Price: n/a

Total Number of Pages: 88

Total Number of Ad Pages: 4

Publisher: Edwin A. Schnepf

Editor: Michael O'Leary

Editorial Concept: How America built the world's greatest air force for WWII.

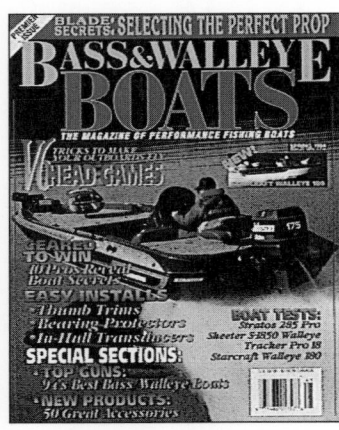

Bass & Walleye Boats

Published by:

Poole Publications

20700 Belshaw Ave.

Carson CA 90746

Date: Spring 1994

Frequency: Quarterly

Cover Price: $2.95

Subscription Price: $9.97

Discount Subscription Price: n/a

Total Number of Pages: 116

Total Number of Ad Pages: 32

Publisher: Wiley Poole

Editor: Bruce W. Smith

Editorial Concept: The magazine of performance fishing boats.

Porthole

Published by:

Panoff Publishing Inc.

10 Fairway Drive, Suite 200

Deerfield Beach FL 33441

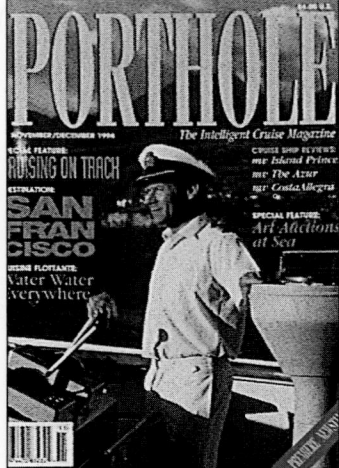

Date: November/December 1994

Frequency: Bimonthly

Cover Price: $6.00

Subscription Price: $35.00

Discount Subscription Price: n/a

Total Number of Pages: 74

Total Number of Ad Pages: 23

Publisher: William Panoff and Douglas Ward

Editor: Douglas Ward

Editorial Concept: News and reviews of luxury travel by cruise ship.

WoodenBoat Magazine's Beautiful Boats

Published by:

WoodenBoat Inc.

P.O. Box 78

Brooklin ME 04616

Date: 1994

Frequency: Special

Cover Price: $5.95

Subscription Price: n/a

Discount Subscription Price: n/a

Total Number of Pages: 168

Total Number of Ad Pages: 18

Publisher: Carl Cramer

Editor: n/a

Editorial Concept: A collection of 20 past pieces from the last 20 years of *WoodenBoat Magazine*.

The Complete Guide to Kayak Touring

Published by:

Canoe American Associates

P.O. Box 3146

Kirkland WA 98083

Date: Spring 1994

Frequency: Special

Cover Price: $3.95

Subscription Price: n/a

Discount Subscription Price: n/a

Total Number of Pages: 84

Total Number of Ad Pages: 30

Publisher: David F. Harrison and Judy C. Harrison

Editor: Nancy Harrison

Editorial Concept: A reference guide to over 40 great spots for kayaking.

Chicago Bride

Published by:

Chicago Bride Inc.

322 South Green St., Suite 406

Chicago IL 60607

Date: 1994

Frequency: Quarterly

Cover Price: $3.95

Subscription Price: $14.00

Discount Subscription Price: n/a

Total Number of Pages: 116

Total Number of Ad Pages: 35

Publisher: Greg Moga

Editor: Sara Sullivan

Editorial Concept: "For brides and grooms in Chicago who want the best of everything for their wedding."

Cincinnati Wedding

Published by:

Marblehead Publications Inc.

P.O. Box 868

Cincinnati OH 45201

Date: Spring/Summer 1994

Frequency: Semiannually

Cover Price: $4.50

Subscription Price: $11.95

Discount Subscription Price: n/a

Total Number of Pages: 108

Total Number of Ad Pages: 31

Publisher: Doug Wolske

Editor: Nita Rollins

Editorial Concept: To help Cincinnati area brides and their families plan a successful wedding.

Annual, Special or Frequency Unknown

Best Weddings Magazine

Published by:

Zentra Publishing Corporation

P.O. Box 7443

Fairfax Station VA 22039

Date: Fall 1994

Frequency: n/a

Cover Price: $3.95

Subscription Price: n/a

Discount Subscription Price: n/a

Total Number of Pages: 146

Total Number of Ad Pages: 107

Publisher: Evan McConnell and Peggi McConnell

Editor: Peggi McConnell

Editorial Concept: An advertising-heavy guide to wedding fashion.

Mid-South Bride

Published by:

MM Corporation

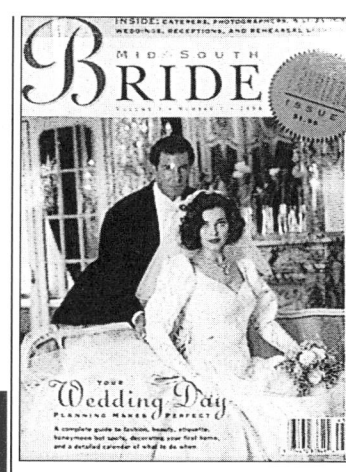

460 Tennessee St.

Memphis TN 38101

Date: 1994

Frequency: Annually

Cover Price: $1.95

Subscription Price: n/a

Discount Subscription Price: n/a

Total Number of Pages: 84

Total Number of Ad Pages: 36

Publisher: Kenneth Neill

Editor: Tim Sampson

Editorial Concept: "A complete guide to making your wedding day perfect."

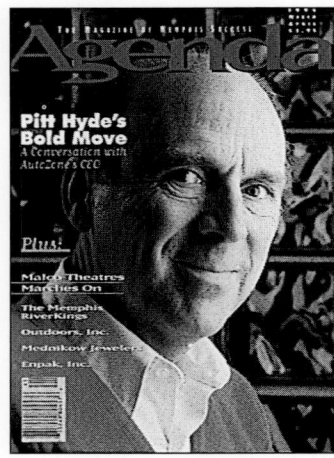

Agenda

Published by:

Towery Publishing Inc.

1835 Union Ave.

Memphis TN 38104

Date: March/April 1994

Frequency: Bimonthly

Cover Price: $1.95

Subscription Price: n/a

Discount Subscription Price: n/a

Total Number of Pages: 44

Total Number of Ad Pages: 18

Publisher: J. Robert Towery

Editor: David Dawson

Editorial Concept: A positive look at Memphis business and business leaders.

Cash Saver

Published by:

HG Publications Inc.

9171 Wilshire Blvd., Suite 300

Beverly Hills CA 90210

Date: January 1994

Frequency: Bimonthly

Cover Price: $2.95

Subscription Price: $9.95

Discount Subscription Price: n/a

Total Number of Pages: 80

Total Number of Ad Pages: 8

Publisher: Larry Flynt

Editor: Michael Goldstein

Editorial Concept: A guide to saving big and having fun doing it.

Electronic Retailing

Published by:

Creative Age Publications Inc.

7628 Densmore Ave.

Van Nuys CA 91406

Date: May 1994

Frequency: Monthly

Cover Price: $5.00

Subscription Price: $44.95

Discount Subscription Price: $22.48

Total Number of Pages: 72

Total Number of Ad Pages: 26

Publisher: Deborah Carver

Editor: Kathy St. Louis

Editorial Concept: New marketing opportunities in direct response TV, infomercials, interactive TV, on-line services, and cable.

Financial Trader

Published by:

Miller Freeman Inc.

600 Harrison St.

San Francisco CA 94107

Date: February/March 1994

Frequency: Bimonthly

Cover Price: $4.95

Subscription Price: $38.00

Discount Subscription Price: $19.95

Total Number of Pages: 40

Total Number of Ad Pages: 11

Publisher: Annie Feldman

Editor: Ivy Schmerken

Editorial Concept: Financial strategies for global trading.

Free Trade News

Published by:

RPM Sales Corporation

No address given

Date: 1994

Frequency: Monthly

Cover Price: $2.00

Subscription Price: $20.00

Discount Subscription Price: n/a

Total Number of Pages: 24

Total Number of Ad Pages: 3

Publisher: RPM Sales Corporation

Editor: Fernando Prado

Editorial Concept: NAFTA-related information updates.

Global Competitor

Published by:

Faulkner & Gray Inc.

Eleven Penn Plaza

New York NY 10001

Date: Winter 1994

Frequency: Quarterly

Cover Price: Subscription only

Subscription Price: $99.00

Discount Subscription Price: n/a

Total Number of Pages: 84

Total Number of Ad Pages: 12

Publisher: Faulkner & Gray Inc.

Editor: Joseph A. Massey and Arpad Von Lazar

Editorial Concept: "To be genuinely useful to the corporate executive trying to navigate the treacherous waters of today's international business."

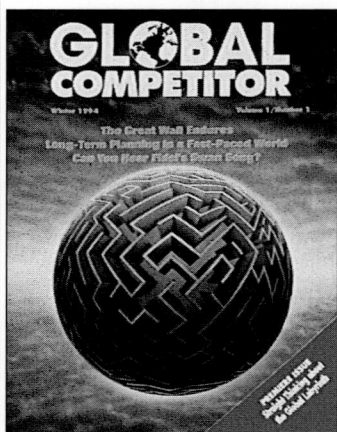

Inc. Technology

Published by:

James J. Spanfeller

488 Madison Ave.

New York NY 10022

Date: 1994

Frequency: Quarterly

Cover Price: $3.00

Subscription Price: n/a

Discount Subscription Price: n/a

Total Number of Pages: 144

Total Number of Ad Pages: 88

Publisher: James J. Spanfeller

Editor: Jeffrey L. Seglin

Editorial Concept: "To provide technology-based ideas and solutions you can apply to your own company."

Information Week

Published by:

CMP Publications Inc.

600 Community Drive

Manhasset NY 11030

Date: May 9, 1994 *(first newsstand issue)*

Frequency: Weekly

Cover Price: $2.95

Subscription Price: $63.95

Discount Subscription Price: $47.95

Total Number of Pages: 104

Total Number of Ad Pages: 56

Publisher: Rebecca S. Barna

Editor: Joel Dreyfuss

Editorial Concept: All the latest in computer news for business and technology managers.

International Businesswoman

Published by:

International Businesswoman Inc.

2049 Calumet Street

Clearwater FL 34625

Date: 1994

Frequency: 5/year

Cover Price: $4.95

Subscription Price: $17.97

Discount Subscription Price: n/a

Total Number of Pages: 156

Total Number of Ad Pages: 42

Publisher: Helen Quin

Editor: Nancy Conrad

Editorial Concept: Business from a woman's perspective.

Japan Related

Published by:

Mangajin Inc.

200 N. Cobb Parkway, Suite 421

Marietta GA 30062

Date: September/October 1994 *(first newsstand issue)*

Frequency: Bimonthly

Cover Price: $4.50

Subscription Price: $25.00

Discount Subscription Price: n/a

Total Number of Pages: 52

Total Number of Ad Pages: 9

Publisher: Vaughn P. Simmons

Editor: Steve Leeper and Elizabeth Baldwin

Editorial Concept: A business-focused magazine on Japanese-American relations.

Marketing Tools

Published by:

American Demographics Inc.

127 W. State St.

Ithaca NY 14850

Date: July/August 1994

Frequency: Bimonthly

Cover Price: $5.00

Subscription Price: $54.00

Discount Subscription Price: $27.00

Total Number of Pages: 80

Total Number of Ad Pages: 29

Publisher: Michelle C. DeChant

Editor: Claudia Montague

Editorial Concept: Tips for marketing in the information age.

Minority Employment Journal

Published by:

C.L. Lovick & Associates

P.O. Box 45273

Los Angeles CA 90045

Date: Spring 1994

Frequency: Quarterly

Cover Price: $2.95

Subscription Price: $12.00

Discount Subscription Price: n/a

Total Number of Pages: 44

Total Number of Ad Pages: 21

Publisher: Calvin L. Lovick

Editor: Angela Cranon

Editorial Concept: "The magazine for minority and women professionals."

Mutual Funds

Published by:

The Institute for Econometric Research

3471 N. Federal

Fort Lauderdale FL 33306

Date: October/November 1994

Frequency: Bimonthly

Cover Price: $2.50

Subscription Price: $12.47

Discount Subscription Price: $9.97

Total Number of Pages: 126

Total Number of Ad Pages: 49

Publisher: Edward C. Frey

Editor: James R. Hagy

Editorial Concept: "Your monthly guide to America's best investments."

The National Home Employment Directory

Published by:

United Marketing and Research Company

P.O. Box 2712

Huntington Beach CA 92647

Date: 1994

Frequency: Bimonthly

Cover Price: $3.95

Subscription Price: $18.00

Discount Subscription Price: n/a

Total Number of Pages: 94

Total Number of Ad Pages: 15

Publisher: Stacy Henderson

Editor: Stacy Henderson

Editorial Concept: "A complete, up-to-date listing for full and part-time home employment opportunities."

The Quality Observer

Published by:

The Quality Observer Corporation

P.O. Box 1111

Fairfax VA 22030

Date: February 1994

(first newsstand issue)

Frequency: Monthly

Cover Price: $4.95

Subscription Price: $79.00

Discount Subscription Price: n/a

Total Number of Pages: 24

Total Number of Ad Pages: 5

Publisher: Quality Observer Corporation

Editor: Kay Moore

Editorial Concept: How business and industry can ensure quality in their operations

U.S./Latin Trade

Published by:

New World Communications Inc.

One Biscayne Tower

2 South Biscayne Blvd., Suite 2950

Miami FL 33131

Date: June 1994

Frequency: Monthly

Cover Price: $3.95

Subscription Price: $36.00

Discount Subscription Price: n/a

Total Number of Pages: 84

Total Number of Ad Pages: 43

Publisher: Richard N. Roffman

Editor: J.P. Faber

Editorial Concept: "The magazine of trade and investment in the Americas."

Annual, Special or Frequency Unknown

Interview Workbook for Professionals

Published by:

Expert Staffing Solution

180A Hamilton Ave., Suite 708

Palo Alto CA 94301

Date: 1994

Frequency: Special

Cover Price: $5.95

Subscription Price: n/a

Discount Subscription Price: n/a

Total Number of Pages: 100

Total Number of Ad Pages: 1

Publisher: Expert Staffing Solution

Editor: Cory Corman

Editorial Concept: A step-by-step look at how to interview successfully for that dream job.

Kiplinger's Mutual Funds '94

Published by:

The Kiplinger Washington Editors

1729 H St. NW

Washington DC 20006

Date: 1994

Frequency: Special

Cover Price: $4.95

Subscription Price: n/a

Discount Subscription Price: n/a

Total Number of Pages: 136

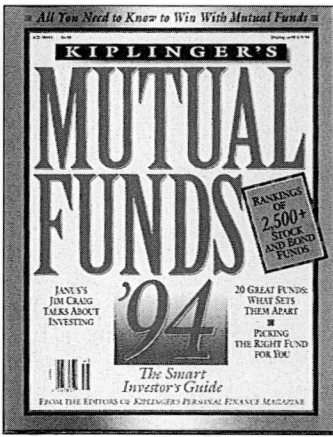

Total Number of Ad Pages: 40

Publisher: Knight A. Kiplinger

Editor: Fred W. Frailey

Editorial Concept: "All you need to know to win with mutual funds."

Babybug

Published by:

Carus Publishing Company

315 Fifth St.

Peru IL 61354

Date: 1994

Frequency: 8/year

Cover Price: $5.00

Subscription Price: $29.97

Discount Subscription Price: n/a

Total Number of Pages: 24

Total Number of Ad Pages: 0

Publisher: Robert W. Harper

Editor: Paula Morrow

Editorial Concept: "The listening and looking magazine for infants and toddlers."

Barney Magazine

Published by:

Welsh Publishing Group

300 Madison Ave.

New York NY 10017

Date: 1994

Frequency: 5/year

Subscription Price: $12.50

Discount Subscription Price: n/a

Total Number of Pages: 64

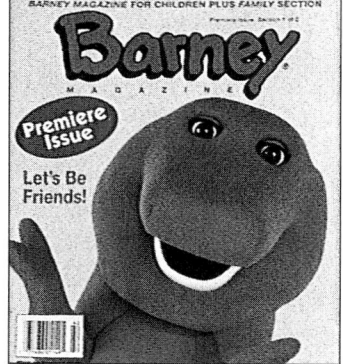

Total Number of Ad Pages: 7

Publisher: Donald E. Welsh

Editor: Margie Larsen

Editorial Concept: A two-part magazine (*Barney Magazine* and *Barney Family Magazine*) designed to help children develop and offer practical advice to parents.

Crayola Kids

Published by:

Meredith Corporation

1912 Grand Ave.

Des Moines IA 5038-3379

Date: April 1994

Frequency: Bimonthly

Cover Price: $2.95

Subscription Price: $19.97

Discount Subscription Price: $14.97

Total Number of Pages: 56

Total Number of Ad Pages: 5

Publisher: Jack Fleisch

Editor: Deborah Gore Ohm

Editorial Concept: Storybooks, crafts, and games to inspire kids to learn.

G.I.R.L.

Published by:

Scholastic Inc.

555 Broadway

New York NY 10012

Date: 1994

Frequency: n/a

Cover Price: $2.50

Subscription Price: n/a

Discount Subscription Price: n/a

Total Number of Pages: 28

Total Number of Ad Pages: 3

and friends and family.

Publisher: Richard K. Delano

Editor: Patricia Levi

Editorial Concept: "Our focus is on the things inside that make you special, like commitment to friends, courage, intelligence, and honor."

Girls' Life

Published by:

Monarch Avalon Inc.

4517 Harford Road

Baltimore MD 21214

Date: August/September 1994

Frequency: Bimonthly

Cover Price: $2.95

Subscription Price: $12.95

Discount Subscription Price: n/a

Total Number of Pages: 76

Total Number of Ad Pages: 10

Publisher: Karen Bokram

Editor: Jean Baer

Editorial Concept: "Treats girls like smart, unique, opinionated, and valuable people," with articles about fashion, sports, reading, horses, the environment,

News Kid

Published by:

Randall Publications

P.O. Box 15563

Beverly Hills CA 90209

Date: January 1994

Frequency: Biweekly

Cover Price: $1.75

Subscription Price: $19.50

Discount Subscription Price: n/a

Total Number of Pages: 12

Total Number of Ad Pages: 0

Publisher: Randall Publications

Editor: Mark R. Lorimer

Editorial Concept: "An educational and entertaining newspaper that informs kids about important events and news."

Outside Kids

Published by:

Mariah Publications Corporation

1165 N. Clark St.

Chicago IL 60610

Date: Spring 1994

Frequency: Quarterly

Cover Price: $1.95

Subscription Price: $9.97

Discount Subscription Price: n/a

Total Number of Pages: 44

Total Number of Ad Pages: 9

Publisher: Mariah Publications

Editor: Lorenzo Burke

Editorial Concept: *Outside*'s magazine for children features articles on rock climbing, street hockey, and animals.

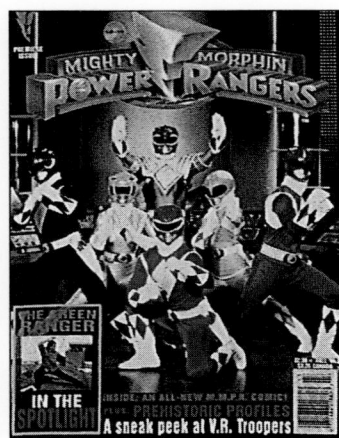

Saban Magazine Mighty Morphin Power Rangers

Published by:

Welsh Publishing Group Inc.

300 Madison Ave.

New York NY 10017

Date: Fall 1994

Frequency: Quarterly

Cover Price: $2.50

Subscription Price: $10.00

Discount Subscription Price: n/a

Total Number of Pages: 36

Total Number of Ad Pages: 13

Publisher: Donald E. Welsh

Editor: Adam Philips

Editorial Concept: "Chock full of great stuff to read and do."

Spider

Published by:

Carus Publishing Company

315 Fifth St.

Peru IL 61354

Date: January 1994

Frequency: Monthly

Cover Price: $3.95

Subscription Price: $29.97

Discount Subscription Price: n/a

Total Number of Pages: 36

Total Number of Ad Pages: 0

Publisher: Robert W. Harper

Editor: Lynn Gutknecht

Editorial Concept: "Specially written for children who have reached that amazing age when they first get excited about reading on their own."

Zoobooks

Published by:

Wildlife Education Ltd.

9820 Willow Creek Road, Suite 300

San Diego CA 92131

Date: 1994

Frequency: Monthly

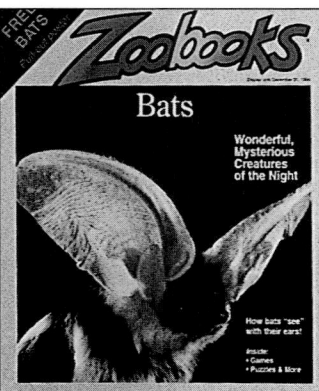

Cover Price: $2.95

Subscription Price: $17.95

Discount Subscription Price: n/a

Total Number of Pages: 18

Total Number of Ad Pages: 0

Publisher: Wildlife Education Ltd.

Editor: John Bonnett Wexo

Editorial Concept: "Colorful, imaginative, scientifically correct *Zoobooks* fascinate children with a new animal every month."

Annual, Special or Frequency Unknown

Fun Pak

Published by:

Hachette Filipacchi Magazines Inc.

1633 Broadway

New York NY 10019

Date: Winter 1994

Frequency: Special

Cover Price: $1.49

Subscription Price: n/a

Discount Subscription Price: n/a

Total Number of Pages: 84

Total Number of Ad Pages: 1

Publisher: Patrice Listfield

Editor: Linda Saltzman

Editorial Concept: Crosswords, word finds, and other games for small children.

Starline Presents Power Heroes and Villains!

Published by:

Starline Publications Inc.

210 Route 4 East, Suite 401

Paramus NJ 07652

Date: 1994

Frequency: Special

Cover Price: $2.95

Subscription Price: n/a

Discount Subscription Price: n/a

Total Number of Pages: 48

Total Number of Ad Pages: 0

Publisher: Starline Publications Inc.

Editor: Ann Leighton

Editorial Concept: Posters, puzzles, games, and articles about the Mighty Morphin Power Rangers and more.

Starline Presents The Mighty Morphin Power Rangers

Published by:

Starline Publications Inc.

210 Route 4 East, Suite 210

Paramus NJ 07652

Date: 1994

Frequency: Special

Cover Price: $2.95

Subscription Price: n/a

Discount Subscription Price: n/a

Total Number of Pages: 52

Total Number of Ad Pages: 0

Publisher: Starline Publications Inc.

Editor: Anne M. Raso

Editorial Concept: Fold-out posters of the show's heroes.

Teen Dream Featuring Mighty Morphin Power Rangers

Published by:

Starline Publications Inc.

210 Route 4 East, Suite 210

Paramus NJ 07652

Date: 1994

Frequency: Special

Cover Price: $2.95

Subscription Price: n/a

Discount Subscription Price: n/a

Total Number of Pages: 52

Total Number of Ad Pages: 0

Publisher: Starline Publications Inc.

Editor: Anne M. Raso

Editorial Concept: Pictures and tidbits about the Power Rangers.

TV Action Fun Presents Mighty Morphin Power Rangers

Published by:

n/a (Distributed by Kuble News)

Date: 1994

Frequency: Special

Cover Price: $1.95

Subscription Price: n/a

Discount Subscription Price: n/a

Total Number of Pages: 16

Total Number of Ad Pages: 0

Publisher: n/a

Editor: n/a

Editorial Concept: Giant fold-out poster, games, quizzes, and information about the Power Rangers.

America's Most Wanted Collectibles

Published by:

America's Most Wanted Collectibles

1400 Cantrell, Suite 332

Little Rock AR 72212

Date: August 1994

Frequency: Monthly

Cover Price: $0.75

Subscription Price: $12.00

Discount Subscription Price: n/a

Total Number of Pages: 32

Total Number of Ad Pages: 32

Publisher: n/a

Editor: n/a

Editorial Concept: Big and easy-to-read ads for various collectibles.

Cards Illustrated

Published by:

Warrior Publications

1920 Highland Ave., Suite 222

Lombard IL 60148

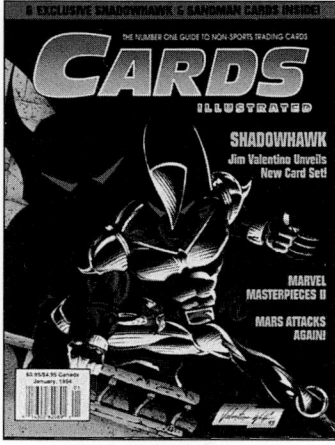

Date: January 1994

Frequency: Monthly

Cover Price: $3.95

Subscription Price: n/a

Discount Subscription Price: n/a

Total Number of Pages: 84

Total Number of Ad Pages: 17

Publisher: Steve Harris

Editor: Don Butler

Editorial Concept: "The number one guide to non-sports trading cards."

Celebrity Collector

Published by:

Celebrity Collector

P.O. Box 1115

Boston MA 02117

Date: Winter 1994

Frequency: Quarterly

Cover Price: $4.95

Subscription Price: $18.00

Discount Subscription Price: n/a

Total Number of Pages: 24

Total Number of Ad Pages: 8

Publisher: George A. Carpinone

Editor: George A. Carpinone

Editorial Concept: "The magazine for collectors of movie, TV, music, and theatre celebrity memorabilia."

Collecting Hollywood

Published by:

American Collectors Exchange

2401 Broad St.

Chattanooga TN 37408

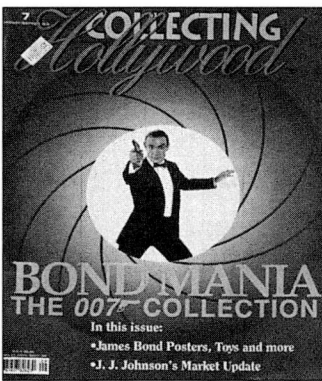

Date: August/September 1994

(first newsstand issue)

Frequency: Bimonthly

Cover Price: $2.95

Subscription Price: $12.00

Discount Subscription Price: n/a

Total Number of Pages: 160

Total Number of Ad Pages: 39

Publisher: Jon R. Warren

Editor: Jon R. Warren

Editorial Concept: "For collectors of Hollywood memorabilia - old and new."

Collector Caps Price Guide

Published by:

Design Marketing International Inc.

P.O. Box 25755

Honolulu HI 96825

Date: Fall 1994

Frequency: Bimonthly

Cover Price: $3.95

Subscription Price: $18.00

Discount Subscription Price: n/a

Total Number of Pages: 78

Total Number of Ad Pages: 42

Publisher: Lionel Takeda and Randall Shiroma

Editor: Judith Nii

Editorial Concept: "The complete guide for milk cap collectors."

Collector Car & Truck Prices

Published by:

VMR International Inc.

41 N. Main St.

North Grafton MA 01536

Date: May 1994

Frequency: Bimonthly

Cover Price: $3.95

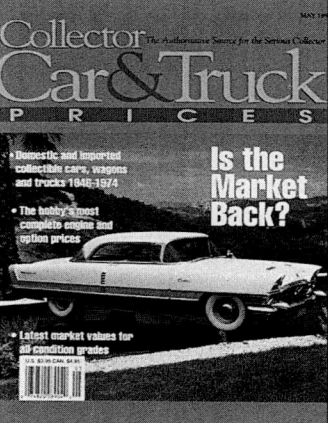

Subscription Price: $14.95

Discount Subscription Price: n/a

Total Number of Pages: 124

Total Number of Ad Pages: 16

Publisher: John Iofolla

Editor: John Iofolla

Editorial Concept: Prices for domestic and imported collectible cars, wagons, and trucks 1946-1974.

Conjure Magazine

Published by:

The Keep of Comics & Games Inc.

2272 Kresga Drive

Amherst OH 44001

Date: November/December 1994

Frequency: Bimonthly

Cover Price: $3.75

Subscription Price: $18.00

Discount Subscription Price: n/a

Total Number of Pages: 68

Total Number of Ad Pages: 12

Publisher: James Grasso

Editor: James Grasso

Editorial Concept: Articles about playing the fantasy game and collecting the cards.

Encyclopedia of Sports Memorabilia and Price Guide

Published by:

LFP Inc.

9171 Wilshire Blvd., Suite 300

Beverly Hills CA 90210

Date: November 1994

Frequency: Bimonthly

Cover Price: $3.99

Subscription Price: $17.95

Discount Subscription Price: n/a

Total Number of Pages: 88

Total Number of Ad Pages: 21

Publisher: Larry Flynt

Editor: Terry Melia

Editorial Concept: "Complete multisport price guide for autographs."

Heroes of the Game

Published by:

Blue Book Publishers Inc.

7807 Girard Ave., Suite 200

La Jolla CA 92037

Date: 1994

Frequency: Quarterly

Cover Price: $5.95

Subscription Price: $32.00

Discount Subscription Price: n/a

Total Number of Pages: 36

Total Number of Ad Pages: 3

Publisher: Blue Book Publishers

Editor: Dianne Gleason

Editorial Concept: "A glossy, upscale look at sports collectibles."

Hollywood Collectibles

Published by:

H&S Media Inc.

3400 Dundee Road

Northbrook IL 60062

Date: February 1994

Frequency: Monthly

Cover Price: $3.95

Subscription Price: $22.00

Discount Subscription Price: n/a

Total Number of Pages: 84

Total Number of Ad Pages: 39

Publisher: Jim Mohr

Editor: Jim Mohr

Editorial Concept: Price guides and strategies for collecting movie memorabilia.

Miller's Barbie Collector

Published by:

Barbara and Dan Miller

West One Sumner, #1

Spokane WA 99204-3661

Date: August/September 1994

Frequency: Bimonthly

Cover Price: $4.75

Subscription Price: $24.00

Discount Subscription Price: n/a

Total Number of Pages: 64

Total Number of Ad Pages: 25

Publisher: Barbara and Dan Miller

Editor: Barbara Miller

Editorial Concept: Articles about collectible Barbie dolls and a current price guide.

Scrye Magazine

Published by:

ILM International Inc.

30617 Highway 19 North, Suite 700

Palm Harbor FL 34684

Date: 1994

Frequency: Bimonthly

Cover Price: $3.50

Subscription Price: $19.00

Discount Subscription Price: n/a

Total Number of Pages: 68

Total Number of Ad Pages: 26

Publisher: J.M. White

Editor: M.E. Campbell

Editorial Concept: "The game card collector's guide."

ShowCase

Published by:

ShowCase Magazine

P.O. Box 2227

Coppell TX 75019

Date: Spring/Summer 1994

Frequency: Quarterly

Cover Price: $4.50

Subscription Price: $18.00

Discount Subscription Price: n/a

Total Number of Pages: 28

Total Number of Ad Pages: 10

Publisher: ShowCase Magazine

Editor: Kelly Walden

Editorial Concept: "Your one-step resource to today's collectibles for today's collector."

Tomart's Action Figure Digest

Published by:

Tomart Publications

3300 Encrete Lane

Dayton OH 45439-1944

Date: 1994 *(first newsstand issue)*

Frequency: Bimonthly

Cover Price: $5.00

Subscription Price: $30.00

Discount Subscription Price: n/a

Total Number of Pages: 60

Total Number of Ad Pages: 18

Publisher: Thomas E. Tumbusch

Editor: T.N. Tumbusch

Editorial Concept: "The most advance news available on the action figure industry."

Tomart's Disneyana Update

Published by:

Tomart Publications

3300 Encrete Lane

Dayton OH 45439-1944

Date: 1994

Frequency: Bimonthly

(first newsstand issue)

Cover Price: $6.00

Subscription Price: $28.00

Discount Subscription Price: n/a

Total Number of Pages: 48

Total Number of Ad Pages: 10

Publisher: Tomart Publications

Editor: Thomas E. Tumbusch

Editorial Concept: "New or coming items you may want to track down for your Disney collection."

Tuff Stuff's Collect!

Published by:

Tuff Stuff Publications Inc.

1934 E. Parham Road

Richmond VA 23228

Date: June 1994

Frequency: Monthly

Cover Price: $3.95

Subscription Price: $23.95

Discount Subscription Price: n/a

Total Number of Pages: 84

Total Number of Ad Pages: 18

Publisher: Tuff Stuff Publications

Editor: Larry Canale

Editorial Concept: "Your guide to non-sports and entertainment cards."

Vintage Gallery Collectible Guitars & Amps

Published by:

Miller Freeman Inc.

600 Harrison St.

San Francisco CA 94107

Date: April 1994

Frequency: Quarterly

Cover Price: $4.95

Subscription Price: n/a

Discount Subscription Price: n/a

Total Number of Pages: 68

Total Number of Ad Pages: 15

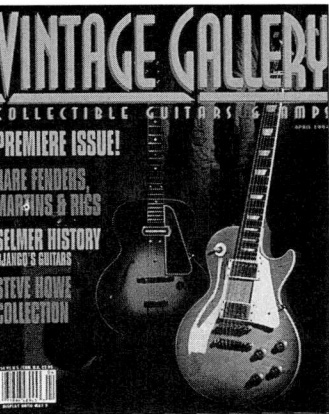

Publisher: Pat Cameron

Editor: Chris Gill

Editorial Concept: High-quality photos and specifications on rare guitars and amplifiers.

Vintage Guitar Classics

Published by:

Vintage Guitar Inc.

201 E. Front Ave.

Bismarck ND 58507-7301

Date: Spring 1994

Frequency: Quarterly

Cover Price: $5.95

Subscription Price: $25.00

Discount Subscription Price: n/a

Total Number of Pages: 76

Total Number of Ad Pages: 0

Publisher: Alan and Cleo Greenwood

Editor: Robert Watkins

Editorial Concept: High-quality photos and technical information on classic collectible guitars.

Boyd's Hockey Card Guide

Published by:

Boyd's Publications

P.O. Box 180

North Tonawanda NY 14120

Date: 1994

Frequency: Special

Cover Price: $4.95

Subscription Price: n/a

Discount Subscription Price: n/a

Total Number of Pages: 132

Total Number of Ad Pages: 0

Publisher: Boyd's Publications

Editor: William E. Paterson

Editorial Concept: Alphabetical, team, and player listings of collectible hockey cards.

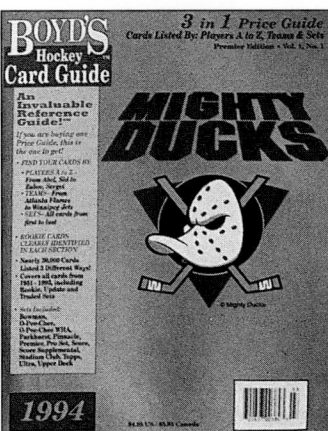

The Comprehensive Guide To Upper Deck Trading Cards

Published by:

Krause Publications Inc.

700 E. State St.

Iola WI 54990

Date: July 1994

Frequency: Special

Cover Price: $3.50

Subscription Price: n/a

Discount Subscription Price: n/a

Total Number of Pages: 88

Total Number of Ad Pages: 14

Publisher: Bob Lemke

Editor: Greg Ambrosius

Editorial Concept: A tribute to Upper Deck's first five years.

Country Accents Christmas Collectibles

Published by:

GCR Publishing Group Inc.

1700 Broadway

New York NY 10019

Date: 1994

Frequency: Annually

Cover Price: $3.95

Subscription Price: n/a

Discount Subscription Price: n/a

Total Number of Pages: 84

Total Number of Ad Pages: 17

Publisher: Charles Goodman

Editor: Cathy Cook

Editorial Concept: "Affordable items that anyone can begin collecting today."

Rodder's Collectibles

Published by:

Challenge Publications Inc.

7950 Deering Ave.

Canoga Park CA 91304

Date: 1994

Frequency: Special

Cover Price: $4.95

Subscription Price: n/a

Discount Subscription Price: n/a

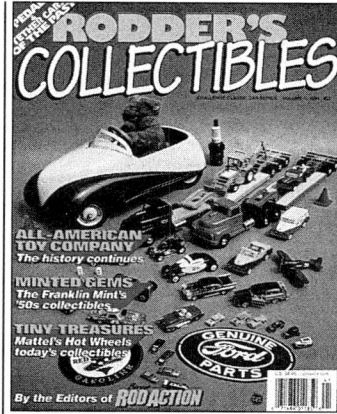

Total Number of Pages: 88

Total Number of Ad Pages: 6

Publisher: Edwin A. Schnepf

Editor: Jon Gobetti

Editorial Concept: Building and collecting miniature and model hot rods.

The Wizard Press Comic Book Price Guide Annual 1995

Published by:

Wizard Press

151 Wells Ave.

Congers NY 10920

Date: November 1994

Frequency: Annually

Cover Price: $12.95

Subscription Price: n/a

Discount Subscription Price: n/a

Total Number of Pages: 290

Total Number of Ad Pages: 19

Publisher: Wizard Press

Editor: John R. Warren

Editorial Concept: An overview to collecting comics and an extensive price guide.

Today's Hottest Collectibles 1994 Annual

Published by:

Krause Publications

700 E. State St.

Iola WI 54990

Date: 1994

Frequency: Annually

Cover Price: $3.50

Subscription Price: n/a

Discount Subscription Price: n/a

Total Number of Pages: 100

Total Number of Ad Pages: 4

Publisher: Greg Smith

Editor: Steve Ellingboe

Editorial Concept: Reprints of articles on collecting dolls, cards, movie memorabilia, and more from the pages of *Today's Collector*.

Triton

Published by:

Attic Books Ltd.

15 Danbury Road

Ridgefield CT 06877

Date: January 1994

Frequency: n/a

Cover Price: $3.50

Subscription Price: $24.99

Discount Subscription Price: n/a

Total Number of Pages: 100

Total Number of Ad Pages: 24

Publisher: Alex Malloy, Stuart Wells, and Roderick Malloy

Editor: Brian Kelly

Editorial Concept: Interviews with comic book writers and artists.

Don Martin Magazine

Published by:

Welsh Publishing Group Inc.

300 Madison Ave.

New York NY 10017

Date: 1994

Frequency: Monthly

Cover Price: $2.50

Subscription Price: n/a

Discount Subscription Price: n/a

Total Number of Pages: 36

Total Number of Ad Pages: 5

Publisher: Donald E. Welsh

Editor: Donna Kamkar

Editorial Concept: Comics by Don Martin.

Inks

Published by:

The Ohio State University Press

1070 Carmack Road

Columbus OH 43210-1002

Date: February 1994

Frequency: 3/year

Cover Price: $8.00

Subscription Price: $20.00

Discount Subscription Price: n/a

Total Number of Pages: 56

Total Number of Ad Pages: 6

Publisher: Ohio State University Press

Editor: Lucy Shelton Caswell

Editorial Concept: An academic look at the social and political importance of comics in our society.

Penthouse Comix

Published by:

Penthouse International Ltd.

1965 Broadway

New York NY 10023-5965

Date: May/June 1994

Frequency: Bimonthly

Cover Price: $4.95

Subscription Price: n/a

Discount Subscription Price: n/a

Total Number of Pages: 100

Total Number of Ad Pages: 13

Publisher: Bob Guccione

Editor: Bob Guccione

Editorial Concept: A collection of sexy comics from the pages of *Penthouse.*

Spider-Man Magazine

Published by:

Marvel Entertainment Group Inc.

387 Park Ave. South

New York NY 10016

Date: March 1994

Frequency: Monthly

Cover Price: $1.95

Subscription Price: $23.40

Discount Subscription Price: n/a

Total Number of Pages: 36

Total Number of Ad Pages: 13

Publisher: Stan Lee

Editor: Michael Teitelbaum

Editorial Concept: Comics, puzzles, and features devoted to the web-slinger.

Annual, Special or Frequency Unknown

Beyond Zero Hour

Published by:

Wizard Press

P.O. Box 656

Yorktown Heights NY 10598-0656

Date: 1994

Frequency: Special

Cover Price: $3.95

Subscription Price: n/a

Discount Subscription Price: n/a

Total Number of Pages: 100

Total Number of Ad Pages: 5

Publisher: Gareb S. Shamus

Editor: Joe Yanarella

Editorial Concept: "A comprehensive look at the history of DC Comics and current story lines."

Comic Book Who's Who

Published by:

Warrior Publications

1920 Highland Ave., Suite 222

Lombard IL 60148

Date: August 1994

Frequency: Special

Cover Price: $3.95

Subscription Price: n/a

Discount Subscription Price: n/a

Total Number of Pages: 100

Total Number of Ad Pages: 4

Publisher: Steve Harris

Editor: Mike Stokes

Editorial Concept: "Complete biographies of the hottest comic book characters."

The Dark Book

Published by:

Wizard Press

P.O. Box 656

Yorktown Heights NY 10598-0656

Date: 1994

Frequency: Special

Cover Price: $3.95

Subscription Price: n/a

Discount Subscription Price: n/a

Total Number of Pages: 132

Total Number of Ad Pages: 11

Publisher: Gareb S. Shamus

Editor: Matthew E. Milliken

Editorial Concept: "A comprehensive look at comic book villains."

Heavy Metal Pin-Up

Published by:

Heavy Metal Magazine

584 Broadway, Suite 608

New York NY 10012

Date: 1994

Frequency: Special

Cover Price: $3.95

Subscription Price: n/a

Discount Subscription Price: n/a

Total Number of Pages: 120

Total Number of Ad Pages: 23

Publisher: Kevin Eastman

Editor: Kevin Eastman

Editorial Concept: A collection of comics from the pages of *Heavy Metal*.

Hero Special Edition — 1993 in Review

Published by:

Warrior Publications

1920 Highland Ave., Suite 222

Lombard IL 60148

Date: February 1994

Frequency: Special

Cover Price: $4.95

Subscription Price: n/a

Discount Subscription Price: n/a

Total Number of Pages: 100

Total Number of Ad Pages: 6

Publisher: Steve Harris

Editor: Marc Camron and Mike Stokes

Editorial Concept: A look back at the year in comic books.

Image Illustrated

Published by:

Warrior Publications

1920 Highland Ave., Suite 222

Lombard IL 60148

Date: September 1994

Frequency: Special

Cover Price: $3.95

Subscription Price: n/a

Discount Subscription Price: n/a

Total Number of Pages: 100

Total Number of Ad Pages: 8

Publisher: Steve Harris

Editor: Mike Stokes

Editorial Concept: A look at the superheros and artists of the upstart Image Comics company.

Pantera

Published by:

Rock-It Comix

26707 W. Agoura Road

Calabasas CA 91302-1960

Date: July 1994

Frequency: n/a

Cover Price: $3.95

Subscription Price: n/a

Discount Subscription Price: n/a

Total Number of Pages: 52

Total Number of Ad Pages: 7

Publisher: Rock-It Comix

Editor: Mark Paniccia

Editorial Concept: A story starring hard rock band Pantera illustrated as a comic.

The Punisher Anniversary Magazine

Published by:

Marvel Comics

387 Park Ave. South

New York NY 10016

Date: February 1994

Frequency: Special

Cover Price: $3.95

Subscription Price: n/a

Discount Subscription Price: n/a

Total Number of Pages: 52

Total Number of Ad Pages: 0

Publisher: Stan Lee

Editor: Steve Saffel

Editorial Concept: A look at the origin and adventures of the rogue comic hero.

X-Men: The Wedding Album

Published by:

Marvel Comics

387 Park Ave. South

New York NY 10016

Date: 1994

Frequency: Special

Cover Price: $2.95

Subscription Price: n/a

Discount Subscription Price: n/a

Total Number of Pages: 36

Total Number of Ad Pages: 0

Publisher: Stan Lee

Editor: Suzanne Gaffney

Editorial Concept: A mock wedding album of the marriage of two superheros.

Access/Visual Basic Advisor

Published by:

Advisor Publications Inc.

4010 Morena Blvd.

San Diego CA 92117

Date: December 1994/January 1995

Frequency: Bimonthly

Cover Price: $4.95

Subscription Price: $35.00

Discount Subscription Price: $29.00

Total Number of Pages: 84

Total Number of Ad Pages: 24

Publisher: William T. Ota

Editor: Michael Groh

Editorial Concept: "Microsoft access...Visual Basic...Office Windows application development guide."

AIXtra: IBM's Magazine for AIX Professionals

Published by:

U.S. Marketing and Services

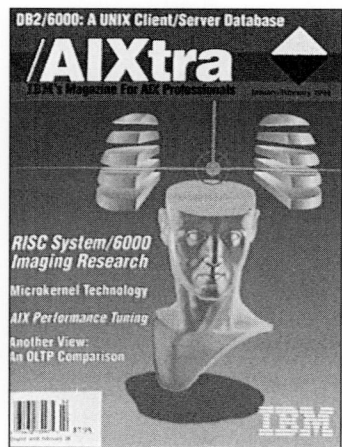

International Business Machines

IBM Corp. – Mail Stop 40-B3-04

One East Kirkwood Boulevard

Roanoke, TX 76299-0015

Date: January/February 1994

(first redesigned issue)

Frequency: Bimonthly

Cover Price: $7.95

Subscription Price: n/a

Discount Subscription Price: n/a

Total Number of Pages: 76

Total Number of Ad Pages: 18

Publisher: Alan E. Hodel

Editor: Alan E. Hodel

Editorial Concept: "IBM's magazine for AIX professionals."

CD ROM Pocket Guide

Published by:

Pemberton Press Inc.

462 Danbury Road

Wilton CT 06897-2126

Date: Summer 1994

Frequency: Quarterly

Cover Price: $5.95

Subscription Price: $16.95

Discount Subscription Price: n/a

Total Number of Pages: 356

Total Number of Ad Pages: 13

Publisher: Adam C. Pemberton

Editor: Richard A. Bowers

Editorial Concept: "America's guide to interactive and multimedia CDs."

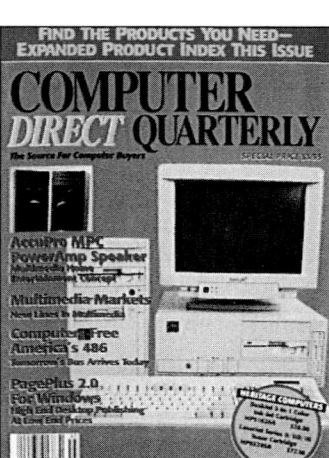

Computer Direct Quarterly

Published by:

Vulcan Publications Inc.

1 Chase Corporate Drive, Suite 300

Birmingham AL 35244

Date: Spring 1994

Frequency: Monthly

Cover Price: $3.95

Subscription Price: n/a

Discount Subscription Price: n/a

Total Number of Pages: 116

Total Number of Ad Pages: 96

Publisher: Brig T. Bearden

Editor: Tanya Thompson

Editorial Concept: Ads, ads, and more ads for people who are ready to buy computers and software.

Computer Life

Published by:

Ziff-Davis Publishing Company

1 Park Ave.

New York NY 10016-5802

Date: October 1994

Frequency: Monthly

Cover Price: $1.95

Subscription Price: $24.97

Discount Subscription Price: $16.97

Total Number of Pages: 200

Total Number of Ad Pages: 107

Publisher: J. Scott Briggs

Editor: Chris Shipley

Editorial Concept: "Writers and editors take you along on their personal journeys through the rapidly unfolding world of new things to do with computers."

dBase Advisor

Published by:

Advisor Communications International Inc.

4010 Morena Blvd., Suite 200

San Diego CA 92117

Date: 1994

Frequency: Bimonthly

Cover Price: $4.95

Subscription Price: $35.00

Discount Subscription Price: $29.00

Total Number of Pages: 60

Total Number of Ad Pages: 23

Publisher: Bill Ota

Editor: John Hawkins

Editorial Concept: "The magazine for using Borland dBase."

dBase Informant

Published by:

Informant Communications Group

10519 E. Stockton Blvd., Suite 142

Elk Grove CA 95624

Date: December 1994

Frequency: Monthly

Cover Price: $4.95

Subscription Price: $44.95

Discount Subscription Price: n/a

Total Number of Pages: 68

Total Number of Ad Pages: 9

Publisher: Mitchell Koulouris

Editor: Jerry Coffey

Editorial Concept: "The complete monthly guide to dBase for Windows development."

Digital Video Magazine

Published by:

TechMedia Publishing Inc.

80 Elm St.

Peterborough NH 03458

Date: June 1994

Frequency: Monthly

Cover Price: $3.95

Subscription Price: $29.97

Discount Subscription Price: $19.97

Total Number of Pages: 100

Total Number of Ad Pages: 42

Publisher: Peter Kamig

Editor: Linda B. Laflamme

Editorial Concept: A somewhat technical journal on combining computer and film technology.

Family PC

Published by:

Jake Winebaum

244 Main St.

Northhampton MA 01060-0929

Date: September/October 1994

Frequency: Bimonthly

Cover Price: $2.95

Subscription Price: $9.95

Discount Subscription Price: n/a

Total Number of Pages: 248

Total Number of Ad Pages: 124

Publisher: Jake Winebaum

Editor: Jake Winebaum

Editorial Concept: "Help you and your kids discover new ways to use your computer."

Full Throttle

Published by:

The Cobb Group

9420 Bunson Parkway, Suite 300

Louisville KY 40220

Date: December/January 1994

Frequency: Bimonthly

Cover Price: $9.00

Subscription Price: $39.00

Discount Subscription Price: n/a

Total Number of Pages: 24

Total Number of Ad Pages: 8

Publisher: Mark Crane and Jan Pyles

Editor: Timothy L. Boone

Editorial Concept: Tips and techniques for using Microsoft's flight simulator.

Home PC

Published by:

CMP Publications Inc.

600 Community Drive

Manhasset NY 11030

Date: June 1994

Frequency: Monthly

Premiere Issue Cover Price: $0.95

Subscription Price: $21.97

Discount Subscription Price: $14.97

Total Number of Pages: 216

Total Number of Ad Pages: 116

Publisher: Dan Schwartz

Editor: Ellen Pearlman

Editorial Concept: Computer entertainment, education, and productivity.

Inter Activity

Published by:

Miller Freeman Inc.

600 Harrison St.

San Francisco CA 94107

Date: November/December 1994

Frequency: Bimonthly

Cover Price: $3.95

Subscription Price: $29.95

Discount Subscription Price: $19.97

Total Number of Pages: 108

Total Number of Ad Pages: 6

Publisher: Pat Cameron

Editor: Dominic Milano

Editorial Concept: "The how-to multimedia magazine."

Interactive Week

Published by:

Interactive Enterprises LLC

100 Quentin Roosevelt Blvd., Suite 508

Garden City NY 11530

Date: October 10, 1994

Frequency: Monthly

Cover Price: $6.00

Subscription Price: $60.00

Discount Subscription Price: n/a

Total Number of Pages: 94

Total Number of Ad Pages: 50

Publisher: Beth Haggerty

Editor: Susan Older

Editorial Concept: "The publication for the information superhighway."

Linux Journal

Published by:

Specialized Systems Consultants Inc.

P.O. Box 85867

Seattle WA 98145-1867

Date: June/July 1994

Frequency: Monthly

Linux Journal

Cover Price: $4.00

Subscription Price: $19.00

Discount Subscription Price: n/a

Total Number of Pages: 48

Total Number of Ad Pages: 8

Publisher: Phil Hughes

Editor: Michael K. Johnson

Editorial Concept: Information for Linux software users.

Maximize: The Practical Guide to Windows

Published by:

Business Computer Publishing Inc.

80 Elm St.

Peterborough NH 03458

Date: November 1994

Frequency: Bimonthly

Cover Price: $4.95

Subscription Price: $15.95

Discount Subscription Price: n/a

Total Number of Pages: 108

Total Number of Ad Pages: 38

Publisher: Stephen Robbins

Editor: Michael J. Comendul

Editorial Concept: The practical guide to using Windows software for business and pleasure.

MicroComputer Journal

Published by:

CQ Communications Inc.

76 N. Broadway

Hicksville NY 11801

Date: January/February 1994

(formerly Computer Craft)

Frequency: Bimonthly

Cover Price: $4.95

Subscription Price: $29.70

Discount Subscription Price: n/a

Total Number of Pages: 116

Total Number of Ad Pages: 23

Publisher: Richard A. Ross

Editor: Art Salsberg

Editorial Concept: "The print forum for the microcomputer professional"

Mobile Office

Published by:

Cowles Business Media

470 Park Ave. South

New York NY 10016

Date: September 1994

Frequency: Monthly

Cover Price: $3.95

Subscription Price: $19.97

Discount Subscription Price: n/a

Total Number of Pages: 136

Total Number of Ad Pages: 66

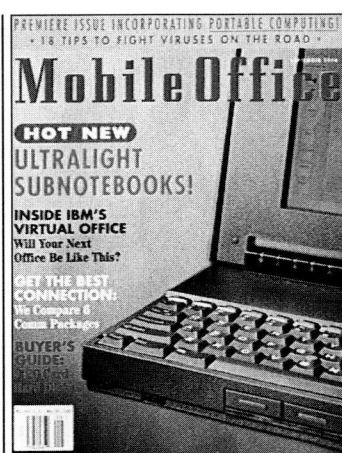

Publisher: Cowles Business Media

Editor: Daniel J. Rosenbaum

Editorial Concept: "A new, definitive guide to portable computing and communications."

Multimedia Schools

Published by:

Online Inc.

462 Danbury Road

Wilton CT 06897-2126

Date: May/June 1994

Frequency: 5/year

Cover Price: $5.95

Subscription Price: $38.00

Discount Subscription Price: n/a

Total Number of Pages: 84

Total Number of Ad Pages: 18

Publisher: Jeffrey K. Pemberton

Editor: Susan Veccia

Editorial Concept: "A practical journal of multimedia, CD-ROM, online, and Internet in K-12."

Multimedium!

Published by:

PennWell Publishing Company

190 Queen Anne Ave. N., Suite 220

Seattle WA 98109

Date: 1994

Frequency: Quarterly

Cover Price: $4.95

Subscription Price: $17.95

Discount Subscription Price: n/a

Total Number of Pages: 150

Total Number of Ad Pages: 25

Publisher: Fritz Feiten

Editor: Ron Wodaski

Editorial Concept: "The multimedia resource for Microsoft Windows."

Morph's Outpost on the Digital Frontier

Published by:

Morph's Outpost Inc.

P.O. Box 578

Orinda CA 94563

Date: April 1994

Frequency: Monthly

Cover Price: $3.95

Subscription Price: $39.95

Discount Subscription Price: $34.99

Total Number of Pages: 36

Total Number of Ad Pages: 18

Publisher: Craig LaGrow

Editor: Doug Millison

Editorial Concept: "The first magazine dedicated to serving, in-depth, the technical, business, and creative needs of the interactive multimedia developer community."

Net Guide

Published by:

CMP Media Inc.

600 Community Drive

Manhasset NY 11030

Date: December 1994

Frequency: Monthly

Cover Price: $2.95

Subscription Price: $22.97

Discount Subscription Price: $14.97

Total Number of Pages: 200

Total Number of Ad Pages: 60

Publisher: Donald F. Tydeman

Editor: Patrice Adcroft

Editorial Concept: "The guide to online services and the Internet."

NetWare Technical Journal

Published by:

McGraw-Hill Inc.

1221 Avenue of the Americas

New York NY 10020

Date: January/February 1994

(first newsstand issue)

Frequency: Bimonthly

Cover Price: $4.95

Subscription Price: $44.95

Discount Subscription Price: $29.95

Total Number of Pages: 100

Total Number of Ad Pages: 39

Publisher: McGraw-Hill Inc.

Editor: Peter Clegg

Editorial Concept: "The latest NetWare information."

Network Administrator

Published by:

R&D Publications Inc.

1601 W. 23rd St., Suite 200

Lawrence KS 66046

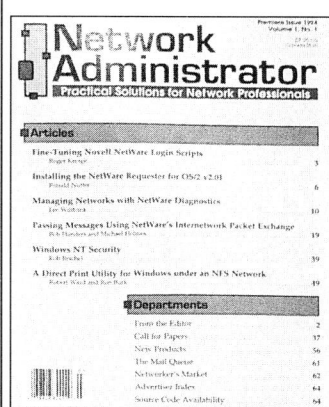

Date: 1994

Frequency: Bimonthly

Cover Price: $7.95

Subscription Price: $39.95

Discount Subscription Price: n/a

Total Number of Pages: 68

Total Number of Ad Pages: 15

Publisher: Robert Ward

Editor: Robert Ward

Editorial Concept: "A forum that working, real-world network administrators can use to exchange information about problems, techniques, and solutions."

PC Bargain Finder

Published by:

Computer Marketing Associates Inc.

770 Washington St., Suite #2

Hulliston MA 01746

Date: June/July 1994

Frequency: Bimonthly

Cover Price: $1.95

Subscription Price: $9.95

Discount Subscription Price: n/a

Total Number of Pages: 100

Total Number of Ad Pages: 20

Publisher: William J. Howell Jr.

Editor: William J. Howell, Jr.

Editorial Concept: "Your source for the best prices on PC products."

PC Graphics & Video

Published by:

Advanstar Communications

7500 Old Oak Blvd.

Cleveland OH 44130

Date: January/February 1994

Frequency: 10/year

Cover Price: $3.95

Subscription Price: $24.95

Discount Subscription Price: n/a

Total Number of Pages: 76

Total Number of Ad Pages: 26

Publisher: Michael L. Forcillo

Editor: Lafe Low

Editorial Concept: Reviews of the latest multimedia products and tips on getting the most out of them.

Pen Computing

Published by:

Pen Computing Inc.

7 Quadrini

Albany NY 12208

Date: August 1994

Frequency: Bimonthly

Cover Price: $3.95

Subscription Price: $24.00

Discount Subscription Price: $18.00

Total Number of Pages: 100

Total Number of Ad Pages: 15

Publisher: Howard Borgen

Editor: Conrad H. Blickenstorfer

Editorial Concept: News and reviews of mobile computing products such as Apple's Newton.

PickWorld

Published by:

PICK Systems

1691 Browning

Irvine CA 92714

Date: May/June 1994 *(first newsstand issue)*

Frequency: Bimonthly

Cover Price: $4.95

Subscription Price: $40.00

Discount Subscription Price: $20.00

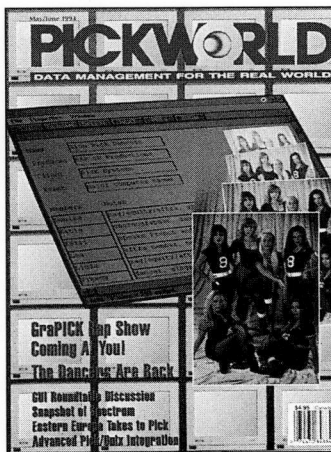

Total Number of Pages: 148

Total Number of Ad Pages: 33

Publisher: PICK Systems

Editor: M. Denis Hill

Editorial Concept: How to make the most of the PICK data management program.

PIX-Elation

Published by:

PIX-Elation

P.O. Box 4139

Highland Park NJ 08904

Date: November 1994

Frequency: Bimonthly

Cover Price: $4.95

Subscription Price: n/a

Discount Subscription Price: n/a

Total Number of Pages: 52

Total Number of Ad Pages: 7

Publisher: Karin August

Editor: Karin August

Editorial Concept: Exploring interactive worlds.

Sco World

Published by:

Venture Publishing Inc.

480 San Antonio Road

Mountain View CA 94040

Date: May 1994

Frequency: Monthly

Cover Price: $2.95

Subscription Price: $17.50

Discount Subscription Price: $15.00

Total Number of Pages: 84

Total Number of Ad Pages: 42

Publisher: Robert A. Billhimer

Editor: Michael J. Burgard

Editorial Concept: "Serving the SCO community in all its diversity."

Unixworld's Open Computing

Published by:

McGraw-Hill Inc.

1900 O'Farrell St.

San Mateo CA 94403-1311

Date: January 1994

Frequency: Monthly

Cover Price: $3.00

Subscription Price: $18.00

Discount Subscription Price: n/a

Total Number of Pages: 124

Total Number of Ad Pages: 61

Publisher: Michela O'Connor Abrams

Editor: Dave Flack

Editorial Concept: McGraw-Hill's magazine of Unix and interoperable solutions.

Annual, Special or Frequency Unknown

Computers & The Family

Published by:

Newsweek Inc.

The Newsweek Building

Livingston NJ 07039

Date: Fall 1994

Frequency: Special

Cover Price: $2.95

Subscription Price: n/a

Discount Subscription Price: n/a

Total Number of Pages: 72

Total Number of Ad Pages: 22

Publisher: Newsweek Inc.

Editor: Maynard Parker

Editorial Concept: "A common sense guide for families considering the purchase of a home computer for work and play."

Dr. Dobb's Information Highway Sourcebook

Published by:

Miller Freeman Inc.

411 Borel Ave.

San Mateo CA 94402-3522

Date: Winter 1994

Frequency: Special

Cover Price: $4.95

Subscription Price: n/a

Discount Subscription Price: n/a

Total Number of Pages: 76

Total Number of Ad Pages: 30

Publisher: Peter Hutchinson

Editor: Jonathon Erickson

Editorial Concept: "Software tools for the professional programmer."

Dr. Dobb's Language Sourcebook

Published by:

Miller Freeman Inc.

411 Borel Ave.

San Mateo CA 94402-3522

Date: Winter 1994

Frequency: Special

Cover Price: $4.95

Subscription Price: n/a

Discount Subscription Price: n/a

Total Number of Pages: 68

Total Number of Ad Pages: 20

Publisher: Peter Hutchinson

Editor: Jonathon Erickson

Editorial Concept: Mastering alternative computer languages.

Dr. Dobb's Sourcebook of Multimedia Programming

Published by:

Miller Freeman Inc.

411 Borel Ave.

San Mateo CA 94402-3522

Date: Winter 1994

Frequency: Special

Cover Price: $4.95

Subscription Price: n/a

Discount Subscription Price: n/a

Total Number of Pages: 84

Total Number of Ad Pages: 14

Publisher: Peter Hutchinson

Editor: Michael Floyd

Editorial Concept: Focusing on multimedia software development.

Edutainment News

Published by:

Edutainment News

8 Digital Drive, Suite 101

Novato CA 94949

Date: August/September 1994

Frequency: n/a

Cover Price: $3.95

Subscription Price: n/a

Discount Subscription Price: n/a

Total Number of Pages: 48

Total Number of Ad Pages: 21

Publisher: Isaac Ash

Editor: Douglas M. Baughman

Editorial Concept: "The best in education and entertainment products."

Family Computing

Published by:

Scholastic Inc.

555 Broadway

New York NY 10022

Date: October 1994

Frequency: Special

Cover Price: Free

Subscription Price: n/a

Discount Subscription Price: n/a

Total Number of Pages: 32

Total Number of Ad Pages: 14

Publisher: Scholastic Inc.

Editor: Nick Sullivan

Editorial Concept: "Resource guide for families looking to make computers an integral part of their children's learning and growth."

Multimedia Before-You-Buy Guide

Published by:

PC World Communications Inc.

501 Second St. #600

San Francisco CA 94107

Date: 1994

Frequency: Special

Cover Price: $4.95

Subscription Price: n/a

Discount Subscription Price: n/a

Total Number of Pages: 130

Total Number of Ad Pages: 42

Publisher: Claudia Smukler

Editor: Vince Broady

Editorial Concept: "How to choose the best system for you."

PC Novice Guide to Software

Published by:

Peed Corporation

120 W. Harvest Drive

Lincoln NE 68501

Date: December 1994

Frequency: Special

Cover Price: $3.95

Subscription Price: n/a

Discount Subscription Price: n/a

Total Number of Pages: 132

Total Number of Ad Pages: 11

Publisher: Peed Corporation

Editor: Alexandra Egan and Nancy Evans

Editorial Concept: "100+ reviews of top-selling programs."

PC Novice Guide to Windows

Published by:

Peed Corporation

120 W. Harvest Drive

Lincoln NE 68501

Date: September/October 1994

Frequency: Special

Cover Price: $3.95

Subscription Price: n/a

Discount Subscription Price: n/a

Total Number of Pages: 148

Total Number of Ad Pages: 8

Publisher: Ronald D. Kobler

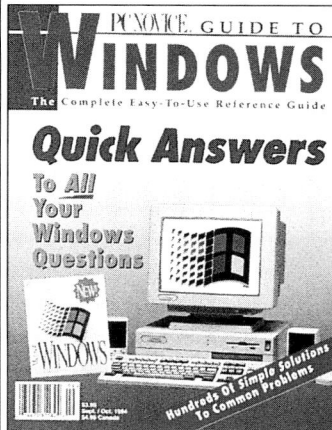

Editor: Alexandra Egan and Nancy Evans

Editorial Concept: "The complete, easy-to-use reference guide with quick answers to all your Windows questions."

Power Windows

Published by:

Harris Publications Inc.

1115 Broadway

New York NY 10010

Date: 1994

Frequency: Annually

Cover Price: $4.95

Subscription Price: n/a

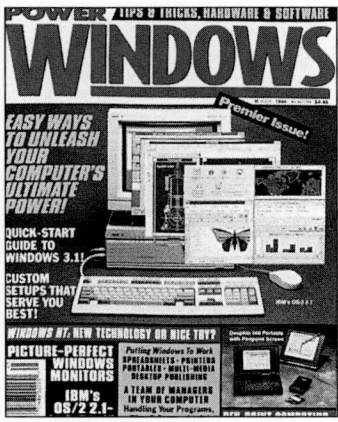

Discount Subscription Price: n/a

Total Number of Pages: 100

Total Number of Ad Pages: 6

Publisher: Stanley R. Harris

Editor: Barry L. Sheer

Editorial Concept: "Easy ways to unleash your computer's ultimate power."

Smalltalk for OS/2

Published by:

Miller Freeman Inc.

600 Harrison St.

San Francisco CA 94107

Date: Fall 1994

Frequency: Special

Cover Price: $9.95

Subscription Price: n/a

Discount Subscription Price: n/a

Total Number of Pages: 60

Total Number of Ad Pages: 8

Publisher: Cathy Passage

Editor: Dick Conklin

Editorial Concept: A technical-minded guide to using the OS/2 software application.

Amiga Game Zone

Published by:

Amiga Game Zone

103 W. California

Urbana IL 61801

Date: 1994

Frequency: Bimonthly

Cover Price: $3.95

Subscription Price: $19.95

Discount Subscription Price: n/a

Total Number of Pages: 44

Total Number of Ad Pages: 8

Publisher: Geoff Miller

Editor: Geoff Miller and Brian Wolsic

Editorial Concept: "America's only Amiga games magazine."

Bead & Button

Published by:

Conterie Press Inc.

P.O. Box 1020

Norwalk CT 06856

Date: February 1994

Frequency: Bimonthly

Cover Price: $3.95

Subscription Price: $19.95

Discount Subscription Price: n/a

Total Number of Pages: 32

Total Number of Ad Pages: 1

Publisher: Lane DeCamp

Editor: Alice Korach

Editorial Concept: How to hand-decorate fancy beads and buttons.

Better Homes and Gardens American Woodcrafts Gallery

Published by:

Meredith Corporation

1912 Grand Ave.

Des Moines IA 50309-3379

Date: Fall/Winter 1994

Frequency: Quarterly

Cover Price: $4.95

Subscription Price: $15.00

Discount Subscription Price: n/a

Total Number of Pages: 100

Total Number of Ad Pages: 5

Publisher: William R. Reed

Editor: Larry Clayton

Editorial Concept: Handcrafted gifts, furnishings, and accessories.

Better Homes and Gardens Floral & Nature Crafts

Published by:

Meredith Corporation

1716 Locust St.

Des Moines IA 50309-3023

Date: May 1994

Frequency: Bimonthly

Cover Price: $4.95

Subscription Price: $29.97

Discount Subscription Price: n/a

Total Number of Pages: 48

Total Number of Ad Pages: 7

Publisher: William R. Reed

Editor: Carl Voss

Editorial Concept: Techniques, materials, designs, and tips.

CD-ROM Entertainment

Published by:

Sendai Publishing Group Inc.

1920 Highland Ave., Suite 222

Lombard IL 60148

Date: May 1994

Frequency: Monthly

Cover Price: Free

Subscription Price: n/a

Discount Subscription Price: n/a

Total Number of Pages: 68

Total Number of Ad Pages: 14

Publisher: Steve Harris

Editor: Steve Honeywell

Editorial Concept: News and reviews on video games played on the CD-ROM format.

Computer Player

Published by:

HG Publications Inc.

9171 Wilshire Blvd., Suite 300

Beverly Hills CA 90210

Date: June 1994

Frequency: Monthly

Cover Price: $4.95

Subscription Price: $24.95

Discount Subscription Price: $19.95

Total Number of Pages: 96

Total Number of Ad Pages: 19

Publisher: Larry Flynt

Editor: Chris Gore

Editorial Concept: Reviews and descriptions of advanced CD-ROM computer games.

Country Home Folk Crafts

Published by:

Meredith Corporation

1716 Locust St.

Des Moines IA 50309-3023

Date: April 1994

Frequency: Bimonthly

Cover Price: $4.95

Subscription Price: $24.97

Discount Subscription Price: $19.97

Total Number of Pages: 32

Total Number of Ad Pages: 0

Publisher: Joseph A. Lagani

Editor: Molly Culbertson

Editorial Concept: Handcraft projects from the early American folk crafts era.

The Crafter

Published by:

Especially For Crafters Inc.

P.O. Box 949

Norwich NY 13815

Date: November 1994 *(first newsstand issue)*

Frequency: Monthly

Cover Price: $1.49

Subscription Price: $11.97

Discount Subscription Price: n/a

Total Number of Pages: 68

Total Number of Ad Pages: 12

Publisher: Especially For Crafters

Editor: Kay Zaia

Editorial Concept: Features cross-stitch, needlepoint, paint, sewing, crafts, and full-size craft patterns.

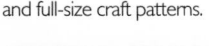

Crafting with Kids

Published by:

MSC Publishing Inc.

243 Newton-Sparta Road

Newton NJ 07860

Date: Winter 1994

Frequency: Semi-annually

Cover Price: $3.95

Subscription Price: n/a

Discount Subscription Price: n/a

Total Number of Pages: 52

Total Number of Ad Pages: 5

Publisher: Jerry Cohen

Editor: Michele Epstein

Editorial Concept: "Latest craft ideas for parties, scouts, camp, or even a rainy day at home."

Dollmaking Crafts & Designs

Published by:

Jones Publishing Inc.

N4750 Aanstad Road

Iola WI 54945-0337

Date: November/December 1994

Frequency: Bimonthly

Cover Price: $3.95

Subscription Price: $17.95

Discount Subscription Price: n/a

Total Number of Pages: 96

Total Number of Ad Pages: 38

Publisher: Scott Kolpien

Editor: Barbara Case

Editorial Concept: The first issue of the combined *Dollmaking* and *Doll Designs* magazines.

The Duelist

Published by:

Wizard of the Coast, Inc.

P.O.Box 707

Renton, WA 98057

Date: Fall 1994

Frequency: Quarterly

Cover Price: $3.50

Subscription Price: $17.95

Discount Subscription Price: n/a

Total Number of Pages: 116

Total Number of Ad Pages: 19

Publisher: n/a

Editor: n/a

Editorial Concept: A guide to playing the Deckmaster role-playing game.

EGM²

Published by:

Sendai Publishing Group Inc.

1920 Highland Ave., Suite 222

Lombard IL 60148

Date: July 1994

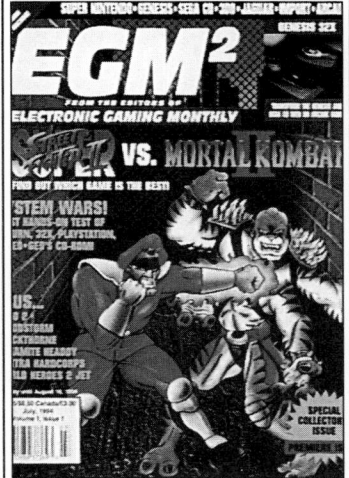

Frequency: Monthly

Cover Price: $4.95

Subscription Price: $28.95

Discount Subscription Price: n/a

Total Number of Pages: 180

Total Number of Ad Pages: 83

Publisher: Steve Harris

Editor: Ed Semrad

Editorial Concept: Tips for playing top video games.

Electronic Entertainment

Published by:

Infotainment World Inc.

951 Mariner's Island Blvd.

San Mateo CA 94404

Date: January 1994

Frequency: Monthly

Cover Price: $3.95

Subscription Price: $24.95

Discount Subscription Price: $19.95

Total Number of Pages: 144

Total Number of Ad Pages: 92

Publisher: Infotainment World Inc.

Editor: Gina Smith

Editorial Concept: "The inside scoop on the hardware, multimedia titles, and games flooding the market."

Express Yourself

Published by:

Meredith Corporation

1716 Locust St.

Des Moines IA 50309

Date: Summer 1994

Frequency: Quarterly

Cover Price: $3.95

Subscription Price: $14.99

Discount Subscription Price: n/a

Total Number of Pages: 36

Total Number of Ad Pages: 2

Publisher: Cindy Sullivan

Editor: Sara Jane Trenen

Editorial Concept: "Over 30 glorious fabric painting projects."

Fine Woodworking's Home Furniture for Woodworkers

Published by:

The Taunton Press Inc.

63 S. Main St.

Newtown CT 06470-5506

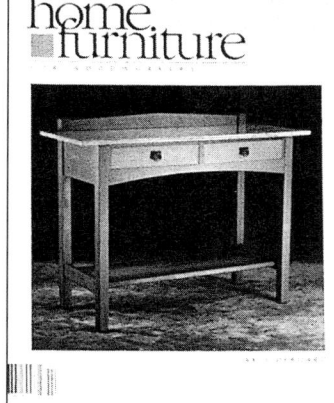

Date: Winter 1994

Frequency: Quarterly

Cover Price: $5.95

Subscription Price: $20.00

Discount Subscription Price: n/a

Total Number of Pages: 112

Total Number of Ad Pages: 17

Publisher: James P. Chiavelli

Editor: Scott Gibson

Editorial Concept: "Your best source for design information."

Game Informer Magazine

Published by:

Sunrise Publications

10120 W. 76th St.

Eden Prairie MN 55344

Date: January/February 1994 *(first newsstand issue)*

Frequency: Bimonthly

Cover Price: $3.95

Subscription Price: $9.88

Discount Subscription Price: n/a

Total Number of Pages: 60

Total Number of Ad Pages: 21

Publisher: Richard A. Cihak

Editor: Elizabeth A. Olson

Editorial Concept: Nintendo and Sega computer game tips and strategies.

Gambler's Guide to Mississippi – Special Tunica Edition

Published by:

Gambler's Guide

3290 New Getwell

Memphis TN

Date: 1994

Frequency: Monthly

Cover Price: Free

Subscription Price: n/a

Discount Subscription Price: n/a

Total Number of Pages: 16

Total Number of Ad Pages: 9

Publisher: Gambler's Guide

Editor: Steve Tamolia

Editorial Concept: "Primary source for complete information on all aspects of the gaming industry in Mississippi."

Historical Gamer

Published by:

Historical Gamer Magazine

99 Shady Lane

Lexington KY 40503

Date: April 1994 *(first newsstand issue)*

Frequency: Bimonthly

Cover Price: n/a

Subscription Price: $25.00

Discount Subscription Price: n/a

Total Number of Pages: 36

Total Number of Ad Pages: 7

Publisher: William S. Biles

Editor: William S. Biles

Editorial Concept: Military history and recreating historic battles.

Lotto World

Published by:

Dynamic World Distributors Inc.

2150 Goodlette Road

Naples FL 33940-4811

Date: August 1994

Frequency: Monthly

Cover Price: $1.50

Subscription Price: $18.00

Discount Subscription Price: n/a

Total Number of Pages: 64

Total Number of Ad Pages: 16

Publisher: Dennis B. Schroeder

Editor: Rich Holman

Editorial Concept: Reports on legally operated state lotteries.

New Type Gaming

Published by:

New Type Gaming

427 Merchant St.

San Francisco CA 94111

Date: 1994

Frequency: Bimonthly

Cover Price: $3.50

Subscription Price: $15.00

Discount Subscription Price: n/a

Total Number of Pages: 28

Total Number of Ad Pages: 1

Publisher: New Type Gaming

Editor: Joe Willis

Editorial Concept: Tips on playing the latest combat and fighting video games.

PC Gamer

Published by:

GP Publications Inc.

2300 Route 208

Fair Lawn NJ 07410

Date: May/June 1994

Frequency: Monthly

Cover Price: $7.95

Subscription Price: $89.95

Discount Subscription Price: $47.95

Total Number of Pages: 124

Total Number of Ad Pages: 37

Publisher: GP Publications Inc.

Editor: Mathew A. Firme and

Stephen Poole

Editorial Concept: Reviews of popular

PC games.

PC Sports and Video Games

Published by:

Cohen and Geller Publishing Group

3322 Sweetwater Springs, Suite 208

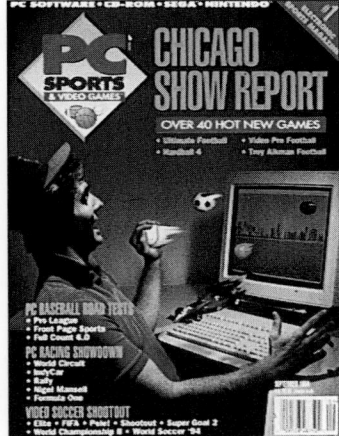

Spring Valley CA 91977

Date: September 1994 (formerly Sports

Game Review)

Frequency: Bimonthly

Cover Price: $3.95

Subscription Price: $14.97

Discount Subscription Price: n/a

Total Number of Pages: 76

Total Number of Ad Pages: 11

Publisher: Cohen and Geller

Publishing Group

Editor: Mark Cohen

Editorial Concept: Reviews of and tips

on playing video games.

Shadis

Published by:

Alderac Entertainment Group

17880 Graystone Ave., #203

Chino Hills CA 91709

Date: January/February 1994

Frequency: Bimonthly

Cover Price: $3.50

Subscription Price: $21.00

Discount Subscription Price: n/a

Total Number of Pages: 100

Total Number of Ad Pages: 33

Publisher: Alderac Entertainment

Group

Editor: Jolly R. Blackburn

Editorial Concept: "The independent

games magazine."

Tips & Tricks

Published by:

LFP Inc.

9171 Wilshire Blvd., Suite 300

Beverly Hills Ca 90210

Date: Spring 1994

Frequency: Quarterly

Cover Price: $4.95

Subscription Price: $19.95

Discount Subscription Price: n/a

Total Number of Pages: 80

Total Number of Ad Pages: 11

Publisher: Larry Flynt

Editor: Chris Gore

Editorial Concept: "A comprehensive

guide to the best cheats, codes, and

strategies for the best video games,

straight from the editors."

Annual, Special or Frequency Unknown

1994-95 Annual Preview Basketball Betting Guide

Published by:

FPG Inc.

4102 E. 7th St.

Long Beach CA 90804

Date: 1994

Frequency: Special

Cover Price: $2.00

Subscription Price: n/a

Discount Subscription Price: n/a

Total Number of Pages: 16

Total Number of Ad Pages: 4

Publisher: FPG Inc.

Editor: Richard L. Thompson and Robert

Wyzkowski

Editorial Concept: An inside look at

sports handicapping services.

Better Homes and Gardens Halloween Tricks and Treats

Published by:

Meredith Corporation

1912 Grand Ave.

Des Moines IA 50309-3379

Date: 1994

Frequency: Special

Cover Price: $4.95

Subscription Price: n/a

Discount Subscription Price: n/a

Total Number of Pages: 68

Total Number of Ad Pages: 4

Publisher: William R. Reed

Editor: Carl Voss

Editorial Concept: Information to

make Halloween crafting easy.

Building Scale R/C Model Warships

Published by:

Challenge Publications Inc.

7950 Deering Ave.

Canoga Park CA 91304

Date: 1994

Frequency: Special

Cover Price: $5.95

Subscription Price: n/a

Discount Subscription Price: n/a

Total Number of Pages: 96

Total Number of Ad Pages: 10

Publisher: Edwin A. Schnepf

Editor: Sydney P. Chivers

Editorial Concept: Building techn.ques for the scale ship modeler.

Classic R/C Models

Published by:

Challenge Publications Inc.

7950 Deering Ave.

Canoga Park CA 91304

Date: 1994

Frequency: Special

Cover Price: $5.95

Subscription Price: n/a

Discount Subscription Price: n/a

Total Number of Pages: 96

Total Number of Ad Pages: 9

Publisher: Edwin A. Schnepf

Editor: Norm Goyer

Editorial Concept: Building and flying miniature aircraft based on classic designs.

Craft & Hobby Catalogs of America

Published by:

LFP Inc.

9171 Wilshire Blvd., Suite 300

Beverly Hills CA 90210

Date: Summer 1994

Frequency: Special

Cover Price: $2.99

Subscription Price: n/a

Discount Subscription Price: n/a

Total Number of Pages: 80

Total Number of Ad Pages: 2

Publisher: Larry Flynt

Editor: Paul Verhelst

Editorial Concept: A listing of available mail-order catalogs for different products.

Crafts Quick and Easy Christmas

Published by:

PJS Publications

News Plaza

P.O. Box 1790

Peoria IL 61656

Date: 1994

Frequency: Special

Cover Price: $3.95

Subscription Price: n/a

Discount Subscription Price: n/a

Total Number of Pages: 100

Total Number of Ad Pages: 5

Publisher: PJS Publications

Editor: Judith Brossart

Editorial Concept: "125 dollar-stretching how-tos, many under $5."

Do-It-Yourself Wood Ideas

Published by:

GCR Publishing Group Inc.

1700 Broadway

New York NY 10019

Date: 1994

Frequency: Annually

Cover Price: $5.95

Subscription Price: n/a

Discount Subscription Price: n/a

Total Number of Pages: 148

Total Number of Ad Pages: 4

Publisher: Charles Goodman

Editor: Ron Renzulli

Editorial Concept: "105 easy-to-make low-budget projects."

Family Fun: Crafts & Hobbies Special Issue

Published by:

Family Fun

P.O. Box 10161

Des Moines IA 50340-0161

Date: 1994

Frequency: Special

Cover Price: $2.50

Subscription Price: n/a

Discount Subscription Price: n/a

Total Number of Pages: 140

Total Number of Ad Pages: 53

Publisher: Kim A. MacLeod

Editor: Alexandra Kennedy

Editorial Concept: "Exciting activities that parents and their children can do together."

Favorite Family Holidays

Published by:

Meredith Corporation

1912 Grand Ave.

Des Moines IA 50309-3379

Date: 1994/95

Frequency: Special

Cover Price: $3.50

Subscription Price: n/a

Discount Subscription Price: n/a

Total Number of Pages: 68

Total Number of Ad Pages: 8

Publisher: Meredith Corporation

Editor: Sara Jean Treinen

Editorial Concept: Holiday decorating ideas.

Folk Art Christmas

Published by:

Meredith Corporation

1716 Locust St.

Des Moines IA 50309-3023

Date: 1994

Frequency: Special

Cover Price: $4.95

Subscription Price: n/a

Discount Subscription Price: n/a

Total Number of Pages: 68

Total Number of Ad Pages: 4

Publisher: William R. Reed

Editor: Carl Voss

Editorial Concept: "A collection of 33 enticing Christmas craft projects."

Game Developer

Published by:

Miller Freeman Inc.

600 Harrison St.

San Francisco CA 94107

Date: 1994

Frequency: n/a

Cover Price: $4.95

Subscription Price: n/a

Discount Subscription Price: n/a

Total Number of Pages: 60

Total Number of Ad Pages: 7

Publisher: Veronica Costanza

Editor: Larry O'Brien

Editorial Concept: The magazine for electronic entertainment professionals.

Games Magazine's 1995 Buyer's Guide to Games

Published by:

B&P Publishing Company Inc.

575 Boylston St.

Boston MA 02116

Date: 1994

Frequency: Annually

Cover Price: $2.95

Subscription Price: n/a

Discount Subscription Price: n/a

Total Number of Pages: 112

Total Number of Ad Pages: 21

Publisher: Alan Segal

Editor: Burt Hochberg

Editorial Concept: "Reviews and ratings of more than 500 of the best games."

Holiday Traditions Folk Santas to Make & Collect

Published by:

MSC Publishing Inc.

243 Newton-Sparta Road

Newton NJ 07860

Date: Winter 1994

Frequency: Special

Cover Price: $4.95

Subscription Price: n/a

Discount Subscription Price: n/a

Total Number of Pages: 68

Total Number of Ad Pages: 2

Publisher: Jerry Cohen

Editor: Michele M. Epstein

Editorial Concept: The 1994 collector edition featuring a gallery of Santa artists.

Home and Country Wood Ornaments

Published by:

MSC Publishing Inc.

243 Newton-Sparta Road

Newton NJ 07860

Date: Winter 1995

Frequency: Special

Cover Price: $4.95

Subscription Price: n/a

Discount Subscription Price: n/a

Total Number of Pages: 68

Total Number of Ad Pages: 1

Publisher: Jerry Cohen

Editor: Robert A. Becker

Editorial Concept: A Christmas woodcrafts special featuring 54 ornaments to make for the tree.

Modeling the Second World War

Published by:

Kalmbach Publishing Company

21027 Crossroads Circle

Waukesha WI 53187

Date: 1994

Frequency: Special

Cover Price: $4.95

Subscription Price: n/a

Discount Subscription Price: n/a

Total Number of Pages: 104

Total Number of Ad Pages: 21

Publisher: Walter J. Mundschau

Editor: Bob Hayden

Editorial Concept: A variety of models of the hardware of WWII.

Mortal Kombat II

Published by:

Prima Publishing

P.O. Box 1260WES

Rocklin CA 95677

Date: 1994

Frequency: Special

Cover Price: n/a

Subscription Price: n/a

Discount Subscription Price: n/a

Total Number of Pages: 100

Total Number of Ad Pages: 0

Publisher: Prima Publishing

Editor: n/a

Editorial Concept: The official guide to playing the popular video game.

Radio Control Sport Flying

Published by:

Air Age Inc.

251 Danbury Road

Wilton CT 06897

Date: January 1994

Frequency: Special

Cover Price: $4.95

Subscription Price: n/a

Discount Subscription Price: n/a

Total Number of Pages: 108

Total Number of Ad Pages: 29

Publisher: Dr. Louis De Francesco

Editor: Tom Atwood

Editorial Concept: Building, detailing,

and flying remote-control model aircraft.

R/C Ship Modeling Special

Published by:

Challenge Publications Inc.

7950 Deering Ave.

Canoga Park CA 91304

Date: 1994

Frequency: Special

Cover Price: $5.95

Subscription Price: n/a

Discount Subscription Price: n/a

Total Number of Pages: 96

Total Number of Ad Pages: 13

Publisher: Edwin A. Schnepf

Editor: Sydney P. Chivers

Editorial Concept: Articles and photos on intricate, detailed ship and submarine models that really float.

The Ultimate Guide to Fighting Games

Published by:

Sendai Publishing Group Inc.

1920 Highland Ave., Suite 222

Lombard IL 60148

Date: Summer 1994

Frequency: Special

Cover Price: $9.95

Subscription Price: n/a

Discount Subscription Price: n/a

Total Number of Pages: 100

Total Number of Ad Pages: 1

Publisher: Steve Harris

Editor: n/a

Editorial Concept: "In-depth tricks, tips, and moves for the hottest fighting games."

The Ultimate PC Gamer's Guide

Published by:

Infotainment World Inc.

951 Mariner's Island Blvd., Suite 700

San Mateo CA 94404

Date: Winter 1994

Frequency: Special

Cover Price: $6.95

Subscription Price: n/a

Discount Subscription Price: n/a

Total Number of Pages: 164

Total Number of Ad Pages: 47

Publisher: Patrick Farrell

Editor: Gregg Keizer

Editorial Concept: Descriptions and reviews of 162 computer games.

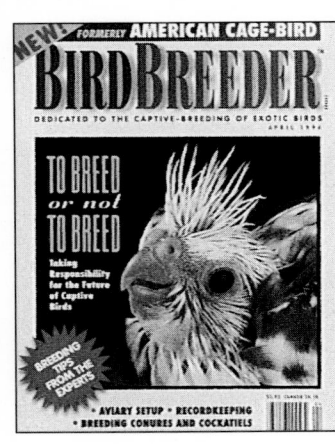

Bird Breeder

Published by:

Fancy Publications Inc.

3 Burroughs

Irvine CA 92718

Date: April 1994

Frequency: Monthly

Cover Price: $3.95

Subscription Price: $29.97

Discount Subscription Price: n/a

Total Number of Pages: 84

Total Number of Ad Pages: 32

Publisher: Norman Ridler

Editor: Kathleen Etchepare

Editorial Concept: "Dedicated to the captive breeding of exotic birds."

Bird World

Published by:

Bird World

850 Park Ave.

Monterey CA 93940

Date: 1994 (first newsstand issue)

Frequency: Bimonthly

Cover Price: $4.50

Subscription Price: $24.00

Discount Subscription Price: n/a

Total Number of Pages: 64

Total Number of Ad Pages: 0

Publisher: D. Stewart Armstrong and Diane Grindol

Editor: D. Stewart Armstrong and Diane Grindol

Editorial Concept: Articles on raising healthy birds.

Captive Breeding

Published by:

Snake Bite Inc.

P.O. Box 87100

Canton MI 48187

Date: July 1994 (first newsstand issue)

Frequency: Quarterly

Cover Price: $7.00

Subscription Price: $20.00

Discount Subscription Price: n/a

Total Number of Pages: 32

Total Number of Ad Pages: 11

Publisher: Richard Aquiline

Editor: Richard Aquiline

Editorial Concept: "Devoted to the captive propagation of reptiles and amphibians."

Exotic Market Review

Published by:

Exotic Market Review

P.O. Box 1203

Bowie TX 76230

Date: August 1994

Frequency: Monthly

Cover Price: $3.00

Subscription Price: $10.00

Discount Subscription Price: n/a

Total Number of Pages: 100

Total Number of Ad Pages: 63

Publisher: Kathy Snider

Editor: Kathy Snider

Editorial Concept: "Bringing you the latest development of the exotic animal industry.

Finch & Canary World

Published by:

Finch & Canary World

850 Park Ave.

Monterey CA 93940

Date: Fall 1994

Frequency: Quarterly

Cover Price: n/a

Subscription Price: $18.00

Discount Subscription Price: n/a

Total Number of Pages: 32

Total Number of Ad Pages: 12

Publisher: D. Stewart Armstrong

Editor: Diane Grindol

Editorial Concept: "This is a magazine dedicated to the interests of all finch, canary, and softbill enthusiasts."

Household Pet Digest

Published by:

Brown Publishing Company Inc.

3900 W. Brown Deer Rd., Suite A175

Milwaukee WI 53209

Date: September 1994

Frequency: Monthly

Cover Price: $2.95

Subscription Price: $16.95

Discount Subscription Price: n/a

Total Number of Pages: 48

Total Number of Ad Pages: 21

Publisher: Brown Publishing

Editor: J. A. Brown

Editorial Concept: "Pet care for the responsible pet owner."

Natural Pet

Published by:

Pet Publications Inc.

P.O. Box 351

Trilby FL 33593-0351

Date: September/October 1994 (first newsstand issue)

Frequency: Bimonthly

Cover Price: $3.50

Subscription Price: $20.00

Discount Subscription Price: $18.00

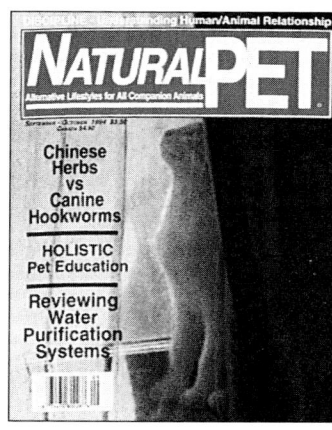

Total Number of Pages: 48

Total Number of Ad Pages: 15

Publisher: Pet Publications Inc.

Editor: Charlene Smith

Editorial Concept: "How to care for your pet's health in a natural, holistic way."

Popular Cats

Published by:

Harris Publications Inc.

1115 Broadway

New York NY 10010

Date: February/March 1994

Frequency: Bimonthly

Cover Price: $2.95

Subscription Price: n/a

Discount Subscription Price: n/a

Total Number of Pages: 76

Total Number of Ad Pages: 16

Publisher: Stanley R. Harris

Editor: Phil Maggitti

Editorial Concept: "To help our readers bring a little comfort into their cat's lives"

Annual, Special or Frequency Unknown

Cat USA 1994 Annual

Published by:

Fancy Publications Inc.

3 Burroughs

Irvine CA 92718

Date: 1994

Frequency: Annually

Cover Price: $5.95

Subscription Price: n/a

Discount Subscription Price: n/a

Total Number of Pages: 132

Total Number of Ad Pages: 52

Publisher: Fancy Publications Inc.

Editor: Debra Phillips-Donaldson

Editorial Concept: Guide to buying and caring for purebred kittens.

Wolf Hybrid Tracker

Published by:

Wolf Hybrid Tracker

4111 NW 10th Terrace

Fort Lauderdale FL 33309

Date: Fall 1994 *(first newsstand issue)*

Frequency: n/a

Cover Price: $4.95

Subscription Price: $28.00

Discount Subscription Price: n/a

Total Number of Pages: 32

Total Number of Ad Pages: 9

Publisher: Timothy Narron

Editor: Vicki Spencer

Editorial Concept: A forum for readers to discuss their wolves and hybrid.

Better Homes & Gardens Craft & Wear

Published by:

Meredith Corporation

1716 Locust St.

Des Moines IA 50309-3023

Date: 1994

Frequency: Bimonthly

Cover Price: $4.95

Subscription Price: $29.97

Discount Subscription Price: $19.97

Total Number of Pages: 32

Total Number of Ad Pages: 7

Publisher: William R. Reed

Editor: Carl Voss

Editorial Concept: "Your pattern source for decorative wearables."

Big Block Quilts

Published by:

Harris Publications Inc.

1115 Broadway

New York NY 10010

Date: Spring 1994

Frequency: Semi-annually

Cover Price: $3.95

Subscription Price: n/a

Discount Subscription Price: n/a

Total Number of Pages: 108

Total Number of Ad Pages: 6

Publisher: Stanley Harris

Editor: Jean Eitel

Editorial Concept: "For quilters who like to make big blocks in pretty patterns for quick and easy quilts."

Country Accents Country Crochet & Crafts

Published by:

GCR Publishing Group Inc.

1700 Broadway

New York NY 10019

Date: 1994

Frequency: Quarterly

Cover Price: $3.95

Subscription Price: n/a

Discount Subscription Price: n/a

Total Number of Pages: 84

Total Number of Ad Pages: 6

Publisher: Charles Goodman

Editor: Barbara Fimbel

Editorial Concept: "Special projects for you to crochet."

Easy-Does-It Needlework & Crafts

Published by:

KC Publishing Inc.

700 W. 47th St., Suite 310

Kansas City MO 64112

Date: April 1994

Frequency: Quarterly

Cover Price: $2.95

Subscription Price: $9.95

Discount Subscription Price: n/a

Total Number of Pages: 68

Total Number of Ad Pages: 10

Publisher: John C. Prebich

Editor: Kay Melchisedech Olson

Editorial Concept: "A broad variety of projects and patterns in easy-on-the-eyes type."

Make Every Day Special

Published by:

Leisure Arts Inc.

5701 Ranch Drive

Little Rock AR 72212

Date: August 1994

Frequency: Bimonthly

Cover Price: $4.00

Subscription Price: $19.97

Discount Subscription Price: $15.00

Total Number of Pages: 36

Total Number of Ad Pages: 6

Publisher: Steve Patterson

Editor: Anne Van Wagner Childs

Editorial Concept: All-new projects for cross-stitch and crochet.

Sewing Decor

Published by:

PJS Publications

News Plaza, P.O. Box 1790

Peoria IL 61656-1790

Date: April 1994

Frequency: Bimonthly

Cover Price: $3.95

Subscription Price: $19.98

Discount Subscription Price: n/a

Total Number of Pages: 84

Total Number of Ad Pages: 14

Publisher: Del Rusher

Editor: Susan Voigt-Reising

Editorial Concept: Home decorating projects for sewers of all skill levels.

The Sewing Room

Published by:

Lynn Carthy Industries Inc.

816 W. Bannock St., Suite 502

Boise ID 83702-5850

Date: November 1994

Frequency: 10/year

Cover Price: $3.95

Subscription Price: $19.97

Discount Subscription Price: n/a

Total Number of Pages: 44

Total Number of Ad Pages: 2

Publisher: Mia C. Crosthwaite

Editor: Mia C. Crosthwaite

Editorial Concept: "To inspire and invigorate the seamstress in all of us."

Annual, Special or Frequency Unknown

Art Quilts

Published by:

Lopez Publications Inc.

111 E. 35th St.

New York NY 10016

Date: Summer 1994

Frequency: Special

Cover Price: $4.95

Subscription Price: n/a

Discount Subscription Price: n/a

Total Number of Pages: 76

Total Number of Ad Pages: 0

Publisher: Adrian B. Lopez

Editor: Karen O'Dowd

Editorial Concept: Patterns and techniques for making beautiful quilts.

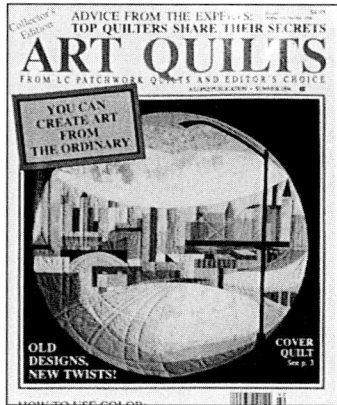

Best of Overall Boys

Published by:

House of White Birches

306 E. Parr Road

Berne IN 46711

Date: 1994

Frequency: Special

Cover Price: $3.95

Subscription Price: n/a

Discount Subscription Price: n/a

Total Number of Pages: 48

Total Number of Ad Pages: 2

Publisher: Carl H. and Arthur K. Muselman

Editor: Sandra Hatch

Editorial Concept: "Fast and fun, easy applique quilting!"

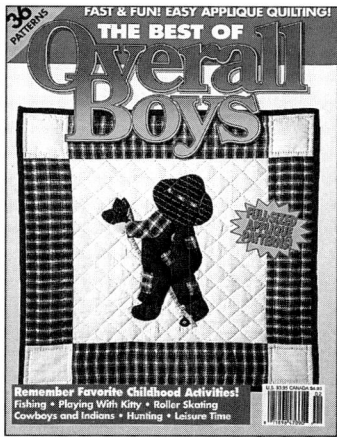

Best of Woman's Day Needlework

Published by:

Hachette Filipacchi Magazines Inc.

1633 Broadway

New York NY 10019

Date: 1994

Frequency: Special

Cover Price: $3.50

Subscription Price: n/a

Discount Subscription Price: n/a

Total Number of Pages: 100

Total Number of Ad Pages: 20

Publisher: Susan S. Buckley

Editor: Yvonne Beecher

Editorial Concept: Cross-stitch, crochet, knitting, and sewing designs.

Date: 1994

Frequency: Annually

Cover Price: $3.95

Subscription Price: n/a

Discount Subscription Price: n/a

Total Number of Pages: 84

Total Number of Ad Pages: 9

Publisher: Charles Goodman

Editor: Deborah Harding

Editorial Concept: "Best bazaar ideas: pins, place mats, pillows, wreaths, hangers, edgings."

Butterfly Quilting Patterns

Published by:

House of White Birches

306 E. Parr Road

Berne IN 46711

Date: 1994

Frequency: Special

Cover Price: $3.95

Subscription Price: n/a

Discount Subscription Price: n/a

Total Number of Pages: 68

Total Number of Ad Pages: 3

Publisher: Carl H. and Arthur K. Muselman

Editor: Sandra Hatch

Editorial Concept: "Delightful quilting patterns."

Country Accents Christmas Crochet

Published by:

GCR Publishing Group Inc.

1700 Broadway

New York NY 10019

Crochet for Bunnies & Bears

Published by:

House of White Birches

306 E. Parr Road

Berne IN 46711

Date: 1994

Frequency: Special

Cover Price: $2.95

Subscription Price: n/a

Discount Subscription Price: n/a

Total Number of Pages: 48

Total Number of Ad Pages: 4

Publisher: Carl H. and Arthur K. Muselman

Editor: Susan Hankins

Editorial Concept: "Precious outfits for plush pals!"

Cross Stitch Sampler's Merry Stitches

Published by:

NKS Publications Inc.

707 Kantz Road

St. Charles IL 69174

Date: 1994

Frequency: Special

Cover Price: $3.95

Subscription Price: n/a

Discount Subscription Price: n/a

Total Number of Pages: 52

Total Number of Ad Pages: 11

Publisher: NKS Publications Inc.

Editor: Deborah Novak

Editorial Concept: "Easy-to-finish holiday projects."

Family Circle Knitting

Published by:

The Family Circle Inc. and Butterick Company Inc.

161 Avenue of the Americas

New York NY 10013

Date: Fall 1994

Frequency: Special

Cover Price: $3.95

Subscription Price: n/a

Discount Subscription Price: n/a

Total Number of Pages: 106

Total Number of Ad Pages: 24

Publisher: Family Circle Inc. and Butterick Company Inc.

Editor: Nancy J. Thomas

Editorial Concept: Knitting instructions and projects.

Fashion Art

Published by:

MSC Publishing Inc.

243 Newton-Sparta Road

Newton NJ 07860

Date: 1994

Frequency: Annually

Cover Price: $4.95

Subscription Price: n/a

Discount Subscription Price: n/a

Total Number of Pages: 52

Total Number of Ad Pages: 4

Publisher: Jerry Cohen

Editor: Camille Pomaco

Editorial Concept: Using crafts and needlework to create wearable fashion.

Fashion Doll Accessories

Published by:

House of White Birches

306 E. Parr Road

Berne IN 46711

Date: 1994

Frequency: Special

Cover Price: $3.95

Subscription Price: n/a

Discount Subscription Price: n/a

Total Number of Pages: 32

Total Number of Ad Pages: 2

Publisher: Carl H. and Arthur K. Muselman

Editor: Laura Scott

Editorial Concept: "Many wonderful and fun accessories for playtime."

Patchwork Crafts

Published by:

MSC Publishing Inc.

243 Newton-Sparta Road

Newton NJ 07860

Date: Summer/Fall 1994

Frequency: Annually

Cover Price: $4.95

Subscription Price: n/a

Discount Subscription Price: n/a

Total Number of Pages: 68

Total Number of Ad Pages: 3

Publisher: Jerry Cohen

Editor: Phyllis K. Barbieri

Editorial Concept: Quilted gifts and decorations.

Quilting for Christmas

Published by:

MSC Publishing Inc.

243 Newton-Sparta Road

Newton NJ 07860

Date: Winter 1994

Frequency: Annually

Cover Price: $4.95

Subscription Price: n/a

Discount Subscription Price: n/a

Total Number of Pages: 68

Total Number of Ad Pages: 5

Publisher: Jerry Cohen

Editor: Phyllis K. Barbieri

Editorial Concept: "Quilted gifts in a wink!"

Victorian Hearts & Flowers

Published by:

Meredith Corporation

1716 Locust St.

Des Moines IA 50309-3023

Date: 1994

Frequency: Annually

Cover Price: $3.95

Subscription Price: n/a

Discount Subscription Price: n/a

Total Number of Pages: 148

Total Number of Ad Pages: 10

Publisher: Meredith Corporation

Editor: Linda True Stueve

Editorial Concept: "The legacy of crafting from the Victorian era – handmade with love."

Vogue Knitting Crochet

Published by:

Butterick Company Inc.

161 Avenue of the Americas

New York NY 10013

Date: 1994

Frequency: Special

Cover Price: $4.95

Subscription Price: n/a

Discount Subscription Price: n/a

Total Number of Pages: 88

Total Number of Ad Pages: 12

Publisher: Art Joinnides

Editor: Nancy J. Thomas

Editorial Concept: "A dozen easy but stylish designs."

Weekend Crochet

Published by:

Harris Publications Inc.

1115 Broadway

New York NY 10010

Date: 1994

Frequency: Annually

Cover Price: $2.95

Subscription Price: n/a

Discount Subscription Price: n/a

Total Number of Pages: 76

Total Number of Ad Pages: 0

Publisher: Stanley R. Harris

Editor: Barbara Jacksier

Editorial Concept: "Complete instructions for 65 easy projects."

Woman's Day Wearable Art

Published by:

Hachette Filipacchi Magazines Inc.

1633 Broadway

New York NY 10019

Date: 1994

Frequency: Special

Cover Price: $3.50

Subscription Price: n/a

Discount Subscription Price: n/a

Total Number of Pages: 100

Total Number of Ad Pages: 14

Publisher: Daniel Filipacchi

Editor: Carolyn M. Gatto

Editorial Concept: Clothes and accessories.

Petersen's Autotronics

Published by:

Petersen Publishing Company

6420 Wilshire Blvd.

Los Angeles CA 90048

Date: May 1994

Frequency: Bimonthly

Cover Price: $3.50

Subscription Price: $12.95

Discount Subscription Price: n/a

Total Number of Pages: 84

Total Number of Ad Pages: 24

Publisher: Bruce Blake

Editor: Ron Cogan

Editorial Concept: "The complete guide to auto sound and accessories."

Satellite Times

Published by:

Grove Enterprises Inc.

P.O. Box 98

Brasstown NC 28902

Date: November/December 1994

Frequency: Bimonthly

Cover Price: $3.50

Subscription Price: $19.95

Discount Subscription Price: n/a

Total Number of Pages: 92

Total Number of Ad Pages: 13

Publisher: Bob Grove

Editor: Larry Van Horn

Editorial Concept: Information for ham radio and satellite enthusiasts.

Annual, Special or Frequency Unknown

Camcorder Buyer's Guide and Handbook

Published by:

Bedford Communications Inc.

150 Fifth Ave.

New York NY 10011

Date: 1994

Frequency: Special

Cover Price: $4.95

Subscription Price: n/a

Discount Subscription Price: n/a

Total Number of Pages: 100

Total Number of Ad Pages: 32

Publisher: Edwin D. Brown

Editor: David Drucker

Editorial Concept: "How to buy top brands for less."

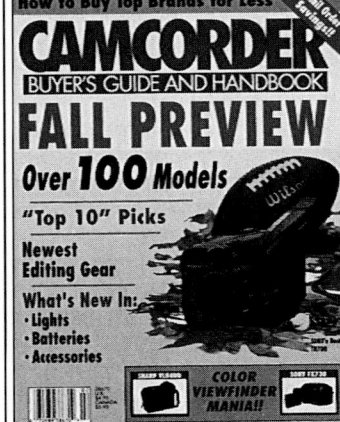

Brewing Techniques

Published by:
New Wine Press Inc.
1127 Lincoln St.
Eugene OR 97401
Date: July/August 1994
Frequency: Bimonthly
Cover Price: $5.50
Subscription Price: $35.00
Discount Subscription Price: $30.00
Total Number of Pages: 60
Total Number of Ad Pages: 18
Publisher: Stephen A. Mallery
Editor: Stephen A. Mallery
Editorial Concept: Recipes and tips for people who brew their own beer.

Cooking Healthy

Published by:
Publications International Ltd.
7373 N. Cicero Ave.
Lincolnwood IL 60646

Date: January 1994
Frequency: 14/year
Cover Price: $2.95
Subscription Price: n/a
Discount Subscription Price: n/a
Total Number of Pages: 100
Total Number of Ad Pages: 2
Publisher: Ivy G. Lester
Editor: Sara Armstrong
Editorial Concept: "Delicious low-fat dishes that capture the flavors of authentic Chinese cooking."

Saveur

Published by:
Meigher Communications L.P.
399 Park Ave.

New York NY 10022-4614
Date: Summer 1994
Frequency: Bimonthly
Cover Price: $5.00
Subscription Price: $28.00
Discount Subscription Price: $24.00
Total Number of Pages: 132
Total Number of Ad Pages: 41
Publisher: Meigher Communications L.P.
Editor: Dorothy Kalins
Editorial Concept: "Tells the life story of food - visiting the places it comes from, meeting the people who create it."

Taunton's Fine Cooking

Published by:
The Taunton Press Inc.
Newtown CT 06470-5506
Date: February/March 1994

Frequency: Bimonthly
Cover Price: $4.95
Subscription Price: $26.00
Discount Subscription Price: n/a
Total Number of Pages: 84
Total Number of Ad Pages: 16
Publisher: Jan Wahlin
Editor: Jan Wahlin
Editorial Concept: Articles and recipes "for people who love to cook."

Annual, Special or Frequency Unknown

America's Best Recipes

Published by:
Southern Living Inc.
2100 Lakeshore Drive
Birmingham AL 35209
Date: Fall 1994
Frequency: n/a
Cover Price: $2.95
Subscription Price: n/a
Discount Subscription Price: n/a

Total Number of Pages: 100
Total Number of Ad Pages: 13
Publisher: Scott Sheppard
Editor: Kaye Mabry Adams
Editorial Concept: "Shortcuts and new ideas to get well-balanced, kind-to-the-budget meals on the table fast."

Amish Favorites

Published by:
House of White Birches
306 E. Parr Road
Berne IN 46711
Date: 1994
Frequency: Special

Cover Price: $1.95
Subscription Price: n/a
Discount Subscription Price: n/a
Total Number of Pages: 68
Total Number of Ad Pages: 4
Publisher: Carl H. and Arthur K. Muselman
Editor: Vivian Rothe
Editorial Concept: "200 authentic Amish recipes."

Bake It Better with Quaker Oats

Published by:
Meredith Publishing Services
1912 Grand Ave.
Des Moines IA 50309-3379
Date: 1994
Frequency: Special
Cover Price: $2.99
Subscription Price: n/a

Discount Subscription Price: n/a

Total Number of Pages: 100

Total Number of Ad Pages: 2

Publisher: Meredith Publishing

Editor: n/a

Editorial Concept: "The Quaker kitchen's favorite and most requested recipes.."

Campbell's Best-Ever Recipes

Published by:

Campbell Soup Company's Publications Center

Campbell Place

Camden NJ 08103-1799

Date: 1994

Frequency: Special

Cover Price: $2.95

Subscription Price: n/a

Discount Subscription Price: n/a

Total Number of Pages: 98

Total Number of Ad Pages: 4

Publisher: Campbell Soup Co.

Editor: Pat Teberg

Editorial Concept: "Both new ideas for the hectic 1990s and time-tested favorites updated for quick and easy preparation."

Campbell's Easy Summer Recipes

Published by:

Meredith Publishing Services

1912 Grand Ave.

Des Moines IA 50309-3379

Date: 1994

Frequency: Special

Cover Price: $2.99

Subscription Price: n/a

Discount Subscription Price: n/a

Total Number of Pages: 100

Total Number of Ad Pages: 4

Publisher: Meredith Publishing

Editor: Pat Teberg

Editorial Concept: "Quick 30-minute suppers."

Casseroles

Published by:

House of White Birches

306 E. Parr Road

Berne IN 46711

Date: 1994

Frequency: Special

Cover Price: $2.50

Subscription Price: n/a

Discount Subscription Price: n/a

Total Number of Pages: 68

Total Number of Ad Pages: 4

Publisher: Carl H. and Arthur K. Muselman

Editor: Peggy Moss

Editorial Concept: "135 tasty recipes to fix in minutes."

Christmas Cookies & Candies

Published by:

House of White Birches

306 E. Parr Road

Berne IN 46711

Date: 1994

Frequency: Special

Cover Price: $1.95

Subscription Price: n/a

Discount Subscription Price: n/a

Total Number of Pages: 68

Total Number of Ad Pages: 5

Publisher: Carl H. and Arthur K. Muselman

Editor: Jeanne Stouffer

Editorial Concept: "145 easy recipes for tempting treats."

Cooking for Two

Published by:

House of White Birches

306 E. Parr Road

Berne IN 46711

Date: 1994

Frequency: Special

Cover Price: $1.95

Subscription Price: n/a

Discount Subscription Price: n/a

Total Number of Pages: 68

Total Number of Ad Pages: 3

Publisher: Carl H. and Arthur K. Muselman

Editor: Shelly Vaughan

Editorial Concept: "Shows you how to cook economically for two in a delightfully delicious way."

Cooking with Meat

Published by:

House of White Birches

306 E. Parr Road

Berne IN 46711

Date: 1994

Frequency: Special

Cover Price: $1.95

Subscription Price: n/a

Discount Subscription Price: n/a

Total Number of Pages: 68

Total Number of Ad Pages: 3

Publisher: Carl H. and Arthur K. Muselman

Editor: Jeanne Stauffer

Editorial Concept: "More than 150 savory recipes."

Country Accents Christmas Baking Ideas

Published by:

GCR Publishing Group Inc.

1700 Broadway

New York NY 10019

Date: 1994

Frequency: Special

Cover Price: $3.95

Subscription Price: n/a

Discount Subscription Price: n/a

Total Number of Pages: 84

Total Number of Ad Pages: 0

Publisher: Charles Goodman

Editor: Devera Pine

Editorial Concept: "Hundreds of festive holiday recipes! Breads! Cakes! Cookies! Chocolates!"

Country Accents Delicious Cookies

Published by:

GCR Publishing Group Inc.

1700 Broadway

New York NY 10019

Date: 1994

Frequency: Annually

Cover Price: $2.95

Subscription Price: n/a

Discount Subscription Price: n/a

Total Number of Pages: 84

Total Number of Ad Pages: 0

Publisher: Charles Goodman

Editor: Marilyn Hansen

Editorial Concept: "135 quick and easy recipes."

Country Accents Light, Fast & Easy Summer Meals in Minutes

Published by:

GCR Publishing Group Inc.

1700 Broadway

New York NY 10019

Date: 1994

Frequency: Annually

Cover Price: $2.95

Subscription Price: n/a

Discount Subscription Price: n/a

Total Number of Pages: 84

Total Number of Ad Pages: 0

Publisher: Charles Goodman

Editor: Sallie Batson

Editorial Concept: "More than 100 of the best warm-weather dishes."

Country Accents Low Calorie Chicken & Fish Recipes

Published by:

GCR Publishing Group Inc.

1700 Broadway

New York NY 10019

Date: 1994

Frequency: Annually

Cover Price: $2.95

Subscription Price: n/a

Discount Subscription Price: n/a

Total Number of Pages: 84

Total Number of Ad Pages: 0

Publisher: Charles Goodman

Editor: Marilyn Hansen

Editorial Concept: "125 delicious dishes."

Country Accents Soups & Salads

Published by:

GCR Publishing Group Inc.

1700 Broadway

New York NY 10019

Date: 1994

Frequency: Annually

Cover Price: $2.95

Subscription Price: n/a

Discount Subscription Price: n/a

Total Number of Pages: 84

Total Number of Ad Pages: 0

Publisher: Charles Goodman

Editor: Sallie Batson

Editorial Concept: "The most exciting recipes ever to pique your appetite."

Country Cooking

Published by:

House of White Birches

306 E. Parr Road

Berne IN 46711

Date: 1994

Frequency: Special

Cover Price: $1.95

Subscription Price: n/a

Discount Subscription Price: n/a

Total Number of Pages: 68

Total Number of Ad Pages: 2

Publisher: Carl H. and Arthur K. Muselman

Editor: Alice Robinson

Editorial Concept: "More than 75 tasty recipes...that represent warmth and comfort."

Country Home Holidays at Home

Published by:

Meredith Corporation

1716 Locust St.

Des Moines IA 50309-3023

Date: 1994

Frequency: Special

Cover Price: $3.95

Subscription Price: n/a

Discount Subscription Price: n/a

Total Number of Pages: 132

Total Number of Ad Pages: 36

Publisher: Joseph A. Lagani

Editor: Molly Culbertson

Editorial Concept: "Lovely menus, delicious recipes, and simple entertaining suggestions."

Country Living Country Cooking

Published by:

Hearst Corporation

959 Eighth Ave.

New York NY 10019

Date: Summer 1994

Frequency: Annually

Cover Price: $2.95

Subscription Price: n/a

Discount Subscription Price: n/a

Total Number of Pages: 130

Total Number of Ad Pages: 24

Publisher: Jay McGill

Editor: Joanne Hayes and Lucy Wing

Editorial Concept: "Lighter in fat and featuring fresh vegetables and whole grains."

Easy Ground Meat Recipes

Published by:

House of White Birches

306 E. Parr Road

Berne IN 46711

Date: 1994

Frequency: Special

Cover Price: $1.95

Subscription Price: n/a

Discount Subscription Price: n/a

Total Number of Pages: 68

Total Number of Ad Pages: 3

Publisher: Carl H. and Arthur K. Muselman

Editor: Ramona Lehrman

Editorial Concept: "Quick and easy throw-together meals...in minutes."

Easy Meals in Minutes

Published by:

NYT Women's Magazines

110 Fifth Ave.

New York NY 10011

Date: 1994

Frequency: Special

Cover Price: $3.50

Subscription Price: n/a

Discount Subscription Price: n/a

Total Number of Pages: 108

Total Number of Ad Pages: 14

Publisher: Marion Aaron

Editor: Sally Koslow

Editorial Concept: "Cook-friendly, delicious, simple, complete menus."

Favorite Cakes

Published by:

House of White Birches

306 E. Parr Road

Berne IN 46711

Date: 1994

Frequency: Special

Cover Price: $2.50

Subscription Price: n/a

Discount Subscription Price: n/a

Total Number of Pages: 68

Total Number of Ad Pages: 4

Publisher: Carl H. and Arthur K. Muselman

Editor: Jeanne Stauffer and Shelly Vaughn

Editorial Concept: "145 delicious desserts for all occasions."

Favorite Slow Cooker Recipes

Published by:

House of White Birches

306 E. Parr Road

Berne IN 46711

Date: 1994

Frequency: Special

Cover Price: $1.95

Subscription Price: n/a

Discount Subscription Price: n/a

Total Number of Pages: 68

Total Number of Ad Pages: 5

Publisher: Carl H. and Arthur K. Muselman

Editor: Peggy Moss

Editorial Concept: "Dozens of delicious recipes."

Favorite Summer Recipes

Published by:

House of White Birches

306 E. Parr Road

Berne IN 46711

Date: 1994

Frequency: Special

Cover Price: $1.95

Subscription Price: n/a

Discount Subscription Price: n/a

Total Number of Pages: 68

Total Number of Ad Pages: 3

Publisher: Carl H. and Arthur K. Muselman

Editor: Jeanne Stauffer

Editorial Concept: "Delicious recipes and sizzling summer treats."

Garlic, Vinegar & Onions

Published by:

Prestige Publications Inc.

P.O. Box 23368

Shawnee Mission KS 66223

Date: 1994

Frequency: Special

Cover Price: $2.95

Subscription Price: n/a

Discount Subscription Price: n/a

Total Number of Pages: 100

Total Number of Ad Pages: 1

Publisher: Russ Moore

Editor: Loralee Baker-Rapue

Editorial Concept: "Historical facts, superstitions, folklore, and delicious recipes."

Good Housekeeping Smart Cooking

Published by:

The Hearst Corporation

959 Eighth Ave.

New York NY 10019

Date: Spring/Summer 1994

Frequency: Annually

Cover Price: $2.95

Subscription Price: n/a

Discount Subscription Price: n/a

Total Number of Pages: 116

Total Number of Ad Pages: 16

Publisher: Alan M. Waxenberg

Editor: Ila Stanger

Editorial Concept: "Light recipes, healthy menus, quick tips."

Grandma's Favorite Recipes

Published by:

House of White Birches

306 E. Parr Road

Berne IN 46711

Date: 1994

Frequency: Special

Cover Price: $1.95

Subscription Price: n/a

Discount Subscription Price: n/a

Total Number of Pages: 68

Total Number of Ad Pages: 2

Publisher: Carl H. and Arthur K. Muselman

Editor: Ramona Lehrman

Editorial Concept: "145 tasty recipes to bring back yesterday."

Great New Tastes with Yogurt

Published by:

Betty Crocker

Food & Publications Center

(No address given.)

Date: 1994

Frequency: Special

Cover Price: $2.95

Subscription Price: n/a

Discount Subscription Price: n/a

Total Number of Pages: 98

Total Number of Ad Pages: 1

Publisher: Betty Crocker Food & Publications Center

Editor: Cathy Swanson

Editorial Concept: Recipes all made with Yoplait yogurt.

Guilt-Free Desserts

Published by:

Southern Living Inc.

2100 Lakeshore Drive

Birmingham AL 35209

Date: 1994

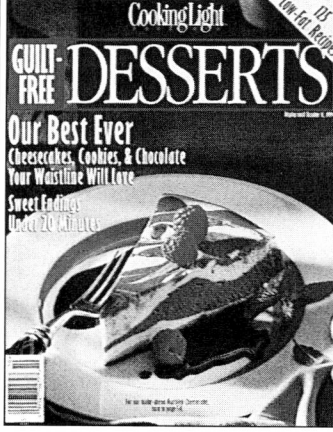

Frequency: Special

Cover Price: $3.95

Subscription Price: n/a

Discount Subscription Price: n/a

Total Number of Pages: 128

Total Number of Ad Pages: 43

Publisher: Jeffrey C. Ward

Editor: Ellen Templeton Carroll

Editorial Concept: Low-calorie, low-fat recipes from the pages of *Cooking Light*.

Low Fat Cookbook

Published by:

GCR Publishing Group Inc.

1700 Broadway

New York NY 10019

Date: 1994

Frequency: Annually

Cover Price: $2.95

Subscription Price: n/a

Discount Subscription Price: n/a

Total Number of Pages: 84

Total Number of Ad Pages: 0

Publisher: Charles Goodman

Editor: Marilyn Hansen

Editorial Concept: "Delicious and healthy recipes."

Pepperidge Farm's Easy Entertaining

Published by:

Meredith Publishing Services

1912 Grand Ave.

Des Moines IA 50309-3379

Date: 1994

Frequency: Special

Cover Price: $2.99

Subscription Price: n/a

Discount Subscription Price: n/a

Total Number of Pages: 96

Total Number of Ad Pages: 2

Publisher: Meredith Publishing Services

Editor: Pat Teberg

Editorial Concept: "Delicious recipes from appetizers to desserts."

Pillsbury Most Requested Recipes – Cookies

Published by:

Pillsbury Publications

200 S. Sixth St.

Minneapolis MN 55402

Date: 1994

Frequency: Special

Cover Price: $2.95

Subscription Price: n/a

Discount Subscription Price: n/a

Total Number of Pages: 100

Total Number of Ad Pages: 1

Publisher: Sally Peters

Editor: Elaine Christiansen

Editorial Concept: "The recipes most requested by callers to Pillsbury's consumer phones."

Pleasing Pasta Recipes

Published by:

House of White Birches

306 E. Parr Road

Berne IN 46711

Date: 1994

Frequency: Special

Cover Price: $1.95

Subscription Price: n/a

Discount Subscription Price: n/a

Total Number of Pages: 68

Total Number of Ad Pages: 3

Publisher: Carl H. and Arthur K. Muselman

Editor: Shelly Vaughan

Editorial Concept: "Delicious recipes for pasta lovers."

Prego Easy Italian Recipes

Published by:

Meredith Custom Publishing

17th St.

Des Moines IA 50336

Date: 1994

Frequency: Special

Cover Price: $2.99

Subscription Price: n/a

Discount Subscription Price: n/a

Total Number of Pages: 96

Total Number of Ad Pages: 2

Publisher: Meredith Publishing

Editor: Pat Teberg

Editorial Concept: "Family favorites, most ready in 30 minutes."

Prevention's Guide to Low-Fat Shopping

Published by:

Rodale Press Inc.

33 E. Minor St.

Emmaus PA 18098

Date: 1994

Frequency: Special

Cover Price: $2.95

Subscription Price: n/a

Discount Subscription Price: n/a

Total Number of Pages: 100

Total Number of Ad Pages: 7

Publisher: Richard Alleger

Editor: Catherine M. Cassidy

Editorial Concept: How to choose the least fatty products.

Recipes Featuring Pillsbury Refrigerated Cookie Dough

Published by:

Pillsbury Publications

200 S. Sixth St.

Minneapolis MN 55402

Date: December 1994

Frequency: Special

Cover Price: $2.95

Subscription Price: n/a

Discount Subscription Price: n/a

Total Number of Pages: 100

Total Number of Ad Pages: 6

Publisher: Sally Peters

Editor: Jackie Sheehan and Betsey Wray

Editorial Concept: Recipes using Pillsbury refrigerated cookie dough.

Slim and Fit Presents Brand Name Calorie Counter

Published by:

Harris Publications Inc.

1115 Broadway

New York NY 10010

Date: 1994

Frequency: Annually

Cover Price: $2.95

Subscription Price: n/a

Discount Subscription Price: n/a

Total Number of Pages: 100

Total Number of Ad Pages: 0

Publisher: Stanley R. Harris

Editor: Diane Lesniewski

Editorial Concept: "Your all-in-one dieting guide so you can find it - fast!"

Strawberries!

Published by:

House of White Birches

306 E. Parr Road

Berne IN 46711

Date: 1994

Frequency: Special

Cover Price: $1.95

Subscription Price: n/a

Discount Subscription Price: n/a

Total Number of Pages: 68

Total Number of Ad Pages: 3

Publisher: Carl H. and Arthur K. Muselman

Editor: Jeanne Stauffer

Editorial Concept: "Delicious recipes using strawberries."

Today's Entertaining

Published by:

Hachette Filipacchi Magazines Inc.

1633 Broadway

New York NY 10019

Date: 1994

Frequency: n/a

Cover Price: $2.95

Subscription Price: n/a

Discount Subscription Price: n/a

Total Number of Pages: 100

Total Number of Ad Pages: 25

Publisher: Susan S. Buckley and Patrice Listfield

Editor: Leah Rosch

Editorial Concept: "Entertaining can, and should, be easy and fun."

Weeknight Meals

Published by:

GCR Publishing Group Inc.

1700 Broadway

New York NY 10019

Date: 1994

Frequency: Special

Cover Price: $2.95

Subscription Price: n/a

Discount Subscription Price: n/a

Total Number of Pages: 84

Total Number of Ad Pages: 0

Publisher: Charles Goodman

Editor: Sallie Batson

Editorial Concept: Fast and easy family meals.

Woman's Day Cookies and Sweet Treats

Published by:

Hachette Filipacchi Magazines Inc.

1633 Broadway

New York NY 10019

Date: 1994

Frequency: Special

Cover Price: $2.75

Subscription Price: n/a

Discount Subscription Price: n/a

Total Number of Pages: 100

Total Number of Ad Pages: 5

Publisher: Hachette Filipacchi

Editor: Lee Randall

Editorial Concept: "Festive family favorites."

Woman's Day Gifts from the Christmas Kitchen

Published by:

Hachette Filipacchi Magazines Inc.

500 W. Putnam Ave.

Greenwich CT 06836

Date: 1994

Frequency: Special

Cover Price: $2.75

Subscription Price: n/a

Discount Subscription Price: n/a

Total Number of Pages: 100

Total Number of Ad Pages: 6

Publisher: Hachette Filipacchi Magazines Inc.

Editor: n/a

Editorial Concept: "Cookies, candies, breads, muffins...sweet treats to give or keep."

Yankee Magazine's Christmas in New England

Published by:

Yankee Publishing Inc.

P.O. Box 400471

Des Moines IA 50340-0471

Date: 1994

Frequency: Special

Cover Price: $3.95

Subscription Price: n/a

Discount Subscription Price: n/a

Total Number of Pages: 116

Total Number of Ad Pages: 30

Publisher: Judson D. Hale Jr.

Editor: Janice Brand

Editorial Concept: "Traditional recipes and festive treats."

The Edge Big Game Fishing Journal

Published by:

Offshore International Publications

2379 Route 34

Manasquan NJ 08736

Date: Fall 1994

Frequency: Quarterly

Cover Price: $4.95

Subscription Price: n/a

Discount Subscription Price: n/a

Total Number of Pages: 116

Total Number of Ad Pages: 33

Publisher: Gary Caputi

Editor: Leonard T. Belcaro

Editorial Concept: Tips, techniques, and procedures from professional anglers around the country.

Fishing World

Published by:

KC Publishing Inc.

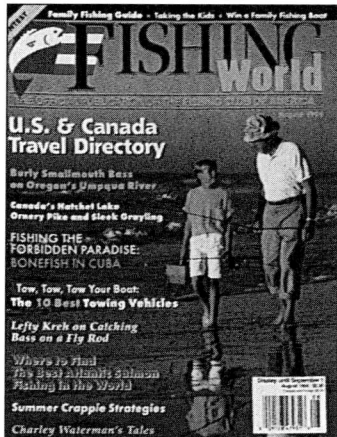

700 W. 47th St., Suite 310

Kansas City MO 64112

Date: August 1994

Frequency: Bimonthly

Cover Price: $2.95

Subscription Price: $12.95

Discount Subscription Price: n/a

Total Number of Pages: 76

Total Number of Ad Pages: 24

Publisher: John C. Prebich

Editor: David J. Richey

Editorial Concept: "The official publication of the Fishing Club of America."

Remington Country

Published by:

Harris Publications Inc.

1115 Broadway

New York NY 10010

Date: 1994

Frequency: Semi-annually

Cover Price: $3.95

Subscription Price: n/a

Discount Subscription Price: n/a

Total Number of Pages: 100

Total Number of Ad Pages: 28

Publisher: Stanley R. Harris

Editor: Lamar Underwood

Editorial Concept: "The hunting magazine that takes you beyond the ordinary."

Rocky Mountain Bowhunter

Published by:

Mountain Publishing Inc.

304 W. Main St.

Grand Junction CO 81505

Date: May/June 1994

(first newsstand issue)

Frequency: Bimonthly

Cover Price: $2.25

Subscription Price: $10.95

Discount Subscription Price: n/a

Total Number of Pages: 44

Total Number of Ad Pages: 17

Publisher: Linda J. Gray

Editor: Dr. N.J. Gray

Editorial Concept: "The bowhunting magazine of the Rocky Mountains."

Western Angler

Published by:

Western Angler Corporation

350 E. Center St., Suite 201

Provo UT 84606

Date: April/May 1994

Frequency: Bimonthly

Cover Price: $2.95

Subscription Price: $12.95

Discount Subscription Price: n/a

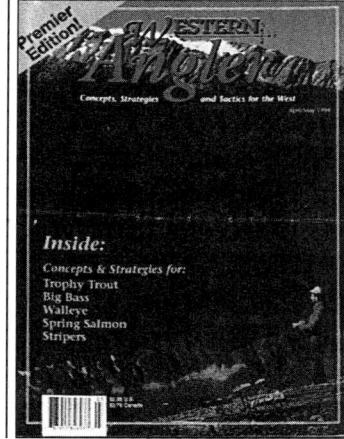

Total Number of Pages: 64

Total Number of Ad Pages: 28

Publisher: Ray Crosby

Editor: Ray Schelble

Editorial Concept: "The absolute best in Western fishing methods, concepts, strategies, and tactics."

Annual, Special or Frequency Unknown

Advanced Bass Strategies

Published by:

Harris Publications Inc.

1115 Broadway

New York NY 10010

Date: March 1994

Frequency: 3/year

Cover Price: $2.95

Subscription Price: n/a

Discount Subscription Price: n/a

Total Number of Pages: 84

Total Number of Ad Pages: 16

Publisher: Stanley R. Harris

Editor: Kim Leighton

Editorial Concept: "Devoted exclusively to the most exciting, diverse, and widespread freshwater fishing in North America."

American Sharpshooter

Published by:

Aquafield Publishing Company

66 W. Gilbert St.

Shrewsbury NJ 07702

Date: 1994

Frequency: n/a

Cover Price: $2.50

Subscription Price: n/a

Discount Subscription Price: n/a

Total Number of Pages: 64

Total Number of Ad Pages: 17

Publisher: Stephen Ferber

Editor: Richard M. Cain

Editorial Concept: Old and new classic guns and knives.

The Fly Fisher's Almanac 1994

Published by:

The Fly Fisher's Almanac Company

P.O. Box 504

Pampton Plains NJ 07444

Date: 1994

Frequency: Annually

Cover Price: $6.95

Subscription Price: n/a

Discount Subscription Price: n/a

Total Number of Pages: 260

Total Number of Ad Pages: 2

Publisher: Eugene M. Casale

Editor: Andrew M. Casale

Editorial Concept: "Everything a fly fisher needs right at your fingertips."

Mossy Oak Full Strut Turkey Hunting

Published by:

Harris Publications Inc.

1115 Broadway

New York NY 10010

Date: 1994

Frequency: Annually

Cover Price: $3.95

Subscription Price: n/a

Discount Subscription Price: n/a

Total Number of Pages: 100

Total Number of Ad Pages: 23

Publisher: Stanley R. Harris

Editor: Kim Leighton

Editorial Concept: "How to find, call, and bag a gobbler this spring."

Scientific Anglers Fly Fishing for Bass & Panfish

Published by:

Aqua-Field Publishing Company

66 W. Gilbert St.

Shrewsbury NJ 07702

Date: 1994

Frequency: Annually

Cover Price: $2.95

Subscription Price: n/a

Discount Subscription Price: n/a

Total Number of Pages: 80

Total Number of Ad Pages: 11

Publisher: Stephen Ferber

Editor: Robert Elman

Editorial Concept: How to catch more bass, panfish, pike, musky, walleye, and other game.

Whitetail Slug Hunter

Published by:

Harris Publications Inc.

1115 Broadway

New York NY 10010

Date: 1994

Frequency: Annually

Cover Price: $3.95

Subscription Price: n/a

Discount Subscription Price: n/a

Total Number of Pages: 100

Total Number of Ad Pages: 20

Publisher: Stanley R. Harris

Editor: Lamar Underwood

Editorial Concept: "The ultimate guide to shotgun deer hunting!"

Whitetail World

Published by:

Krause Publications Inc.

700 E. State St.

Ida WI 54990

Date: 1994

Frequency: Special

Cover Price: $3.95

Subscription Price: n/a

Discount Subscription Price: n/a

Total Number of Pages: 84

Total Number of Ad Pages: 3

Publisher: Debbie Knauer

Editor: Patrick Durkin

Editorial Concept: Photographic facts for white-tailed deer hunters.

Garden Design

Published by:

Meigher Communications, L.P.

100 Avenue of the Americas

New York NY 10013

Date: April/May 1994

Frequency: Bimonthly

Cover Price: $5.00

Subscription Price: $28.00

Discount Subscription Price: $24.00

Total Number of Pages: 140

Total Number of Ad Pages: 53

Publisher: Arthur H. Loomis

Editor: Dorothy Kalins

Editorial Concept: "To celebrate the gardener as artist and writer, philosopher and photographer, horticulturist and nurturer."

Annual, Special or Frequency Unknown

Country Accents Gardens & Decks

Published by:

GCR Publishing Group Inc.

1700 Broadway

New York NY 10019

Date: 1994

Frequency: Annually

Cover Price: $3.95

Subscription Price: n/a

Discount Subscription Price: n/a

Total Number of Pages: 84

Total Number of Ad Pages: 10

Publisher: Charles Goodman

Editor: Ron Renzulli

Editorial Concept: "Ideas for improving the exterior of your house and property."

Country Home & Garden

Published by:

Prestige Publications Inc.

4151 Knob Drive

Eagan MN 55122

Date: 1994

Frequency: Special

Cover Price: $3.95

Subscription Price: n/a

Discount Subscription Price: n/a

Total Number of Pages: 84

Total Number of Ad Pages: 8

Publisher: Prestige Publications Inc.

Editor: n/a

Editorial Concept: "Tips for successful gardening of flowers and vegetables."

Easy Lawn & Garden

Published by:

Aquafield Publishing Company

66 W. Gilbert St.

Shrewsbury NJ 07702

Date: 1994

Frequency: n/a

Cover Price: $2.95

Subscription Price: n/a

Discount Subscription Price: n/a

Total Number of Pages: 84

Total Number of Ad Pages: 17

Publisher: Stephen Ferber

Editor: Edward Montague

Editorial Concept: "How to plan and execute your dream landscape."

Everything You Need to Know about Gardening

Published by:

Prestige Publications

P.O. Box 23368

Shawnee Mission KS 66223

Date: 1994

Frequency: Special

Cover Price: $3.95

Subscription Price: n/a

Discount Subscription Price: n/a

Total Number of Pages: 84

Total Number of Ad Pages: 2

Publisher: Russ Moore

Editor: Lucinda Spencer

Editorial Concept: "Everything you need to know about gardening."

Rodale's Organic Flower Gardening

Published by:

Rodale Press Inc.

33 E. Minor St.

Emmaus PA 18098

Date: Spring 1994

Frequency: Annually

Cover Price: $2.95

Subscription Price: n/a

Discount Subscription Price: n/a

Total Number of Pages: 100

Total Number of Ad Pages: 19

Publisher: Barbara R. Newton

Editor: Mike McGrath

Editorial Concept: "Your chemical-free guide to fabulous flower gardening."

Weekend Gardening

Published by:

Harris Publications Inc.

1115 Broadway

New York NY 10010

Date: 1994

Frequency: Annually

Cover Price: $3.95

Subscription Price: n/a

Discount Subscription Price: n/a

Total Number of Pages: 84

Total Number of Ad Pages: 2

Publisher: Stanley R. Harris

Editor: Diane Morelli

Editorial Concept: Tips for first-time and part-time gardeners.

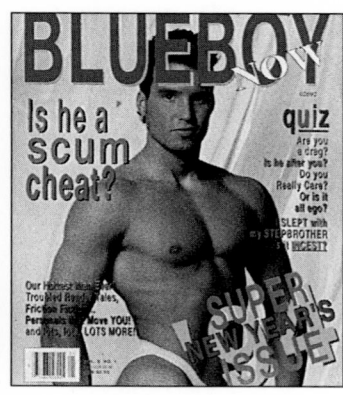

Blueboy Now

Published by:

Leemar Publishing Inc.

28 W. 25th St., 7th Floor

New York NY 10010

Date: 1994

Frequency: 9/year

Cover Price: $5.95

Subscription Price: $75/12 issues

Discount Subscription Price: n/a

Total Number of Pages: 100

Total Number of Ad Pages: 32

Publisher: Casey Lee Klinger

Editor: Robert Leighton

Editorial Concept: "A hot shower of way cool dudes, perverse, digestible hardcore stories, and more."

Girl Friends

Published by:

Girlfriends Magazine

P.O. Box 713

Half Moon Bay CA 94019

Date: July 1994

Frequency: Bimonthly

Cover Price: $4.95

Subscription Price: $24.00

Discount Subscription Price: n/a

Total Number of Pages: 52

Total Number of Ad Pages: 7

Publisher: Erin Findlay

Editor: Heather Findlay

Editorial Concept: "*Girlfriends*' mission is to cover lesbian culture, politics, and sexuality in a beautifully designed, color, glossy format."

The Harvard Gay and Lesbian Review

Published by:

Harvard Gay and Lesbian Caucus

Box 1809

Cambridge MA 02238

Date: Summer 1994

(first newsstand issue)

Frequency: Quarterly

Cover Price: $5.00

Subscription Price: $16.00

Discount Subscription Price: n/a

Total Number of Pages: 48

Total Number of Ad Pages: 3

Publisher: Harvard Gay and Lesbian Caucus

Editor: Richard Schneider Jr.

Editorial Concept: Features essays, book reviews, and memoirs.

Honcho Overload

Published by:

Overload Company

462 Broadway, 4th Floor

New York NY 10013

Date: February 1994

Frequency: 9/year

Cover Price: $4.50

Subscription Price: $31.95

Discount Subscription Price: n/a

Total Number of Pages: 180

Total Number of Ad Pages: 11

Publisher: Overload Company

Editor: Aaron Travis

Editorial Concept: "The emphasis is on gay men's erotic fiction that goes beyond the everyday sexual experience."

In Uniform

Published by:

A.M. Publications

P.O. Box 3226

Portland OR 97208

Date: August 1994

Frequency: Quarterly

Cover Price: $5.95

Subscription Price: $24.00

Discount Subscription Price: n/a

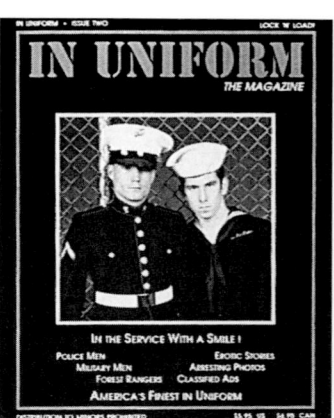

Total Number of Pages: 76

Total Number of Ad Pages: 15

Publisher: Andy Mangels

Editor: Andy Mangels

Editorial Concept: "Committed to promoting the gay and lesbian community and the uniform/leather/ S&M/fetish community at large."

Indulge

Published by:

In Touch Inc.

13122 Saticoy St.

North Hollywood CA 91605

Date: Fall 1994

Frequency: Quarterly

Cover Price: $5.95

Subscription Price: $29.94/6 issues

Discount Subscription Price: n/a

Total Number of Pages: 68

Total Number of Ad Pages: 18

Publisher: In Touch Inc.

Editor: Darrell Roberts

Editorial Concept: Explicit pictorials of nude men for a gay audience.

Latin Men

Published by:

Heat Publications Inc.

462 Broadway, 4th Floor

New York NY 10013

Date: 1994

Frequency: Quarterly

Cover Price: $5.99

Subscription Price: n/a

Discount Subscription Price: n/a

Total Number of Pages: 100

Total Number of Ad Pages: 3

Publisher: Jay Epstein

Editor: Blade Brice

Editorial Concept: Explicit nude pictorials of Latin hunks for gay men.

Male Cherries

Published by:

Thrust Industries Inc.

208 E. 51st St., Suite 228

New York NY 10022

Date: January 1994

Frequency: Bimonthly

Cover Price: $3.95

Subscription Price: $19.95

Discount Subscription Price: n/a

Total Number of Pages: 132

Total Number of Ad Pages: 5

Publisher: Thrust Industries Inc.

Editor: n/a

Editorial Concept: "Hopeful young bucks and the men who break them in."

Annual, Special or Frequency Unknown

Bear Tales

Published by:

First Hand Ltd.

310 Cedar Lane

Teaneck NJ 07666

Date: January 1994

Frequency: Special

Cover Price: $4.95

Subscription Price: n/a

Discount Subscription Price: n/a

Total Number of Pages: 132

Total Number of Ad Pages: 22

Publisher: Jackie Lewis

Editor: Dave Babbitt

Editorial Concept: Sex tales told by and targeted at the rugged gay man.

Cherry Tales

Published by:

First Hand Ltd.

310 Cedar Lane

Teaneck NJ 07666

Date: March 1994

Frequency: Special

Cover Price: $4.95

Subscription Price: n/a

Discount Subscription Price: n/a

Total Number of Pages: 132

Total Number of Ad Pages: 26

Publisher: Jackie Lewis

Editor: William Spencer

Editorial Concept: "All new sex tales, plus the best of your letters."

Cowpoke Tales

Published by:

First Hand Ltd.

310 Cedar Lane

Teaneck NJ 07666

Date: May 1994

Frequency: Special

Cover Price: $4.95

Subscription Price: n/a

Discount Subscription Price: n/a

Total Number of Pages: 132

Total Number of Ad Pages: 29

Publisher: Jackie Lewis

Editor: Bob Harris

Editorial Concept: "All new sex tales, plus the best of your letters."

Jockstrap Tales

Published by:

First Hand Ltd.

310 Cedar Lane

Teaneck NJ 07666

Date: July 1994

Frequency: Special

Cover Price: $4.95

Subscription Price: n/a

Discount Subscription Price: n/a

Total Number of Pages: 132

Total Number of Ad Pages: 24

Publisher: Jackie Lewis

Editor: Dave Babbitt

Editorial Concept: Tales of gay sex with a sports theme.

Locker Room Tales

Published by:

First Hand Ltd.

310 Cedar Lane

Teaneck NJ 07666

Date: December 1994

Frequency: Special

Cover Price: $4.95

Subscription Price: n/a

Discount Subscription Price: n/a

Total Number of Pages: 132

Total Number of Ad Pages: 22

Publisher: Jackie Lewis

Editor: Nick Roberts

Editorial Concept: "All new sex tales plus the best of your letters."

Tearoom Tales

Published by:

First Hand Ltd.

310 Cedar Lane

Teaneck NJ 07666

Date: November 1994

Frequency: Special

Cover Price: $4.95

Subscription Price: n/a

Discount Subscription Price: n/a

Total Number of Pages: 132

Total Number of Ad Pages: 29

Publisher: Jackie Lewis

Editor: Bill Jaeger

Editorial Concept: Explicit sex tales, drawings, and letters of gay sex.

Telephone Tales

Published by:

First Hand Ltd.

310 Cedar Lane

Teaneck NJ 07666

Date: September 1994

Frequency: Special

Cover Price: $4.95

Subscription Price: n/a

Discount Subscription Price: n/a

Total Number of Pages: 132

Total Number of Ad Pages: 23

Publisher: Jackie Lewis

Editor: William Spencer

Editorial Concept: "All new sex tales, plus your hottest letters."

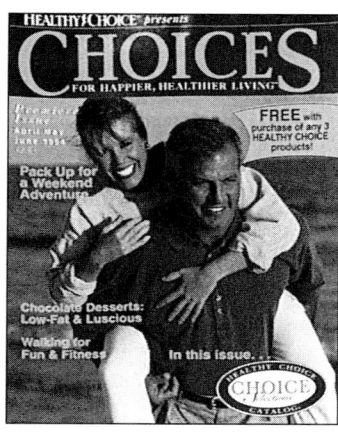

Choices for Happier, Healthier Living

Published by:

Time Inc. Ventures Custom Publishing

2100 Lakeshore Drive

Birmingham AL 35209

Date: Spring 1994

Frequency: Quarterly

Cover Price: $2.50

Subscription Price: n/a

Discount Subscription Price: n/a

Total Number of Pages: 52

Total Number of Ad Pages: 14

Publisher: Dianne Mooney

Editor: Cathy A. Wesler, R.D.

Editorial Concept: "Written expressly for people who enjoy eating Healthy Choice products."

éternelle

Published by:

éternelle Magazine Company

P.O. Box 1646

Los Altos CA 94023

Date: Spring 1994

Frequency: Quarterly

Cover Price: $3.50

Subscription Price: $18.00

Discount Subscription Price: n/a

Total Number of Pages: 44

Total Number of Ad Pages: 10

Publisher: Valerie Foster

Editor: Laura Dayton

Editorial Concept: A woman's publication geared toward exercise and cosmetic advice on looking young.

Fabio's Healthy Bodies

Published by:

Stingray Publishing Company Inc.

153 Merrick Road, Suite 244

Merrick NY 11566

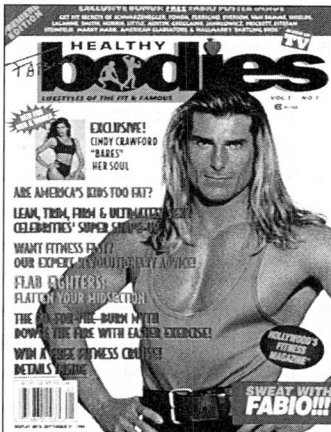

Date: Summer 1994

Frequency: Bimonthly

Cover Price: $2.95

Subscription Price: $16.50

Discount Subscription Price: n/a

Total Number of Pages: 60

Total Number of Ad Pages: 17

Publisher: Steve Raimondi

Editor: Jeff Everson

Editorial Concept: "Lifestyles of the fit and famous."

Health Counselor

Published by:

Impakt Communications Inc.

P.O. Box 12496

Green Bay WI 54307-2496

Date: February 1994

Frequency: Bimonthly

Cover Price: $2.95

Subscription Price: $18.00

Discount Subscription Price: n/a

Total Number of Pages: 48

Total Number of Ad Pages: 9

Publisher: Karolyn A. Gazella

Editor: Karolyn A. Gazella

Editorial Concept: "To provide accurate and useful information to the consumer about advances and alternatives in the field of natural health and nutrition."

The Home Fitness Buyers Guide

Published by:

Waters Onigman & Associates

1 Union Ave.

Sudbury MA 01776-2246

Date: Winter 1994

Frequency: Quarterly

Cover Price: $4.95

Subscription Price: $15.80

Discount Subscription Price: n/a

Total Number of Pages: 100

Total Number of Ad Pages: 30

Publisher: Craig R. Waters and Marc Onigman

Editor: Craig R. Waters

Editorial Concept: "Entirely devoted to home fitness equipment."

Home Gym and Fitness

Published by:

Inside Sports Inc.

990 Grove St.

Evanston IL 60201

Date: Summer 1994

Frequency: Quarterly

Cover Price: $2.95 (special offer)

Subscription Price: $14.95

Discount Subscription Price: $9.97

Total Number of Pages: 84

Total Number of Ad Pages: 27

Publisher: Jerry L. Croft

Editor: Larry Burke

Editorial Concept: Features, profiles, and instructional articles for Americans interested in maintaining good health, personal fitness, and conditioning in their own homes.

Lifetime Fitness

Published by:

Publications Partners Inc.

4151 Knob Drive

Eagan MN 55122

Date: October 1994

Frequency: Quarterly

Cover Price: $2.95

Subscription Price: $9.95

Discount Subscription Price: n/a

Total Number of Pages: 84

Total Number of Ad Pages: 9

Publisher: Russ Moore

Editor: Tony Grundhauser

Editorial Concept: "Dedicated to fitness and health news for men and women over 35 who seek the joys and benefits an active, healthy lifestyle can deliver."

Mississippi Healthscope 2000

Published by:

R&M Publications

No address given.

Date: Summer 1994

Frequency: Quarterly

Cover Price: $2.95

Subscription Price: $10.00

Discount Subscription Price: n/a

Total Number of Pages: 48

Total Number of Ad Pages: 16

Publisher: Joe and Billie Moan

Editor: Pat Coggin

Editorial Concept: "To bring together Mississippi health-care consumers with Mississippi health-care providers."

Plus Voice

Published by:

Plus Voice Magazine Inc.

29 S. LaSalle St., Suite 1150

Chicago IL 60603

Date: January/February 1994

Frequency: Bimonthly

Cover Price: $1.95

Subscription Price: $30.00

Discount Subscription Price: n/a

Total Number of Pages: 84

Total Number of Ad Pages: 30

Publisher: Joseph Crump

Editor: Brett Grodeck

Editorial Concept: Health, activism, and lifestyle for individuals affected by the AIDS virus.

POZ

Published by:

Strubco Inc.

349 W. 12th St.

New York NY 10014

Date: April/May 1994

Frequency: Bimonthly

Cover Price: $3.50

Subscription Price: $19.95

Discount Subscription Price: n/a

Total Number of Pages: 68

Total Number of Ad Pages: 12

Publisher: Sean O'Brien Strub

Editor: Sean O'Brien Strub

Editorial Concept: "To cover AIDS from the eyes of everyone affected by the disease, including families, friends, neighbors, co-workers, and caregivers."

The Right Stuff

Published by:

The Right Stuff

P.O. Box 2176

Terre Haute IN 47802

Date: December 1994

Frequency: Monthly

Cover Price: $2.95

Subscription Price: $19.95

Discount Subscription Price: n/a

Total Number of Pages: 58

Total Number of Ad Pages: 13

Publisher: The Right Stuff

Editor: Erette Labuzan

Editorial Concept: Training and nutrition tips for serious, competition-level bodybuilders.

Scientific American Science & Medicine

Published by:

Scientific American Inc.

415 Madison Ave.

New York NY 10017-1111

Date: March/April 1994

Frequency: Bimonthly

Cover Price: $9.95

Subscription Price: $59.00

Discount Subscription Price: n/a

Total Number of Pages: 92

Total Number of Ad Pages: 16

Publisher: John J. Moeling Jr.

Editor: Albert E. Maier

Editorial Concept: "To review, over time, the entire scientific foundation of clinical medicine."

Urban Fitness

Published by:

Urban Fitness

Suite 2200, U.S. Bank Tower

1420 Fifth Ave.

Seattle WA 98101

Date: September/October 1994

Frequency: Bimonthly

Cover Price: $4.95

Subscription Price: $20.79

Discount Subscription Price: n/a

Total Number of Pages: 140

Total Number of Ad Pages: 0

Publisher: Jim L. Herman

Editor: Jim L. Herman

Editorial Concept: "A new magazine for a healthy lifestyle, aimed primarily but not exclusively at gay men and women."

Annual, Special or Frequency Unknown

The American Guide

Published by:

American Guide

P.O. Box 2924

Clearwater FL 34617

Date: 1994

Frequency: Special

Cover Price: $1.95

Subscription Price: $7.50

Discount Subscription Price: n/a

Total Number of Pages: 36

Total Number of Ad Pages: 0

Publisher: American Guide

Editor: n/a

Editorial Concept: "A simple explanation of President Clinton's Health Security Act."

Best Home Remedies

Published by:

Rodale Press Inc.

33 E. Minor St.

Emmaus PA 18098

Date: 1994

Frequency: Special

Cover Price: $2.95

Subscription Price: n/a

Discount Subscription Price: n/a

Total Number of Pages: 98

Total Number of Ad Pages: 5

Publisher: Richard Alleger

Editor: Catherine M. Cassidy

Editorial Concept: "Practical advice on combatting stress, treating health maladies at home, losing weight, and buying the most nutritious foods possible."

Bodywise Presents Fat Buster Diet & Exercise Program

Published by:

Prestige Publications Inc.

7726 W. 152nd St.

Overland Park KS 66223

Date: 1994

Frequency: Special

Cover Price: $3.95

Subscription Price: n/a

Discount Subscription Price: n/a

Total Number of Pages: 132

Total Number of Ad Pages: 0

Publisher: Russ Moore

Editor: Lucinda Spencer

Editorial Concept: Tips and recipes to lose weight on the fat buster diet.

Family Circle's 500 Weight-Loss Secrets

Published by:

NYT Women's Magazines

110 Fifth Ave.

New York NY 10011

Date: 1994

Frequency: Special

Cover Price: $2.95

Subscription Price: n/a

Discount Subscription Price: n/a

Total Number of Pages: 100

Total Number of Ad Pages: 6

Publisher: Marion Aaron

Editor: Nancy Clark

Editorial Concept: Shaping up and staying slim.

A Great Body by Summer

Published by:

GCR Publishing Group Inc.

1700 Broadway

New York NY 10019

Date: 1994

Frequency: Special

Cover Price: $2.95

Subscription Price: n/a

Discount Subscription Price: n/a

Total Number of Pages: 68

Total Number of Ad Pages: 0

Publisher: Charles Goodman

Editor: Claudia Bernstein

Editorial Concept: "Get your hips, thighs, tummy, bust, and bottom in shape - fast."

Kathy Smith's In Shape for Summer

Published by:

Southern Progress Corporation

2100 Lakeshore Drive

Birmingham AL 35209

Date: 1994

Frequency: Special

Cover Price: $2.95

Subscription Price: n/a

Discount Subscription Price: n/a

Total Number of Pages: 114

Total Number of Ad Pages: 45

Publisher: Jeffrey C. Ward

Editor: Mary Kay Culpepper

Editorial Concept: Fitness tips from exercise guru Kathy Smith.

Molding Mighty Abdominals

Published by:

Chelo Publishing Inc.

350 Fifth Ave.

New York NY 10118

Date: 1994

Frequency: Special

Cover Price: $4.95

Subscription Price: n/a

Discount Subscription Price: n/a

Total Number of Pages: 164

Total Number of Ad Pages: 2

Publisher: Cheh N. Low

Editor: Mark Ritter

Editorial Concept: "For men who want a great midsection."

Muscle & Fitness and Flex Present Arnold the Icon

Published by:

I. Brute Enterprises Inc.

21100 Erwin St.

Woodland Hills CA 91367

Date: Spring 1994

Frequency: Special

Cover Price: $3.95

Subscription Price: n/a

Discount Subscription Price: n/a

Total Number of Pages: 188

Total Number of Ad Pages: 65

Publisher: Joe Weider

Editor: n/a

Editorial Concept: "A loving look at Arnold Schwarzenegger's career, plus his tips for body building to the max."

New Body's Firm and Flatten Your Stomach

Published by:

GCR Publishing Inc.

1700 Broadway

New York NY 10019

Date: 1994

Frequency: Special

Cover Price: $2.95

Subscription Price: n/a

Discount Subscription Price: n/a

Total Number of Pages: 68

Total Number of Ad Pages: 2

Publisher: Charles Goodman

Editor: Lisa Klugman

Editorial Concept: "Quick and easy ways to narrow your waist."

New Body's Home Remedies

Published by:

CGR Publishing Group Inc.

1700 Broadway

New York NY 10019

Date: 1994

Frequency: Special

Cover Price: $2.95

Subscription Price: n/a

Discount Subscription Price: n/a

Total Number of Pages: 68

Total Number of Ad Pages: 0

Publisher: Charles Goodman

Editor: Sallie Batson

Editorial Concept: "To share a wealth of traditional folk medicine from a variety of cultures."

New Body's Fat, Cholesterol, Sodium & Calorie Counter

Published by:

GCR Publishing Group Inc.

1700 Broadway

New York NY 10019

Date: 1994

Frequency: Special

Cover Price: $2.95

Subscription Price: n/a

Discount Subscription Price: n/a

Total Number of Pages: 68

Total Number of Ad Pages: 0

Publisher: Charles Goodman

Editor: Sallie Batson

Editorial Concept: How to pick healthy foods.

New Body's Stress Reduction & Weight Loss Workbook

Published by:

GCR Publishing Group Inc.

1700 Broadway

New York NY 10019

Date: 1994

Frequency: Special

Cover Price: $2.95

Subscription Price: n/a

Discount Subscription Price: n/a

Total Number of Pages: 68

Total Number of Ad Pages: 0

Publisher: Charles Goodman

Editor: Lisa Klugman

Editorial Concept: "To help reduce your weight, improve health, and reduce stress levels."

New Body's Thin Forever

Published by:

GCR Publishing Group Inc.

1700 Broadway

New York NY 10019

Date: 1994

Frequency: Annually

Cover Price: $2.95

Subscription Price: n/a

Discount Subscription Price: n/a

Total Number of Pages: 68

Total Number of Ad Pages: 0

Publisher: Charles Goodman

Editor: Lisa Klugman

Editorial Concept: Tips to boost your willpower and lose weight.

Prevention's Guide to Stress-Free Living

Published by:

Rodale Press Inc.

33 E. Minor St.

Emmaus PA 18098

Date: 1994

Frequency: Special

Cover Price: $2.95

Subscription Price: n/a

Discount Subscription Price: n/a

Total Number of Pages: 100

Total Number of Ad Pages: 3

Publisher: Richard Alleger

Editor: Catherine M. Cassidy

Editorial Concept: "Practical ways to reduce stress and its negative effects in every area of your life."

Prevention's Guide to Health for Men Only

Published by:

Rodale Press Inc.

33 E. Minor St.

Emmaus PA 18098

Date: 1994

Frequency: Special

Cover Price: $2.95

Subscription Price: n/a

Discount Subscription Price: n/a

Total Number of Pages: 100

Total Number of Ad Pages: 6

Publisher: Richard Alleger

Editor: Catherine M. Cassidy

Editorial Concept: "Comprehensive coverage of every health topic important to men."

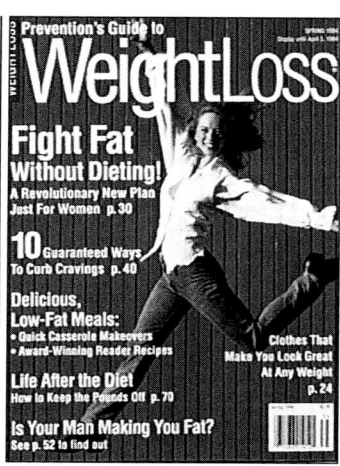

Prevention's Guide to Weight Loss

Published by:

Rodale Press Inc.

33 E. Minor St.

Emmaus PA 18098

Date: Spring 1994

Frequency: Annually

Cover Price: $2.95

Subscription Price: n/a

Discount Subscription Price: n/a

Total Number of Pages: 82

Total Number of Ad Pages: 13

Publisher: Richard Alleger

Editor: Catherine M. Cassidy

Editorial Concept: "To increase your knowledge of health developments and disease prevention."

Shape Presents Living Fit

Published by:

Shape Magazine Inc.

21100 Erwin St.

Woodland Hills CA 91367

Date: Winter 1994

Frequency: Special

Cover Price: $2.95

Subscription Price: n/a

Discount Subscription Price: n/a

Total Number of Pages: 132

Total Number of Ad Pages: 32

Publisher: Joe Weider

Editor: Barbara S. Harris

Editorial Concept: A guide to fitness at any age.

Travel Fit

Published by:

Prestige Publications Inc.

4151 Knob Drive

Eagen MN 55122

Date: 1994

Frequency: Special

Cover Price: $2.95

Subscription Price: n/a

Discount Subscription Price: n/a

Total Number of Pages: 100

Total Number of Ad Pages: 4

Publisher: Russ Moore

Editor: Tony Grundhauser

Editorial Concept: "How to get away from it all without losing your fitness goals."

American Builder

Published by:

Transcontinental Publishing Inc.

P.O. Box 45454

Phoenix AZ 85016

Date: March 1994

Frequency: Monthly

Cover Price: Free

Subscription Price: n/a

Discount Subscription Price: n/a

Total Number of Pages: 28

Total Number of Ad Pages: 12

Publisher: Pam Simmons

Editor: Laura J. Kress

Editorial Concept: News of the residential building industry for home builders, remodelers, and architects.

Better Homes and Gardens Home Products Guide

Published by:

Meredith Corporation

1716 Locust St.

Des Moines IA 50309-3023

Date: Spring/Summer 1994

Frequency: Semi-annually

Cover Price: $3.95

Subscription Price: n/a

Discount Subscription Price: n/a

Total Number of Pages: 148

Total Number of Ad Pages: 19

Publisher: Steven B. Levinson

Editor: Kathie Kull

Editorial Concept: "The best of what's new for your home."

Builder's Square Home Image Magazine

Published by:

The Summit Group

1227 W. Magnolia

Fort Worth TX 76104

Date: November/December 1994

Frequency: Bimonthly

Cover Price: $3.50

Subscription Price: $15.95

Discount Subscription Price: n/a

Total Number of Pages: 84

Total Number of Ad Pages: 34

Publisher: Mark Hulme

Editor: Jim Moore

Editorial Concept: "The best and brightest new concepts in home construction, decor, and style."

Country Accents Kitchens and Baths

Published by:

GCR Publishing Group Inc.

1700 Broadway

New York NY 10019

Date: 1994

Frequency: Quarterly

Cover Price: $3.50

Subscription Price: n/a

Discount Subscription Price: n/a

Total Number of Pages: 84

Total Number of Ad Pages: 6

Publisher: Charles Goodman

Editor: Richard M. Braun

Editorial Concept: Country-style design ideas for kitchens and baths.

Country Rooms

Published by:

GCR Publishing Group Inc.

1700 Broadway

New York NY 10019

Date: Summer 1994

Frequency: Quarterly

Cover Price: $3.50

Subscription Price: n/a

Discount Subscription Price: n/a

Total Number of Pages: 84

Total Number of Ad Pages: 10

Publisher: Charles Goodman

Editor: Jill Harbers

Editorial Concept: Country-inspired decorating for every room of the house.

Home Design Quarterly

Published by:

Southern Living Inc.

2100 Lakeshore Drive

Birmingham AL 35209

Date: 1994

Frequency: Quarterly

Cover Price: $4.95

Subscription Price: n/a

Discount Subscription Price: n/a

Total Number of Pages: 132

Total Number of Ad Pages: 9

Publisher: Burton Craige

Editor: Ann H. Harvey

Editorial Concept: A broad election of

upscale home designs, plus a variety of decorating features.

Home Items for Sale

Published by:

HIFS Magazine

No address given.

Date: June 1994

Frequency: 3/month

Cover Price: $0.46

Subscription Price: n/a

Discount Subscription Price: n/a

Total Number of Pages: 12

Total Number of Ad Pages: 8

Publisher: Curtis and Donna Gelston

Editor: Donna Gelston

Editorial Concept: Picture ads featuring used furniture and home items for sale in the Memphis area.

Home Plans

Published by:

JCP Publications

34 Industrial Park Place

Middletown CT 06457

Date: Spring 1994

Frequency: Quarterly

Cover Price: $3.95

Subscription Price: n/a

Discount Subscription Price: n/a

Total Number of Pages: 196

Total Number of Ad Pages: 10

Publisher: JCP Publications

Editor: Pamela Robertson

Editorial Concept: "Custom home

designs to suit every style and budget."

House Plans & Products

Published by:

Cahners Publishing Company

275 Washington St.

Newton MA 02158-1630

Date: 1994

Frequency: Bimonthly

Cover Price: $4.95

Subscription Price: $30.00

Discount Subscription Price: n/a

Total Number of Pages: 188

Total Number of Ad Pages: 14

Publisher: Peter T. Orsi

Editor: Ed Fitch

Editorial Concept: 200 new house plans.

Lake Home

Published by:

Blue Water Communications Inc.

137 N. Main St.

West Bend WI 53095

Date: March/April 1994

Frequency: Bimonthly

Cover Price: $4.95

Subscription Price: $19.95

Discount Subscription Price: n/a

Total Number of Pages: 60

Total Number of Ad Pages: 6

Publisher: Frank DeRaimo

Editor: David Rank

Editorial Concept: The lakeshore lifestyle magazine for the owner of inland waterfront property.

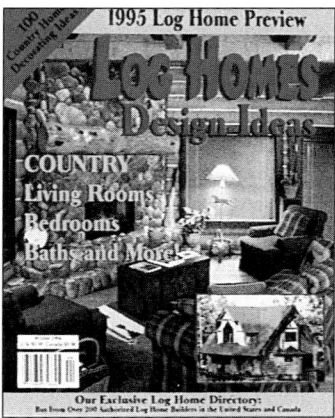

Log Homes Design Ideas

Published by:

H&S Media Inc.

3400 Dundee Road

Northbrook IL 60062

Date: Winter 1994

Frequency: Quarterly

Cover Price: $3.95

Subscription Price: $15.00

Discount Subscription Price: n/a

Total Number of Pages: 132

Total Number of Ad Pages: 50

Publisher: H&S Media Inc.

Editor: Jim Mohr

Editorial Concept: "Design ideas for a perfect log home."

Low-Budget Home Plans

Published by:

Home Planners Inc.

3275 W. Ina Road, Suite 110

Tucson AZ 85741

Date: Spring/Summer 1994

Frequency: Semi-annually

Cover Price: $3.95

Subscription Price: n/a

Discount Subscription Price: n/a

Total Number of Pages: 196

Total Number of Ad Pages: 3

Publisher: Rickard D. Bailey

Editor: Amanda Shaver

Editorial Concept: Blueprints for 180 easy-to-build houses.

The National Locksmith's Crime Prevention

Published by:

National Publishing Company

1533 Burgundy Parkway

Streamwood IL 60107

Date: Summer 1994

Frequency: Quarterly

Cover Price: $2.50

Subscription Price: n/a

Discount Subscription Price: n/a

Total Number of Pages: 32

Total Number of Ad Pages: 10

Publisher: Marc Goldberg

Editor: Marc Goldberg

Editorial Concept: "The consumer guide to home, vehicle, and personal safety."

Practical Home Automation

Published by:

Practical Home Automation

3043 S. Laredo Circle

Aurora CO 80013

Date: August/September 1994

Frequency: Bimonthly

Cover Price: $3.95

Subscription Price: n/a

Discount Subscription Price: n/a

Total Number of Pages: 36

Total Number of Ad Pages: 9

Publisher: Practical Home Automation

Editor: Malcolm MacLeod

Editorial Concept: "The hands-on magazine of 21st-century living."

Scenic Style Home Plans

Published by:

Home Styles Publishing and Marketing Inc.

P.O. Box 50670

Minneapolis MN 55405

Date: 1994

Frequency: Quarterly

Cover Price: $4.95

Subscription Price: n/a

Discount Subscription Price: n/a

Total Number of Pages: 228

Total Number of Ad Pages: 5

Publisher: Roger W. Heegaard

Editor: Pamela Robertson

Editorial Concept: More than 200 blueprints for vacation-style homes.

Southern Living Decorating Step-By-Step

Published by:

Southern Living Inc.

2100 Lakeshore Drive

Birmingham AL 35209

Date: 1994

Frequency: Bimonthly

Cover Price: $4.95

Subscription Price: $19.95

Discount Subscription Price: n/a

Total Number of Pages: 48

Total Number of Ad Pages: 4

Publisher: Scott Sheppard

Editor: John Alex Floyd Jr.

Editorial Concept: "Ideas to bring the decorator look to your home without the expense."

Today's Lifestyles Home Plans

Published by:

Homestyles Publishing and Marketing

P.O. Box 50670

Minneapolis MN 55405

Date: 1994

Frequency: Quarterly

Cover Price: $3.95

Subscription Price: $20.00

Discount Subscription Price: n/a

Total Number of Pages: 324

Total Number of Ad Pages: 1

Publisher: Roger W. Heegaard

Editor: Diane Talmage

Editorial Concept: Classic Eurostyle designs.

Town & Country Home Designs Countrypolitan Home Plans

Published by:

Homestyles Publishing and Marketing

P.O. Box 50670

Minneapolis MN 55405

Date: 1994

Frequency: Quarterly

Cover Price: $5.95

Subscription Price: $17.00

Discount Subscription Price: n/a

Total Number of Pages: 292

Total Number of Ad Pages: 12

Publisher: Roger W. Heegaard

Editor: Dianne Talmage

Editorial Concept: More than 275 best-selling dream homes.

101 Affordable Ways to Protect Your Home

Published by:

Challenge Publications Inc.

7950 Deering Ave.

Canoga Park CA 91304

Date: 1994

Frequency: Special

Cover Price: $5.95

Subscription Price: n/a

Discount Subscription Price: n/a

Total Number of Pages: 88

Total Number of Ad Pages: 4

Publisher: Edwin A. Schnepf

Editor: Brian Hemsworth

Editorial Concept: De-emphasizing guns in favor of safer protection measures.

Better Homes and Gardens Editor's Choice Home Plans

Published by:

Meredith Corporation

1716 Locust St.

Des Moines IA 50309-3023

Date: 1994

Frequency: Special

Cover Price: $3.95

Subscription Price: n/a

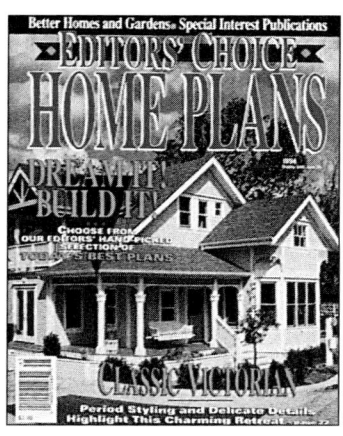

Discount Subscription Price: n/a

Total Number of Pages: 196

Total Number of Ad Pages: 10

Publisher: Meredith Corporation

Editor: Joe Hawkins

Editorial Concept: "A hand-picked selection of today's best plans."

Better Homes and Gardens Leisure & Outdoor Products Guide

Published by:

Meredith Corporation

1716 Locust St.

Des Moines IA 50309-3023

Date: 1994

Frequency: Annually

Cover Price: $3.95

Subscription Price: n/a

Discount Subscription Price: n/a

Total Number of Pages: 148

Total Number of Ad Pages: 5

Publisher: Steven Levinson

Editor: Miriam Strum

Editorial Concept: A review of leisure products.

Better Homes and Gardens Your New Home Planning Guide

Published by:

Meredith Corporation

1716 Locust St.

Des Moines IA 50309-3023

Date: Spring1994

Frequency: Special

Cover Price: $3.95

Subscription Price: n/a

Discount Subscription Price: n/a

Total Number of Pages: 132

Total Number of Ad Pages: 9

Publisher: Stephen B. Levinson

Editor: n/a

Editorial Concept: How to find and buy your own home.

Country Accents Windows & Walls

Published by:

GCR Publishing Group Inc.

1700 Broadway

New York NY 10019

Date: 1994

Frequency: Annually

Cover Price: $3.50

Subscription Price: n/a

Discount Subscription Price: n/a

Total Number of Pages: 84

Total Number of Ad Pages: 12

Publisher: Charles Goodman

Editor: Deborah Harding

Editorial Concept: "Impressive results with a minimum of fuss."

Country Living Dream Homes

Published by:

Hearst Corporation

959 Eighth Ave.

New York NY 10019

Date: 1994

Frequency: Annually

Cover Price: $2.95

Subscription Price: n/a

Discount Subscription Price: n/a

Total Number of Pages: 164

Total Number of Ad Pages: 18

Publisher: Jay McGill

Editor: Nancy Memit Soriano

Editorial Concept: "Over 120 house plans you can buy."

Guns for Home Defense

Published by:

Challenge Publications Inc.

7950 Deering Ave.

Canoga Park CA 91304

Date: 1994

Frequency: Special

Cover Price: $5.95

Subscription Price: n/a

Discount Subscription Price: n/a

Total Number of Pages: 96

Total Number of Ad Pages: 5

Publisher: Edwin A. Schnepf

Editor: Joe Poyer

Editorial Concept: Handguns for defending your home against intruders.

Muir's Original Log Structures Restoration Guide for Builders and Buyers

Published by:

Muir Publishing Company Inc.

164 Middle Creek Road

Cosby TN 37722

Date: 1994

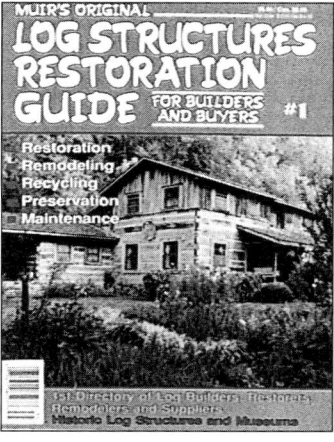

Frequency: Special

Cover Price: $8.95

Subscription Price: n/a

Discount Subscription Price: n/a

Total Number of Pages: 148

Total Number of Ad Pages: 25

Publisher: Doris L. Muir

Editor: Alan C. Pape

Editorial Concept: How to take care of a log building .

New Products for Your Home

Published by:

Harris Publications Inc.

1115 Broadway

New York NY 10010

Date: 1994

Frequency: Annually

Cover Price: $3.95

Subscription Price: n/a

Discount Subscription Price: n/a

Total Number of Pages: 116

Total Number of Ad Pages: 8

Publisher: Stanley R. Harris

Editor: Barbara Jacksier

Editorial Concept: "Newest home products available now."

Old House Interiors

Published by:

Dovetale Publishers

2 Main St.

Gloucester MA 01930

Date: Summer 1994

Frequency: Annually

Cover Price: $4.00

Subscription Price: n/a

Discount Subscription Price: n/a

Total Number of Pages: 116

Total Number of Ad Pages: 50

Publisher: William J. O'Donnell

Editor: Patricia Poore

Editorial Concept: A decorating and architecture source with a historical view.

Southern Living Idea House Magazine and Resource Guide

Published by:

Southern Living Inc.

2100 Lakeshore Drive

Birmingham AL 35209

Date: 1994

Frequency: Special

Cover Price: $3.95

Subscription Price: n/a

Discount Subscription Price: n/a

Total Number of Pages: 116

Total Number of Ad Pages: 31

Publisher: Scott Sheppard

Editor: Bill McDougald

Editorial Concept: Decorating and design ideas from the model home at Opryland in Nashville.

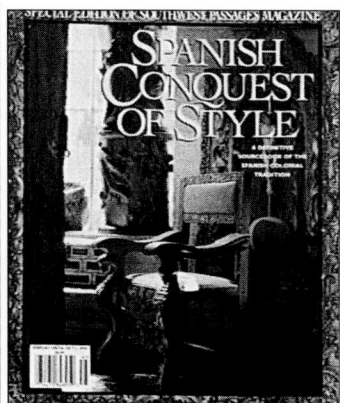

Spanish Conquest of Style

Published by:

El Zaguan Publishing Company

P.O. Box 44338

Phoenix AZ 85064

Date: 1994

Frequency: Special

Cover Price: $4.95

Subscription Price: n/a

Discount Subscription Price: n/a

Total Number of Pages: 68

Total Number of Ad Pages: 27

Publisher: Manya Winsted

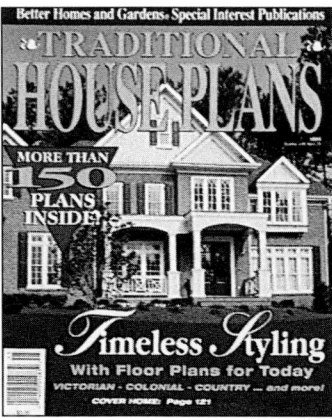

Editor: Manya Winsted

Editorial Concept: The Spanish colonial tradition.

Traditional House Plans

Published by:

Meredith Corporation

1716 Locust St.

Des Moines IA 50309-3023

Date: 1994

Frequency: Annually

Cover Price: $3.95

Subscription Price: n/a

Discount Subscription Price: n/a

Total Number of Pages: 196

Total Number of Ad Pages: 6

Publisher: Stephen B. Levinson

Editor: William J. Yates

Editorial Concept: More than 150 floor plans for several different styles of homes.

Woman's Day Classic Series Additions & Decks

Published by:

Hachette Filipacchi Magazines Inc.

1633 Broadway

New York NY 10019

Date: 1994

Frequency: Annually

Cover Price: $3.50

Subscription Price: n/a

Discount Subscription Price: n/a

Total Number of Pages: 132

Total Number of Ad Pages: 19

Publisher: Susan S. Buckley

Editor: Joe Carter

Editorial Concept: Possibilities for expanding a home.

Woman's Day Weekend Decorating Projects

Published by:

Hachette Filipacchi Magazines Inc.

1633 Broadway

New York NY 10019

Date: 1994

Frequency: Annually

Cover Price: $3.50

Subscription Price: n/a

Discount Subscription Price: n/a

Total Number of Pages: 132

Total Number of Ad Pages: 21

Publisher: Susan S. Buckley

Editor: Maureen Mullin Klein

Editorial Concept: "A magazine full of stunning photography on home decorating projects."

Woman's Day Weekend Home Improvement Projects

Published by:

Hachette Filipacchi Magazines Inc.

1633 Broadway

New York NY 10019

Date: 1994

Frequency: Special

Cover Price: $3.50

Subscription Price: n/a

Discount Subscription Price: n/a

Total Number of Pages: 132

Total Number of Ad Pages: 24

Publisher: Susan S. Buckley

Editor: Olivia Bell Buehl

Editorial Concept: "Fast fix-ups for every room with step-by-step instructions."

Wood Magazine's Best Outdoor Projects

Published by:

Meredith Corporation

1912 Grand Ave.

Des Moines IA 50309

Date: Spring/Summer 1994

Frequency: Special

Cover Price: $4.95

Subscription Price: n/a

Discount Subscription Price: n/a

Total Number of Pages: 100

Total Number of Ad Pages: 14

Publisher: William R. Reed

Editor: Larry Clayton

Editorial Concept: "The all-time best outdoor furniture pieces from past issues of *Wood* and our sister publication, *Weekend Woodworking Projects*."

The Comedy Magazine

Published by:

Quality Services Company

5290 Overpass Road

Santa Barbara CA 93111

Date: March/April 1994

Frequency: Bimonthly

Cover Price: $4.95

Subscription Price: $19.95

Discount Subscription Price: n/a

Total Number of Pages: 100

Total Number of Ad Pages: 10

Publisher: Walter Jurek

Editor: Walter Jurek

Editorial Concept: "This magazine won't solve the budget deficit or solve the problems of the world. The real goal is to have you come away...with a smile on your face."

Laugh Factory

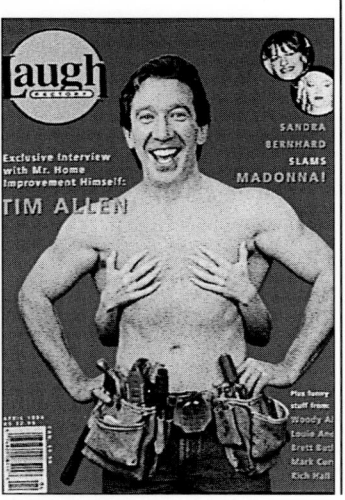

Published by:

L.F. Inc.

8001 Sunset Blvd.

Los Angeles CA 90046

Date: April 1994

Frequency: Monthly

Cover Price: $2.95

Subscription Price: $26.40

Discount Subscription Price: n/a

Total Number of Pages: 100

Total Number of Ad Pages: 20

Publisher: Jamie Masada

Editor: Sabrina LaBow

Editorial Concept: "Celebrates those who make us laugh and feel joy."

Lighter Times

Published by:

Lighter Times Publishing

2929 Second Ave. North

Seattle WA 98109

Date: November 1994

Frequency: Monthly

Cover Price: $2.95

Subscription Price: $26.95

Discount Subscription Price: n/a

Total Number of Pages: 40

Total Number of Ad Pages: 0

Publisher: V.S. Skip Schermer

Editor: Stan Snow

Editorial Concept: Strange and offbeat news stories from around the country.

The Big Clinton Joke Book

Published by:

Slick Times

P.O. Box 1710

Valley Center CA 92082

Date: 1994

Frequency: Special

Cover Price: $7.95

Subscription Price: n/a

Discount Subscription Price: n/a

Total Number of Pages: 148

Total Number of Ad Pages: 2

Publisher: Michael Dalton Johnson

Editor: Michael Dalton Johnson

Editorial Concept: "Hundreds of jokes, cartoons, and satirical articles...the worst of *Slick Times*."

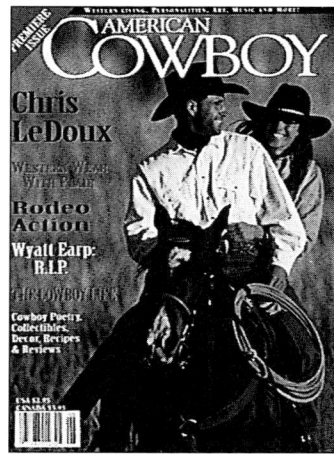

American Cowboy

Published by:

Web Publications Inc.

650 Westlake Drive, Suite 100

Wichita KS 67209

Date: May/June 1994

Frequency: Bimonthly

Cover Price: $2.95

Subscription Price: $16.95

Discount Subscription Price: n/a

Total Number of Pages: 108

Total Number of Ad Pages: 40

Publisher: William E. Bales

Editor: Jesse Mullins

Editorial Concept: "Features Western living, personalities, art, and music...the magazine that captures the romance of the American West."

Biracial Child

Published by:

Interrace Inc.

P.O. Box 12048

Atlanta GA 30355

Date: Winter 1994

Frequency: Quarterly

Cover Price: $3.95

Subscription Price: $20.00

Discount Subscription Price: n/a

Total Number of Pages: 24

Total Number of Ad Pages: 0

Publisher: Gabe Grosz and Candy Mills Grosz

Editor: Candy Mills Grosz

Editorial Concept: "The nation's first magazine for parents of biracial and multiracial children, transracial adoptive parents, and interracial stepfamilies."

Caribbean Heritage

Published by:

Arawak Communications

P.O. Box 921946

Sylmar CA 91392-1946

Date: July 1994

Frequency: Bimonthly

Cover Price: $2.50

Subscription Price: $9.75

Discount Subscription Price: n/a

Total Number of Pages: 52

Total Number of Ad Pages: 9

Publisher: Arawak Communications

Editor: Marva Griffiths Herman

Editorial Concept: "The magazine for the people and friends of the Caribbean."

Creative Retirement

Published by:

Vacation Publications Inc.

1502 Augusta, Suite 415

Houston TX 77057

Date: Winter 1994

Frequency: Quarterly

Cover Price: $2.95

Subscription Price: $11.80

Discount Subscription Price: $9.95

Total Number of Pages: 68

Total Number of Ad Pages: 18

Publisher: Alan Fox

Editor: Mary Lu Abbott

Editorial Concept: "To explore the most promising new approaches to life after work."

Departures

Published by:

American Express Publishing Corp.

1120 Avenue of the Americas

New York NY 10036

Date: April 1994 *(first newsstand issue)*

Frequency: Monthly

Cover Price: $2.95

Subscription Price: $18.00

Discount Subscription Price: n/a

Total Number of Pages: 122

Total Number of Ad Pages: 48

Publisher: Ed Kelly

Editor: Gary Walther

Editorial Concept: "Connoisseurship of the good life."

Dragazine

Published by:

Dragazine

P.O. Box 691664

West Hollywood CA 90069

Date: 1994

Frequency: Biannually

Cover Price: $5.95

Subscription Price: $10.95

Discount Subscription Price: n/a

Total Number of Pages: 48

Total Number of Ad Pages: 4

Publisher: Lois Commondenominator

Editor: Lois Commondenominator

Editorial Concept: "The magazine for Halloweeners and Inbetweeners" - all about transvestites.

German Life

Published by:

Zeitgeist Publishing

1 Corporate Drive

Grantsville MD 21536

Date: July 1994

Frequency: Bimonthly

Cover Price: $3.95

Subscription Price: $19.95

Discount Subscription Price: $15.95

Total Number of Pages: 76

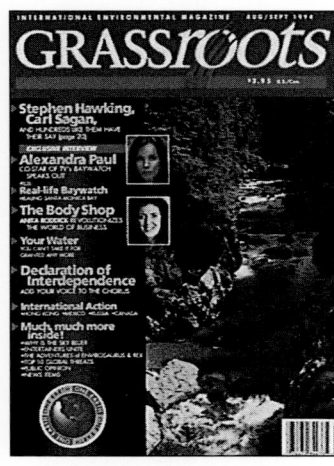

Total Number of Ad Pages: 16

Publisher: Lisa A. Fitzpatrick

Editor: Michael Koch

Editorial Concept: "To relay all sides of German culture" - for Americans of German descent.

Grassroots

Published by:

Grassroots Publishing Ltd.

250 H St.

Blaine WA 98231-8110

Date: August/September 1994

Frequency: Bimonthly

Cover Price: $3.95

Subscription Price: $24.00

Discount Subscription Price: n/a

Total Number of Pages: 64

Total Number of Ad Pages: 3

Publisher: Rick McLean

Editor: Wendy Rennison

Editorial Concept: International environmental magazine"

The Lumpen Times

Published by:

Lumpen Media Group

2558 W. Armitage Ave.

Chicago IL 60647

Date: 1994

Frequency: Monthly

Cover Price: $3.00

Subscription Price: $25.00

Discount Subscription Price: n/a

Total Number of Pages: 50

Total Number of Ad Pages: 9

Publisher: The Lumpen Times

Editor: Ed Marszewski, Chris Molnar, Leslie Stella

Editorial Concept: A music, arts, and culture journal for slackers.

Marriage

Published by:

International Marriage Encounter

955 Lake Drive

Saint Paul MN 55120

Date: March/April 1994 (formerly Marriage Encounter)

Frequency: 9/year

Cover Price: $2.00

Subscription Price: $17.00

Discount Subscription Price: n/a

Total Number of Pages: 44

Total Number of Ad Pages: 1

Publisher: Jerry Sexton

Editor: Krysta Eryn Kavenaugh

Editorial Concept: "To share the vision of the infinite potential of marriage"

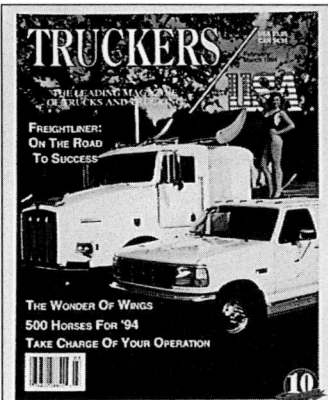

New Truckers USA

Published by:

BPS Inc.

P.O. Box 3168

Tuscaloosa AL 35403

Date: February/March 1994

Frequency: Bimonthly

Cover Price: $3.95

Subscription Price: $19.95

Discount Subscription Price: n/a

Total Number of Pages: 84

Total Number of Ad Pages: 17

Publisher: BPS Inc.

Editor: Dave Adams

Editorial Concept: Articles on controlling costs, making the most of life on the road, new equipment, and trucking history.

Practical Homeschooling

Published by:

Home Life

P.O. Box 1250

Fenton MO 63026-1850

Date: Summer 1994

(first newsstand issue)

Frequency: Quarterly

Cover Price: $5.00

Subscription Price: $15.00

Discount Subscription Price: n/a

Total Number of Pages: 100

Total Number of Ad Pages: 34

Publisher: Mary Pride

Editor: Mary Pride

Editorial Concept: "For better education right now."

Psychology Digest

Published by:

Sussex Publishers Inc.

24 E. 23rd St.

New York NY 10010

Date: Summer 1994

Frequency: Bimonthly

Cover Price: $3.00

Subscription Price: $18.00

Discount Subscription Price: $15.97

Total Number of Pages: 84

Total Number of Ad Pages: 16

Publisher: John Colman

Editor: James C. Mauro

Editorial Concept: A digest of material affecting psychology and human behavior.

Q-VO Magazine

Published by:

Q-VO Magazine

745 E. Valley Blvd.

San Gabriel CA 91776

Date: 1994

Frequency: Quarterly

Cover Price: $4.95

Subscription Price: n/a

Discount Subscription Price: n/a

Total Number of Pages: 100

Total Number of Ad Pages: 8

Publisher: Benjamin F. Hernandez

Editor: Teresa R. Hernandez

Editorial Concept: Music, women, politics, and culture for the Chicano community.

The Sandwich Generation

Published by:

Carol Abaya Associates

P.O. Box 132

Wickatunk NJ 07765

Date: Summer 1994

Frequency: Quarterly

Cover Price: $2.50

Subscription Price: $12.00

Discount Subscription Price: n/a

Total Number of Pages: 32

Total Number of Ad Pages: 9

Publisher: Carol Abaya

Editor: Carol Abaya

Editorial Concept: A magazine on the problems faced by adults caring for aging parents.

Troika

Published by:

Lone Trout Publications Inc.

P.O. Box 1006

Weston CT 06883

Date: Summer 1994

Frequency: Quarterly

Cover Price: $3.00

Subscription Price: $10.00

Discount Subscription Price: n/a

Total Number of Pages: 98

Total Number of Ad Pages: 53

Publisher: Eric S. Meadow

Editor: Celia R. Meadow

Editorial Concept: "An upscale and thoughtful general interest magazine."

U.S. Immigrant

Published by:

Dennis Carey

P.O. Box 257

Woodland Hills CA 91365-0257

Date: 1994

Frequency: Monthly

Cover Price: $2.50

Subscription Price: $24.00

Discount Subscription Price: n/a

Total Number of Pages: 40

Total Number of Ad Pages: 0

Publisher: Dennis Carey

Editor: n/a

Editorial Concept: A current review

and analysis of immigrant rights.

Wilma Russell's Cowboys & Country

Published by:

Wilma Russell

131 E. Exchange #202

Fort Worth TX 76106

Date: Winter 1994

Frequency: Semi-annually

Cover Price: $4.95

Subscription Price: $9.00

Discount Subscription Price: n/a

Total Number of Pages: 116

Total Number of Ad Pages: 32

Publisher: Wilma Russell

Editor: Wilma Russell

Editorial Concept: Cowboys and country.

Yolk

Published by:

InformAsian Media Inc.

P.O. Box 861555

Los Angeles CA 90086-1555

Date: 1994

Frequency: Quarterly

Cover Price: $3.95

Subscription Price: n/a

Discount Subscription Price: n/a

Total Number of Pages: 76

Total Number of Ad Pages: 13

Publisher: InformAsian Media Inc.

Editor: Philip W. Chung

Editorial Concept: "American pop culture from a distinctly Asian-American perspective."

Your Next Party!

Published by:

Miller Freeman Inc.

1515 Broadway

New York NY 10036

Date: Fall 1994

Frequency: Quarterly

Cover Price: $0.99

Subscription Price: n/a

Discount Subscription Price: n/a

Total Number of Pages: 36

Total Number of Ad Pages: 14

Publisher: Steve Silberberg

Editor: Tania M. McMenamin

Editorial Concept: "Party ideas, craft projects, recipes, decorating suggestions, gift-wrapping instructions, favor-making tips and more."

Can This Marriage Be Saved?

Published by:

Meredith Corporation

1716 Locust St.

Des Moines IA 50309-3023

Date: 1994

Frequency: Special

Cover Price: $2.95

Subscription Price: n/a

Discount Subscription Price: n/a

Total Number of Pages: 100

Total Number of Ad Pages: 25

Publisher: Donna Galotti

Editor: Carolyn Noyes

Editorial Concept: Stories of love and marriage from the *Ladies' Home Journal's* most popular column.

Frost's Summer Camp Guide

Published by:

Frost Publications

50 Parkhill Road

Harrington Park NJ 07640

Date: 1994

Frequency: Special

Cover Price: $4.95

Subscription Price: n/a

Discount Subscription Price: n/a

Total Number of Pages: 100

Total Number of Ad Pages: 11

Publisher: Don Frost

Editor: Marcia Frost

Editorial Concept: A parent's guide to Northeast day and overnight camps for 1994.

Home Defense/Personal Safety

Published by:

Petersen Publishing Company

6420 Wilshire Blvd.

Los Angeles CA 90048

Date: 1994

Frequency: Special

Cover Price: $3.95

Subscription Price: n/a

Discount Subscription Price: n/a

Total Number of Pages: 100

Total Number of Ad Pages: 4

Publisher: Doug Hamlin

Editor: Todd Smith

Editorial Concept: Fear-inspired articles on how to beat burglars, prevent rape, avoid muggings, and tips on when it's legal to use lethal force.

Parties for Kids

Published by:

Publications International Ltd.

No address given.

Date: 1994

Frequency: Special

Cover Price: $2.95

Subscription Price: n/a

Discount Subscription Price: n/a

Total Number of Pages: 100

Total Number of Ad Pages: 0

Publisher: Publications International Ltd.

Editor: Rorena Rekenthaler

Editorial Concept: Innovative theme parties for boys and girls of all ages.

Private Colleges and Universities

Published by:

Carnegie Communications Inc.

750 Third Ave.

New York NY 10017

Date: 1994

Frequency: Special

Cover Price: $4.95

Subscription Price: n/a

Discount Subscription Price: n/a

Total Number of Pages: 196

Total Number of Ad Pages: 0

Publisher: Robert L. Leyburn

Editor: Paul D. Adams

Editorial Concept: "Profiles on 72 private colleges, plus tips on how to get into the elite school of your choice."

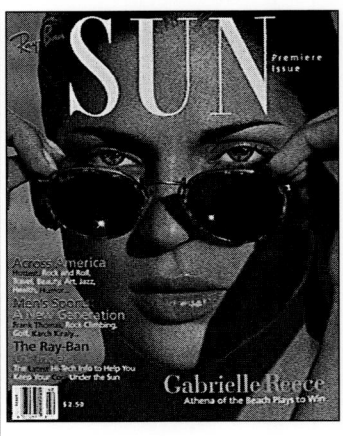

Ray-Ban Sun

Published by:

Hachette Filipacchi Magazines Inc.

1633 Broadway

New York NY 10019

Date: 1994

Frequency: n/a

Cover Price: $2.50

Subscription Price: n/a

Discount Subscription Price: n/a

Total Number of Pages: 116

Total Number of Ad Pages: 27

Publisher: Hachette Filipacchi

Editor: Jean-Louis Ginibre

Editorial Concept: "Designed to entertain, educate, and celebrate the power and life force of our brightest star - the sun."

TV Guide Parents' Guide to Children's Entertainment

Published by:

News America Publications Inc.

100 Matsonford Road

Radnor PA 19088

Date: Holiday 1994

Frequency: Special

Cover Price: $2.95

Subscription Price: n/a

Discount Subscription Price: n/a

Total Number of Pages: 100

Total Number of Ad Pages: 26

Publisher: Mary G. Berner

Editor: Cathy Cavender and Greg Fagan

Editorial Concept: "Best holiday gifts - 86 toys, 72 videos, 35 books, 58 computer games, 17 movies."

Winter Fun

Published by:

Time Inc. Ventures

301 Howard St., 17th Floor

San Francisco CA 94105

Date: 1994

Frequency: Special

Cover Price: $1.95

Subscription Price: n/a

Discount Subscription Price: n/a

Total Number of Pages: 76

Total Number of Ad Pages: 30

Publisher: Carol A. Smith

Editor: Steven Reddicliffe

Editorial Concept: Outdoor and indoor winter fun projects from the editors of *Parenting* magazine.

Worldwide Holiday Shopping Guide

Published by:

National Publications Sales Agency

1610 E. 79th St.

Chicago IL 60649

Date: Winter 1994

Frequency: Special

Cover Price: $9.95

Subscription Price: n/a

Discount Subscription Price: n/a

Total Number of Pages: 196

Total Number of Ad Pages: 60

Publisher: Donald C. Walker

Editor: Donald C. Walker

Editorial Concept: "A shopping and travel guide geared toward upscale African-Americans."

Absolute Magnitude

Published by:

D.N.A. Publishing

P.O. Box 13

Greenfield MA 01302-0013

Date: Fall/Winter 1994

(formerly Harsh Mistress)

Frequency: Quarterly

Cover Price: $4.00

Subscription Price: $14.00

Discount Subscription Price: n/a

Total Number of Pages: 100

Total Number of Ad Pages: 5

Publisher: D.N.A. Publishing

Editor: Warren Lapine

Editorial Concept: Science fiction short stories.

Affaire de Coeur

Published by:

Affaire de Coeur Inc.

3976 Oak Hill Road

Oakland CA 94605-4931

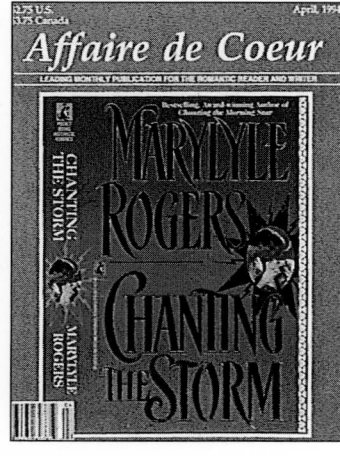

Date: April 1994

(first national newsstand issue)

Frequency: Monthly

Cover Price: $2.75

Subscription Price: $30.00

Discount Subscription Price: n/a

Total Number of Pages: 60

Total Number of Ad Pages: 11

Publisher: Louise B. Snead

Editor: Louise B. Snead

Editorial Concept: "For the romantic reader and writer."

Creative Screenwriting

Published by:

Creative Screenwriters Group

816 E. St. NE, Suite 201

Washington DC 20002

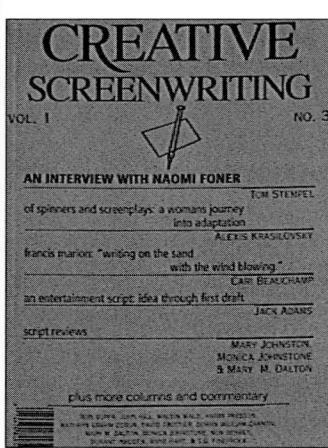

Date: Fall 1994

Frequency: Quarterly

Cover Price: $8.50

Subscription Price: $35.00

Discount Subscription Price: n/a

Total Number of Pages: 134

Total Number of Ad Pages: 4

Publisher: Creative Screenwriters Group

Editor: Erik N. Bauer

Editorial Concept: "Critical, theoretical, historical, and practical essays on all aspects of writing for TV and the movies."

Delirium

Published by:

Delirium Inc.

779 Riverside Drive #A-11

New York NY 10032

Date: October 1994

Frequency: Quarterly

Cover Price: $4.00

Subscription Price: $14.00

Discount Subscription Price: n/a

Total Number of Pages: 68

Total Number of Ad Pages: 12

Publisher: Delirium Inc.

Editor: Sophie Diamantis

Editorial Concept: "Stories, poetry, and music reviews for those fascinated with the dark side of life."

Louis L'Amour Western Magazine

Published by:

Dell Magazines

1540 Broadway

New York NY 10036

Date: 1994

Frequency: Bimonthly

Cover Price: $2.95

Subscription Price: $17.70

Discount Subscription Price: $14.97

Total Number of Pages: 114

Total Number of Ad Pages: 36

Publisher: Christoph Haas-Heye

Editor: Elana Lore

Editorial Concept: "A selection of the finest western fiction being written today."

Mindsparks

Published by:

Molecudyne Research

P.O. Box 1379

Laurel MD 20725-1379

Date: 1994 *(first newsstand issue)*

Frequency: Bimonthly

Cover Price: $3.95

Subscription Price: $23.00

Discount Subscription Price: n/a

Total Number of Pages: 48

Total Number of Ad Pages: 2

Publisher: Molecudyne Research

Editor: Catherine Asaro

Editorial Concept: "The magazine of science and science fiction."

Pirate Writings Magazine

Published by:

Pirate Writings Publishing

53 Whitman Ave.

Islip NY 11751

Date: Summer 1994

Frequency: Quarterly

Cover Price: $4.99

Subscription Price: $14.50

Discount Subscription Price: $13.75

Total Number of Pages: 68

Total Number of Ad Pages: 6

Publisher: Pirate Writings Publishing

Editor: Ed McFaddon

Editorial Concept: Tales of fantasy, mystery, and science fiction.

Plot

Published by:

Calypso Publishing

P.O. Box 1351

Sugar Land TX 77487

Date: 1994

Frequency: Quarterly

Cover Price: $3.95

Subscription Price: $12.00

Discount Subscription Price: n/a

Total Number of Pages: 52

Total Number of Ad Pages: 0

Publisher: Calypso Publishing

Editor: Teresa Williams

Editorial Concept: Fantasy, science fiction, horror, and suspense short fiction.

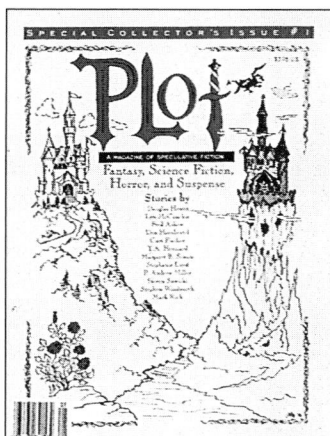

Romantic Interludes

Published by:

Charter Publishing Inc.

P.O. Box 760

Germantown MD 20875

Date: June/July 1994

Frequency: Bimonthly

Cover Price: $3.25

Subscription Price: $18.00

Discount Subscription Price: n/a

Total Number of Pages: 100

Total Number of Ad Pages: 8

Publisher: Bill Cummings

Editor: Wilma Leber

Editorial Concept: "The best in romantic short fiction."

Stories Good 'n' Short

Published by:

Stories Good 'n' Short Inc.

1250 Humbolt St., Suite 905

Denver CO 80218-2416

Date: January/February 1994

Frequency: Bimonthly

Cover Price: $6.95

Subscription Price: $29.95

Discount Subscription Price: n/a

Total Number of Pages: 52

Total Number of Ad Pages: 5

Publisher: Todd Lederman

Editor: Rene Cohen

Editorial Concept: Short fiction.

Wicked Mystic

Published by:

Fuck That Weak Shit Press

P.O. Box 3087

Astoria NY 11103

Date: Summer 1994

Frequency: Quarterly

Cover Price: $5.95

Subscription Price: $23.00

Discount Subscription Price: n/a

Total Number of Pages: 72

Total Number of Ad Pages: 6

Publisher: Victor Chin

Editor: Andre Scheluchin

Editorial Concept: "In-your-face horror" fiction, art, and poetry.

Annual, Special or Frequency Unknown

Artes International

Published by:

The Ecco Press

100 W. Broad St.

Hopewell NJ 08525

Date: 1994

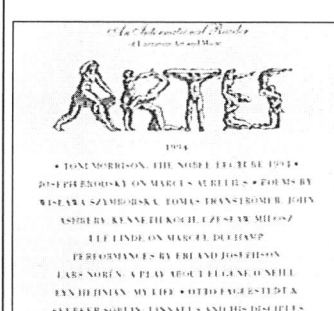

Frequency: Annually

Cover Price: $15.00

Subscription Price: n/a

Discount Subscription Price: n/a

Total Number of Pages: 154

Total Number of Ad Pages: 1

Publisher: The Ecco Press

Editor: Gunner Harding and Bengt Jangfeldt

Editorial Concept: "An international reader of literature, art, and music."

Unshaved Truths

Published by:

Fringeware Inc.

2507 Roehampton Drive

Austin TX 78745-6964

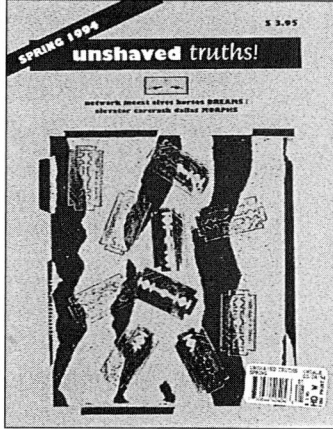

Date: Spring 1994

Frequency: n/a

Cover Price: $3.95

Subscription Price: n/a

Discount Subscription Price: n/a

Total Number of Pages: 56

Total Number of Ad Pages: 3

Publisher: Fringeware Inc.

Editor: Jon Lebkowsky

Editorial Concept: Stories, essays, and more.

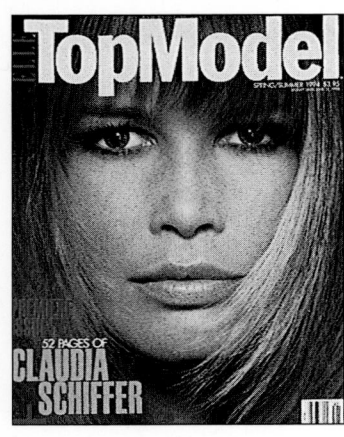

Elle Top Model

Published by:

Elle Publishing, L.P.

1633 Broadway

New York NY 10019

Date: Spring/Summer 1994

Frequency: Quarterly

Cover Price: $3.95

Subscription Price: n/a

Discount Subscription Price: n/a

Total Number of Pages: 100

Total Number of Ad Pages: 15

Publisher: Elle Publishing LP

Editor: Jean-Dominique Bauby

Editorial Concept: "Readers of *Elle Top Model* will share the secrets of these famed beauties and find out what the life of a model is really like."

In Style

Published by:

Time Inc.

1271 Avenue of the Americas

New York NY 10020

Date: June 1994

Frequency: Monthly

Cover Price: $2.95

Subscription Price: $19.97

Discount Subscription Price: n/a

Total Number of Pages: 132

Total Number of Ad Pages: 35

Publisher: Ann W. Jackson

Editor: Martha Nelson

Editorial Concept: "An intimate look at celebrity lifestyles in vivid pictures and inside stories that will move, amuse, and inform you."

Latin Style

Published by:

Latin Style Magazine

P.O. Box 2969

Venice CA 90294

Date: August 1994

Frequency: Monthly

Cover Price: $2.50

Subscription Price: $20.00

Discount Subscription Price: n/a

Total Number of Pages: 96

Total Number of Ad Pages: 36

Publisher: Walter Martinez

Editor: Walter Martinez

Editorial Concept: Entertainment, celebrities, and fashion for the Latin-American community.

People Today Secrets

Published by:

Scope Publications Inc.

NW 17th Way, Suite 600

Ft. Lauderdale FL 33309

Date: July 1994

Frequency: Bimonthly

Cover Price: $3.95

Subscription Price: $29.70

Discount Subscription Price: n/a

Total Number of Pages: 82

Total Number of Ad Pages: 1

Publisher: David Harvard

Editor: Sheila Tyler

Editorial Concept: A celebrity mag that attempts to go more in-depth than other star-driven publications.

Surface

Published by:

Surface Publishing Inc.

1388 Haight St.

San Francisco CA 94117

Date: Winter 1994 *(first newsstand issue)*

Frequency: Quarterly

Cover Price: $4.00

Subscription Price: $16.00

Discount Subscription Price: n/a

Total Number of Pages: 44

Total Number of Ad Pages: 6

Publisher: Richard Klein

Editor: n/a

Editorial Concept: "Avant-garde fashion, photography, and culture for the tragically hip."

Action Heroes '94

Published by:

Jacobs Publications

475 Park Ave. South, 8th Floor

New York NY 10016

Date: 1994

Frequency: Special

Cover Price: $4.95

Subscription Price: n/a

Discount Subscription Price: n/a

Total Number of Pages: 68

Total Number of Ad Pages: 9

Publisher: Norman Jacobs

Editor: David McDonnell

Editorial Concept: Articles and photographs of the biggest action stars from the biggest action films.

All Talk

Published by:

K-III Magazines Corporation

717 Fifth Ave.

New York NY 10010

Date: November/December 1994

Frequency: n/a

Cover Price: $2.50

Subscription Price: n/a

Discount Subscription Price: n/a

Total Number of Pages: 64

Total Number of Ad Pages: 6

Publisher: Linda Vaughan

Editor: Jason Bonderoff

Editorial Concept: "All the stars, all the news, all the gossip."

Baywatch: Special Photo Tribute

Published by:

Ashley Communications Inc.

P.O. Box 1053

Malibu CA 90265

Date: October 1994

Frequency: Special

Cover Price: $4.95

Subscription Price: n/a

Discount Subscription Price: n/a

Total Number of Pages: 48

Total Number of Ad Pages: 2

Publisher: Ashley Communications

Editor: n/a

Editorial Concept: "A T&A photo tribute to the wildly popular TV show."

Daytime TV's Greatest Stories

Published by:

The Sterling MacFadden Partnership

233 Park Ave. South

New York NY 10003

Date: May 1994

Frequency: Annually

Cover Price: $2.95

Subscription Price: n/a

Discount Subscription Price: n/a

Total Number of Pages: 84

Total Number of Ad Pages: 10

Publisher: The Sterling MacFadden Partnership

Editor: Lucille Giordana

Editorial Concept: Color pinups and fun features about the stars of "General Hospital."

Elizabeth Taylor - Portrait of a Legend

Published by:

Meredith Corporation

1716 Locust St.

Des Moines IA 50309-3023

Date: 1994

Frequency: Special

Cover Price: $2.95

Subscription Price: n/a

Discount Subscription Price: n/a

Total Number of Pages: 100

Total Number of Ad Pages: 9

Publisher: Donna Galotti

Editor: Carolyn Noyes

Editorial Concept: "A loving look at the career and life of the film actress."

Elvis Presley Astrological Profile

Published by:

Lifestyles International Inc.

25680 W. 12 Mile Road

Southfield MI 48304-1184

Date: 1994

Frequency: Special

Cover Price: $3.95

Subscription Price: n/a

Discount Subscription Price: n/a

Total Number of Pages: 52

Total Number of Ad Pages: 1

Publisher: Lifestyles International Inc.

Editor: n/a

Editorial Concept: "Elvis's astrological horoscope and psychological profile."

Globe Special: Jackie

Published by:

No information given.

Date: 1994

Frequency: Special

Cover Price: $2.25

Subscription Price: n/a

Discount Subscription Price: n/a

Total Number of Pages: 48

Total Number of Ad Pages: 3

Publisher: n/a

Editor: n/a

Editorial Concept: A look at the life and times of Jackie Kennedy Onassis.

Jackie, the Last Lady of Camelot

Published by:

LFP Inc.

9171 Wilshire Blvd., Suite 300

Beverly Hills CA 90210

Date: 1994

Frequency: Special

Cover Price: $3.95

Subscription Price: n/a

Discount Subscription Price: n/a

Total Number of Pages: 80

Total Number of Ad Pages: 0

Publisher: Larry Flynt

Editor: Chris Gore

Editorial Concept: A memorial to Jackie Kennedy Onassis.

Ladies' Home Journal Special: Barbara Walter's Best Interviews

Published by:

Meredith Corporation

1716 Locust St.

Des Moines IA 50309-3023

Date: 1994

Frequency: Special

Cover Price: $2.95

Subscription Price: n/a

Discount Subscription Price: n/a

Total Number of Pages: 100

Total Number of Ad Pages: 13

Publisher: Myrna Blyth

Editor: Carolyn Noyes

Editorial Concept: Barbara Walter's top interviews.

Ladies' Home Journal Special: Close-Up - TV's Leading Ladies

Published by:

Meredith Corporation

1716 Locust St.

Des Moines IA 50309-3023

Date: 1994

Frequency: Special

Cover Price: $2.95

Subscription Price: n/a

Discount Subscription Price: n/a

Total Number of Pages: 100

Total Number of Ad Pages: 14

Publisher: Donna Galotti

Editor: Carolyn Noyes

Editorial Concept: Saluting the women of TV.

Ladies' Home Journal Special: Jackie - A Remembrance of a Great Lady

Published by:

Meredith Corporation

1716 Locust St.

Des Moines IA 50309-3023

Date: 1994

Frequency: Special

Cover Price: $3.95

Subscription Price: n/a

Discount Subscription Price: n/a

Total Number of Pages: 100

Total Number of Ad Pages: 11

Publisher: Donna Galotti

Editor: Carolyn Noyes

Editorial Concept: A look in words and pictures at the life of Jacqueline Bouvier Kennedy Onassis.

Love, Marriage and Divorce Scandals of the Rich and Famous

Published by:

National Enquirer Inc.

Lantana FL 33464

Date: 1994

Frequency: Special

Cover Price: $2.50

Subscription Price: n/a

Discount Subscription Price: n/a

Total Number of Pages: 76

Total Number of Ad Pages: 7

Publisher: National Enquirer Inc.

Editor: Mike Nevard

Editorial Concept: "The title says it all."

Marilyn

Published by:

Starlog Group Inc.

475 Park Ave. South

New York Ny 10016

Date: 1994

Frequency: Special

Cover Price: $11.95

Subscription Price: n/a

Discount Subscription Price: n/a

Total Number of Pages: 92

Total Number of Ad Pages: 5

Publisher: Norman Jacobs

Editor: Milburn Smith

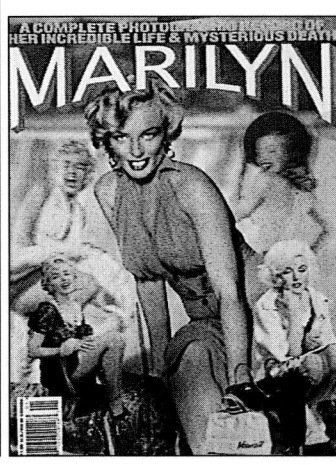

Editorial Concept: "The complete photographic record of her incredible life and mysterious death."

Michael Jackson & His Famous Family

Published by:

The Sterling/MacFadden Partnership

233 Park Ave. South

New York NY 10003

Date: March 1994

Frequency: Special

Cover Price: $3.95

Subscription Price: n/a

Discount Subscription Price: n/a

Total Number of Pages: 94

Total Number of Ad Pages: 9

Publisher: The Sterling/MacFadden Partnership

Editor: Ellen Jurcsak

Editorial Concept: "Pictures and articles about entertainment's first family and other media stars."

National Enquirer Special: Oprah - This Is Your Life

Published by:

Enquirer/Star Group Inc.

600 SE Coast Ave.

Lantana FL 33462

Date: Fall 1994

Frequency: Special

Cover Price: $2.50

Subscription Price: n/a

Discount Subscription Price: n/a

O.J. Simpson - Looking Back

Published by:

H&S Media Inc.

3400 Dundee Road

Northbrook IL 60062

Date: 1994

Frequency: Special

Cover Price: $4.95

Subscription Price: n/a

Discount Subscription Price: n/a

Total Number of Pages: 100

Total Number of Ad Pages: 0

Publisher: H&S Media Inc.

Editor: n/a

Editorial Concept: "Thousands of O.J. Simpson football records and exclusive photos."

Total Number of Pages: 76

Total Number of Ad Pages: 6

Publisher: Enquirer/Star Group Inc.

Editor: n/a

Editorial Concept: "Her money... her loves...her diets...her views on men, marriage, babies, and God."

O.J. Simpson: From Triumph to Tragedy

Published by:

L.F.P. Inc.

9171 Wilshire Blvd., Suite 300

Beverly Hills CA 90210

Date: 1994

Frequency: Special

Cover Price: $3.95

Subscription Price: n/a

Discount Subscription Price: n/a

Total Number of Pages: 80

Total Number of Ad Pages: 0

Publisher: Larry Flynt

Editor: Terry Melia

Editorial Concept: "To provide readers with a sense of history regarding O.J."

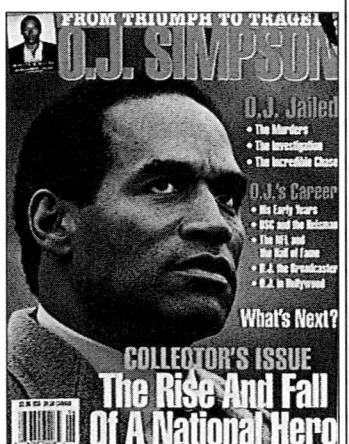

People Weekly Commemorative Issue Tribute: Jacqueline Kennedy Onassis

Published by:

Time Inc.

Rockefeller Center

New York NY 10020-1393

Date: Summer 1994

Frequency: Special

Cover Price: $3.95

Subscription Price: n/a

Discount Subscription Price: n/a

Total Number of Pages: 100

Total Number of Ad Pages: 40

Publisher: Nora P. McAniff

Editor: Landon Y. Jones Jr.

Editorial Concept: A tribute to the late first lady.

Soap Opera Digest Wedding Extra

Published by:

K-III Magazine Corporation

45 W. 25th St.

New York NY 10010

Date: Winter 1994

Frequency: Special

Cover Price: $2.25

Subscription Price: n/a

Discount Subscription Price: n/a

Total Number of Pages: 68

Total Number of Ad Pages: 5

Publisher: Linda Vaughn

Editor: Donna Hoke Kahwaty

Editorial Concept: A fan's look at celebrated soap-opera weddings.

Soap Opera Digest Wedding Spectacular

Published by:

K-III Magazine Corporation

717 Fifth Ave.

New York NY 10010

Date: Summer 1994

Frequency: Special

Cover Price: $2.50

Subscription Price: n/a

Discount Subscription Price: n/a

Total Number of Pages: 68

Total Number of Ad Pages: 4

Publisher: Linda Vaughn

Editor: Donna Hoke Kahwaty

Editorial Concept: Celebrity love and scandal.

Starline Presents A Tribute to Jonathan Brandis and Friends

Published by:

Starline Publications Inc.

210 Route 4 East, Suite 410

Paramus NJ 07652

Date: 1994

Frequency: Special

Cover Price: $3.50

Subscription Price: n/a

Discount Subscription Price: n/a

Total Number of Pages: 68

Total Number of Ad Pages: 6

Publisher: Scott Mitchell Figman

Editor: Anne M. Raso

Editorial Concept: Photos and stories about the teen heartthrob.

Starline Presents A Tribute to Jonathan Brandis & Joey Lawrence

Published by:

Starline Publications Inc.

210 Route 4 East, Suite 401

Paramus NJ 07652

Date: 1994

Frequency: Special

Cover Price: $3.50

Subscription Price: n/a

Discount Subscription Price: n/a

Total Number of Pages: 68

Total Number of Ad Pages: 4

Publisher: Scott Mitchell Figman

Editor: Anne M. Raso

Editorial Concept: Photos and stories about the teen heartthrobs.

Star Special Memorial Issue: Jackie

Published by:

Enquirer/Star Group Inc.

600 SE Coast Ave.

Lantana FL 33462

Date: 1994

Frequency: Special

Cover Price: $3.50

Subscription Price: n/a

Discount Subscription Price: n/a

Total Number of Pages: 76

Total Number of Ad Pages: 0

Publisher: n/a

Editor: n/a

Editorial Concept: "Over 200 memorable photos."

A Tribute to Days of Our Lives

Published by:

Starline Publications Inc.

210 Route 4 East, Suite 401

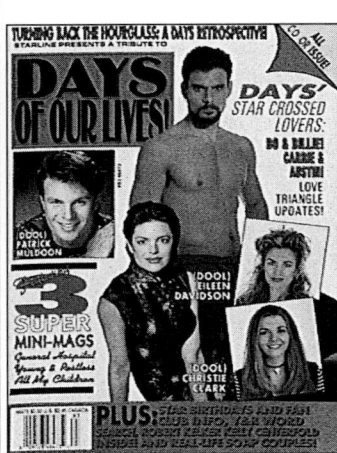

Paramus NJ 07652

Date: 1994

Frequency: Special

Cover Price: $3.50

Subscription Price: n/a

Discount Subscription Price: n/a

Total Number of Pages: 68

Total Number of Ad Pages: 0

Publisher: Starline Publications Inc.

Editor: Anne M. Raso

Editorial Concept: Articles and color photos about the stars of this soap opera.

A Tribute to Jackie

Published by:

Lopez Publications Inc.

152 Madison Ave., Suite 906

New York NY 10016

Date: 1994

Frequency: Special

Cover Price: $3.95

Subscription Price: n/a

Discount Subscription Price: n/a

Total Number of Pages: 68

Total Number of Ad Pages: 5

Publisher: Adrian B. Lopez

Editor: Holly Garrison

Editorial Concept: More than 30 years of photos and stories of Jackie Kennedy Onassis from *Lady's Circle*.

Image

Published by:

Image Inc.

11012 Ventura Blvd.

Studio City CA 91604

Date: October 1994

Frequency: Bimonthly

Cover Price: $2.95

Subscription Price: $15.95

Discount Subscription Price: n/a

Total Number of Pages: 64

Total Number of Ad Pages: 8

Publisher: J. Edward Giles III, J.D.

Editor: Meredith C. Beal

Editorial Concept: Upscale fashion and lifestyle for black men.

New Body Bikini Girls

Published by:

GCR Publishing Group Inc.

1700 Broadway

New York NY 10019

Date: 1994

Frequency: Quarterly

Cover Price: $4.95

Subscription Price: n/a

Discount Subscription Price: n/a

Total Number of Pages: 68

Total Number of Ad Pages: 0

Publisher: Charles Goodman

Editor: Jane Miller

Editorial Concept: "Hot babes showing off their assets in the latest bikini styles from Venus swimwear."

New Man

Published by:

Strang Communications

600 Rinehart Road

Lake Mary FL 32746

Date: July/August 1994

Frequency: Bimonthly

Cover Price: $2.95

Subscription Price: $15.00

Discount Subscription Price: n/a

Total Number of Pages: 96

Total Number of Ad Pages: 41

Publisher: Stephen Strang

Editor: Brian Peterson

Editorial Concept: "To introduce men to real Christianity and masculinity."

New Rave

Published by:

AmLon Publishing Group

7060 Hollywood Blvd., Suite 805

Hollywood CA 90028

Date: August 1994

Frequency: Monthly

Cover Price: $4.99

Subscription Price: $39.95

Discount Subscription Price: n/a

Total Number of Pages: 132

Total Number of Ad Pages: 26

Publisher: Hank Londoner

Editor: Larry Wichman

Editorial Concept: "The MTV of men's magazines: sex, fun, and rock 'n' roll... raunchier than *Playboy* and younger than *Penthouse*."

Platinum Perspectives

Published by:

Platinum Media Group

7301 Topanga Canyon Blvd.

Canoga Park CA 91303

Date: June 1994

Frequency: 11/year

Cover Price: $4.95

Subscription Price: $27.95

Discount Subscription Price: $25.95

Total Number of Pages: 150

Total Number of Ad Pages: 28

Publisher: David Rafael

Editor: Trevor Miller

Editorial Concept: "An upscale men's publication in which the style of the photography is just as important in the pictorials as the nude models."

Annual, Special or Frequency Unknown

Gallery Centerfolds

Published by:

Montcalm Publishing Corporation

401 Park Ave. South

New York NY 10016

Date: Winter 1994

Frequency: Special

Cover Price: $5.95

Subscription Price: n/a

Discount Subscription Price: n/a

Total Number of Pages: 100

Total Number of Ad Pages: 9

Publisher: n/a

Editor: n/a

Editorial Concept: A collection of nude pictorials of past *Gallery* magazine centerfolds.

International Pets

Published by:

Girls of Penthouse Publications Inc.

1965 Broadway

New York NY 10023

Date: October 1994

Frequency: Special

Cover Price: $5.50

Subscription Price: n/a

Discount Subscription Price: n/a

Total Number of Pages: 116

Total Number of Ad Pages: 21

Publisher: Bob Guccione

Editor: Don Myers

Editorial Concept: "High-quality nude pictorials of seven women from around the world."

Men's Journal
Equipment Guide

Published by:

Men's Journal Company L.P.

1290 Avenue of the Americas

New York NY 10104-0298

Date: 1994

Frequency: Special

Cover Price: $3.95

Subscription Price: n/a

Discount Subscription Price: n/a

Total Number of Pages: 184

Total Number of Ad Pages: 68

Publisher: Mark E. MacDonald

Editor: James Kaminsky

Editorial Concept: "The consummate resource for the right stuff and the best deals - the greatest sports gear, electronics, and more."

Alaska People Magazine

Published by:

Alaska People Magazine

P.O. Box 190648, Dept. A

Anchorage AK 99519

Date: July/August 1994

Frequency: Bimonthly

Cover Price: $2.95

Subscription Price: $19.95

Discount Subscription Price: $15.00

Total Number of Pages: 48

Total Number of Ad Pages: 17

Publisher: Jim Rosen and Yvonne Akai Evans

Editor: Yvonne Akai Evans

Editorial Concept: "To introduce the delightful and inspiring stories of the people who share the state of being . . . Alaskan."

Alaskan Exposure

Published by:

B-Mark Company

1330 E. Huffman Road #434

Anchorage AK 99515

Date: Spring 1994 (first newsstand issue)

Frequency: Quarterly

Cover Price: $3.95

Subscription Price: $12.65

Discount Subscription Price: n/a

Total Number of Pages: 52

Total Number of Ad Pages: 8

Publisher: B-Mark Company

Editor: Robert A. Olson, Kathy Pitchford

Editorial Concept: "Expose yourself to the real Alaska and its talented people."

Big Sky Journal

Published by:

Spring Creek Publishing Inc.

P.O. Box 1837

Bozeman MT 59771-9975

Date: Spring 1994

Frequency: Quarterly

Cover Price: $4.95

Subscription Price: $15.00

Discount Subscription Price: n/a

Total Number of Pages: 86

Total Number of Ad Pages: 26

Publisher: David McCumber

Editor: David McCumber

Editorial Concept: "The very best of Montana journalism and art and fiction."

Branson Getaway Guide 1994

Published by:

Action Publications Inc.

621 W. Plainview Road

Springfield MO 65810-2419

Date: Spring 1994

Frequency: Semi-annually

Cover Price: $6.95

Subscription Price: n/a

Discount Subscription Price: n/a

Total Number of Pages: 156

Total Number of Ad Pages: 16

Publisher: Jim and Janet Peters

Editor: n/a

Editorial Concept: "Your guide to America's most amazing vacation spot."

Carolina Style

Published by:

Carolina Style Inc.

3975-B Market

Wilmington NC 28405

Date: 1994

Frequency: Monthly

Cover Price: $3.50

Subscription Price: $24.00

Discount Subscription Price: $18.00

Total Number of Pages: 114

Total Number of Ad Pages: 20

Publisher: Stuart F. Slater

Editor: Anthony S. Policastro

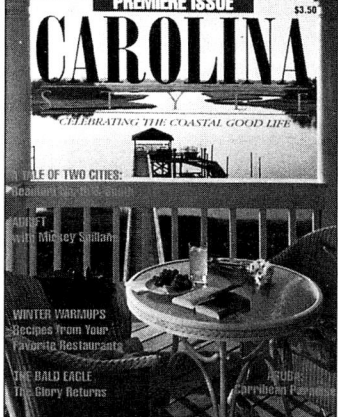

Editorial Concept: A celebration of the coastal good life.

Houston Life

Published by:

Houston Metropolitan Ltd.

P.O. Box 25386

Houston TX 77265

Date: Feb. 20 - March 19, 1994

Frequency: Monthly

Cover Price: Free

Subscription Price: n/a

Discount Subscription Price: n/a

Total Number of Pages: 170

Total Number of Ad Pages: 72

Publisher: Mark B. Inabnit

Editor: Maria Ross

Editorial Concept: "The magazine for better living in Houston."

Know Tampa Bay

Published by:

New South Publishing Inc.

7840 Roswell Road, Suite 328

Atlanta GA 30350

Date: Spring 1994

Frequency: Quarterly

Cover Price: $3.50

Subscription Price: n/a

Discount Subscription Price: n/a

Total Number of Pages: 68

Total Number of Ad Pages: 23

Publisher: Susan Thompson

Editor: Stephen Morrill

Editorial Concept: An overview of Tampa Bay for people relocating to the area.

Empires, Eagles & Lions

Published by:

The Emperor's Headquarters

5744 W. Irving Road

Chicago IL 60634

Date: March/April 1994

(first newsstand issue)

Frequency: Bimonthly

Cover Price: $6.00

Subscription Price: $33.00

Discount Subscription Price: n/a

Total Number of Pages: 64

Total Number of Ad Pages: 5

Publisher: The Emperor's Headquarters

Editor: Jean A. Lochet

Editorial Concept: "Dedicated to Napoleonic history and wargaming."

Great Sea Sagas of WWII

Published by:

Challenge Publications Inc.

7950 Deering Ave.

Canoga Park CA 91304

Date: Winter 1994

Frequency: Quarterly

Cover Price: $5.95

Subscription Price: $12.95

Discount Subscription Price: n/a

Total Number of Pages: 96

Total Number of Ad Pages: 8

Publisher: Edwin A. Schnepf

Editor: Edwin A. Schnepf

Editorial Concept: WWII naval stories.

Guns and Gear

Published by:

Guns and Gear Magazine

7040 W. Palmetto Road

Boca Raton FL 33433

Date: February 1994

Frequency: Bimonthly

Cover Price: $4.95

Subscription Price: $29.70

Discount Subscription Price: n/a

Total Number of Pages: 84

Total Number of Ad Pages: 12

Publisher: David Harvard

Editor: Jerry Gerardi

Editorial Concept: Reviews of handguns and ammo.

Handgun Times

Published by:

Handgun Times

7040 W. Palmetto Park Road

Boca Raton FL 33433

Date: March 1994

Frequency: Bimonthly

Cover Price: $4.95

Subscription Price: $29.70

Discount Subscription Price: n/a

Total Number of Pages: 84

Total Number of Ad Pages: 13

Publisher: David Harvard

Editor: Jerry Gerardi

Editorial Concept: "To provide you with more editorial paper on handguns than any other newsstand magazine."

The Handgunner's Journal

Published by:

The Handgunner's Journal

7040 W. Palmetto Park Road

Boca Raton FL 33433

Date: March 1994

Frequency: Bimonthly

Cover Price: $4.95

Subscription Price: $29.70

Discount Subscription Price: n/a

Total Number of Pages: 84

Total Number of Ad Pages: 13

Publisher: David Harvard

Editor: Jerry Gerardi

Editorial Concept: "Expert commentary on handguns of all types."

Official Black Book's Gun Guide

Published by:

Official Black Book's Gun Guide

7040 W. Palmetto Park Road

Boca Raton FL 33433

Date: February 1994

Frequency: Bimonthly

Cover Price: $4.95

Subscription Price: $29.70

Discount Subscription Price: n/a

Total Number of Pages: 84

Total Number of Ad Pages: 5

Publisher: David Harvard

Editor: Jerry Gerardi

Editorial Concept: "Expert commentary on handguns of all types."

Rifle and Shotgun Sport Shooting

Published by:

Nat Com Inc.

5300 CityPlex Tower

2448 E. 81st St.

Tulsa OK 74137

Date: August 1994

Frequency: Bimonthly

Cover Price: $2.95

Subscription Price: $13.95

Discount Subscription Price: n/a

Total Number of Pages: 72

Total Number of Ad Pages: 21

Publisher: Gerald W. Pope

Editor: Lawrence Taylor

Editorial Concept: "Improving your shooting, no matter what your target."

Soldier of Fortune's Fighting Firearms

Published by:

Omega Group Limited

P.O. Box 693

Boulder CO 80306

Date: Spring 1994

Frequency: Quarterly

Cover Price: $3.95

Subscription Price: n/a

Discount Subscription Price: n/a

Total Number of Pages: 84

Total Number of Ad Pages: 10

Publisher: Robert K. Brown

Editor: Robert K. Brown

Editorial Concept: "New, in-depth, up-to-date, information for the growing number of military firearm users and enthusiasts."

Annual, Special or Frequency Unknown

Aces and Aircraft of the Great War

Published by:

Challenge Publications Inc.

7950 Deering Ave.

Canoga Park CA 91304

Date: 1994

Frequency: Special

Cover Price: $5.95

Subscription Price: n/a

Discount Subscription Price: n/a

Total Number of Pages: 96

Total Number of Ad Pages: 6

Publisher: Edwin A. Schnepf

Editor: Edwin A. Schnepf

Editorial Concept: Stories of the pilots and planes of WWII.

Airborne Attack WWII

Published by:

Challenge Publications Inc.

7950 Deering Ave.

Canoga Park CA 91304

Date: 1994

Frequency: Special

Cover Price: $5.95

Subscription Price: n/a

Discount Subscription Price: n/a

Total Number of Pages: 96

Total Number of Ad Pages: 6

Publisher: Edwin A. Schnepf

Editor: Joe Poyer

Editorial Concept: An account in words and pictures of the airborne warfare of WWII.

Banned Guns!

Published by:

Challenge Publications Inc.

7950 Deering Ave.

Canoga Park CA 91304

Date: 1994

Frequency: Special

Cover Price: $5.95

Subscription Price: n/a

Discount Subscription Price: n/a

Total Number of Pages: 88

Total Number of Ad Pages: 8

Publisher: Edwin A. Schnepf

Editor: Joe Poyer

Editorial Concept: "Buyers guide to an endangered species!"

Battle Stations

Published by:

Challenge Publications Inc.

7950 Deering Ave.

Canoga Park CA 91304

Date: 1994

Frequency: Special

Cover Price: $5.95

Subscription Price: n/a

Discount Subscription Price: n/a

Total Number of Pages: 96

Total Number of Ad Pages: 7

Publisher: Edwin A. Schnepf

Editor: Edwin A. Schnepf

Editorial Concept: Twelve action-packed naval war stories mostly from WWII.

Battleships at War!

Published by:

Challenge Publications Inc.

7950 Deering Ave.

Canoga Park CA 91304

Date: 1994

Frequency: Special

Cover Price: $5.95

Subscription Price: n/a

Discount Subscription Price: n/a

Total Number of Pages: 132

Total Number of Ad Pages: 4

Publisher: Edwin A. Schnepf

Editor: Edwin A. Schnepf

Editorial Concept: Stories and pictures of military battleships from around the world.

Custom Combat Handguns

Published by:

Harris Publications Inc.

1115 Broadway

New York NY 10010

Custom Combat HANDGUNS

Date: 1994

Frequency: Annually

Cover Price: $4.50

Subscription Price: n/a

Discount Subscription Price: n/a

Total Number of Pages: 100

Total Number of Ad Pages: 19

Publisher: Stanley R. Harris

Editor: Harry Kane

Editorial Concept: "Making your handgun the most powerful weapon it can be."

D-Day

Published by:

Starlog Telecommunications Inc.

475 Park Ave. South

New York NY 10016

Date: 1994

Frequency: Special

Cover Price: $4.95

Subscription Price: n/a

Discount Subscription Price: n/a

Total Number of Pages: 84

Total Number of Ad Pages: 2

Publisher: Norman Jacobs

Editor: Michael Benson

Editorial Concept: The Allied invasion at Normandy on the 50th anniversary.

Great Naval Battles of the Civil War

Published by:

Challenge Publications Inc.

7950 Deering Ave.

Canoga Park CA 91304

Date: 1994

Frequency: Special

Cover Price: $5.95

Subscription Price: n/a

Discount Subscription Price: n/a

Total Number of Pages: 96

Total Number of Ad Pages: 10

Publisher: Edwin A. Schnepf

Editor: Edwin A. Schnepf

Editorial Concept: Stories and art depicting the real-life drama of Civil War gunboats and ironclads.

Guns and Ammo High-Tech Firearms

Published by:

Petersen Publishing Company

6420 Wilshire Blvd.

Los Angeles CA 90048-5515

Date: 1994

Frequency: Annually

Cover Price: $3.95

Subscription Price: n/a

Discount Subscription Price: n/a

Total Number of Pages: 100

Total Number of Ad Pages: 3

Publisher: Doug Hamlin

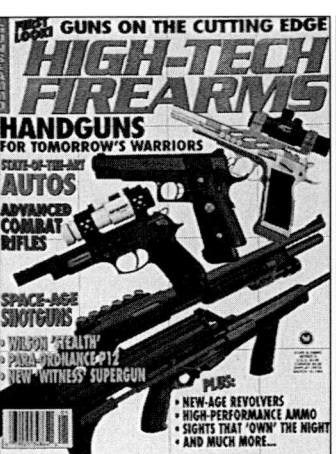

Editor: Phil Spangenberger

Editorial Concept: "Guns on the cutting edge" - new-age revolvers, advanced combat rifles, and space-age shotguns.

Guns and Ammo Rifles and Cartridges For Big Game

Published by:

Peterson Publishing Company

6420 Wilshire Blvd.

Los Angeles CA 90048

Date: 1994

Frequency: Special

Cover Price: $3.95

Subscription Price: n/a

Discount Subscription Price: n/a

Total Number of Pages: 100

Total Number of Ad Pages: 4

Publisher: Thomas J. Siatos

Editor: Todd Smith

Editorial Concept: The guns and bullets used to bring down buck, bear, moose, etc.

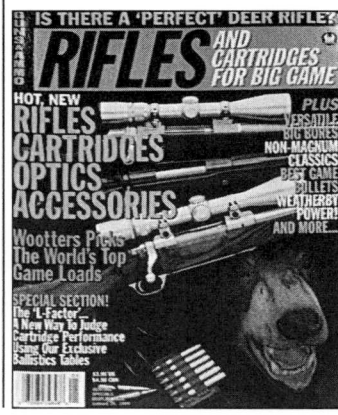

Guns and Ammo Shooting Tips

Published by:

Petersen Publishing Company

6420 Wilshire Blvd.

Los Angeles CA 90048

Date: 1994

Frequency: Special

Cover Price: $3.95

Subscription Price: n/a

Discount Subscription Price: n/a

Total Number of Pages: 100

Total Number of Ad Pages: 5

Publisher: Doug Hamlin

Editor: Jerry Lee

Editorial Concept: "Gun and ammo experts share their shooting secrets."

Handgun Shootout!

Published by:

Petersen Publishing Company

6420 Wilshire Blvd.

Los Angeles CA 90048-5515

Date: 1994

Frequency: Special

Cover Price: $3.95

Subscription Price: n/a

Discount Subscription Price: n/a

Total Number of Pages: 100

Total Number of Ad Pages: 3

Publisher: Doug Hamlin

Editor: Jerry Lee

Editorial Concept: Comparisons and reviews of different makes and models of handguns.

Frequency: n/a

Cover Price: $3.95

Subscription Price: n/a

Discount Subscription Price: n/a

Total Number of Pages: 84

Total Number of Ad Pages: 12

Publisher: Stephen Ferber

Editor: Robert Elman

Editorial Concept: "Shooting as it relates to law enforcement, combat, and self-defense."

Publisher: Edwin A. Schnepf

Editor: Edwin A. Schnepf

Editorial Concept: "13 exciting true tales of daring submarine raids."

Perils of the Deep

Published by:

Challenge Publications Inc.

7950 Deering Ave.

Canoga Park CA 91304

Date: 1994

Frequency: Special

Cover Price: $5.95

Subscription Price: n/a

Discount Subscription Price: n/a

Total Number of Pages: 96

Total Number of Ad Pages: 8

Sigarms Handgunning

Published by:

Aqua-Field Publishing Company

66 W. Gilbert St.

Shrewsbury NJ 07702

Date: 1994

Submarine Raiders of World War II

Published by:

Challenge Publications Inc.

7950 Deering Ave.

Canoga Park CA 91304

Date: 1994

Frequency: Special

Cover Price: $5.95

Subscription Price: n/a

Discount Subscription Price: n/a

Total Number of Pages: 96

Total Number of Ad Pages: 7

Publisher: Edwin A. Schnepf

Editor: Edwin A. Schnepf

Editorial Concept: True stories of danger and disaster on the high reef.

Target: Japan!

Published by:

Challenge Publications Inc.

7950 Deering Ave.

Canoga Park CA 91304

Date: 1994

Frequency: Special

Cover Price: $5.95

Subscription Price: n/a

Discount Subscription Price: n/a

Total Number of Pages: 96

Total Number of Ad Pages: 15

Publisher: Edwin A. Schnepf

Editor: Michael O'Leary

Editorial Concept: "WWII special: the U.S. Army Air Force and U.S. Navy strike back at the Japanese empire."

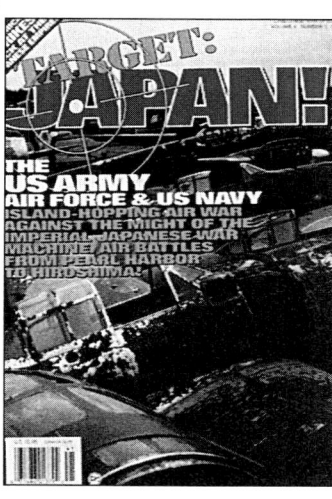

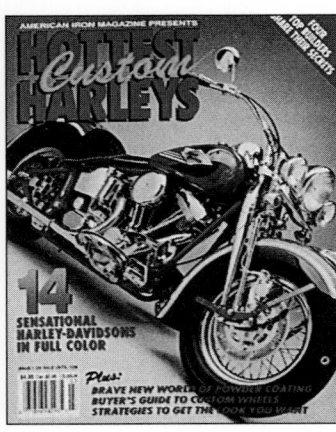

American Iron Magazine Presents Hottest Custom Harleys

Published by:

TAM Communications Inc.

6 Prowitt St.

Norwalk CT 06855

Date: 1994

Frequency: 9/Year

Cover Price: $4.95

Subscription Price: n/a

Discount Subscription Price: n/a

Total Number of Pages: 96

Total Number of Ad Pages: 14

Publisher: Buzz Kanter

Editor: Buzz Kanter

Editorial Concept: High-quality photos and articles on customized Harley-Davidson motorcycles.

American Rider

Published by:

TL Enterprises Inc.

3601 Calle Tecate

Camarillo TX

Date: Winter 1994

Frequency: Quarterly

Cover Price: $3.50

Subscription Price: $14.00

Discount Subscription Price: $9.98

Total Number of Pages: 108

Total Number of Ad Pages: 34

Publisher: Joseph E. McNeill Jr.

Editor: Buzz Buzzelli

Editorial Concept: " To bring the highest quality magazine to today's Harley-Davidson rider."

Early Riders

Published by:

Paisano Publications Inc.

28210 Dorothy Drive

Agoura Hills CA 91301-2693

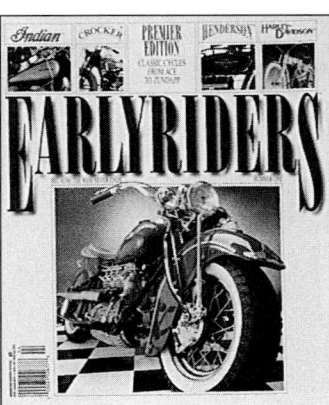

Date: Fall 1994

Frequency: Quarterly

Cover Price: $4.95

Subscription Price: $13.95

Discount Subscription Price: n/a

Total Number of Pages: 100

Total Number of Ad Pages: 26

Publisher: Joe Teresi

Editor: Joe Teresi

Editorial Concept: "Classic cycles from Ace to Zudapp."

Hot Rod Harleys

Published by:

Petersen Publishing Company

6420 Wilshire Blvd.

Los Angeles CA 90048

Date: March 1994

Frequency: Bimonthly

Cover Price: $2.95

Subscription Price: $13.95

Discount Subscription Price: $11.95

Total Number of Pages: 84

Total Number of Ad Pages: 22

Publisher: John Dianna

Editor: Erik Falconer

Editorial Concept: "How to build a head-snapping customized Harley, plus pictures of the finished product."

Renegade XPress

Published by:

RX Publishing Inc.

North Miami Beach FL 33269

Date: March1994 *(formerly Rider's Xchange)*

Frequency: Monthly

Cover Price: $3.95

Subscription Price: $25.00

Discount Subscription Price: n/a

Total Number of Pages: 116

Total Number of Ad Pages: 40

Publisher: Clayton R. Douglas

Editor: Bea Ralph

Editorial Concept: News about motorcycle rallies and biker issues from around the country.

VQ

Published by:

Paisano Publications Inc.

28210 Dorothy Drive

Agoura Hills CA 91301

Date: April 1994

Frequency: Quarterly

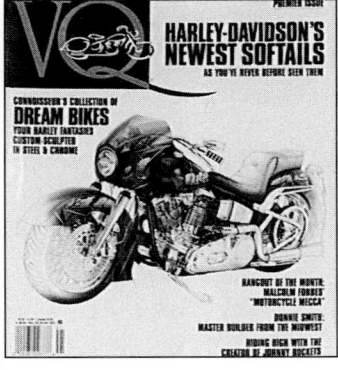

Cover Price: $5.95

Subscription Price: $16.50

Discount Subscription Price: n/a

Total Number of Pages: 100

Total Number of Ad Pages: 24

Publisher: Joe Teresi

Editor: Dick Teresi

Editorial Concept: "High-quality pictures and articles about customized motorcycles."

Annual, Special or Frequency Unknown

American Iron Magazine Presents Thunder Alley

Published by:

TAM Communications Inc.

6 Prowitt St.

Norwalk CT 06855

Date: 1994

Frequency: n/a

Cover Price: $4.95

Subscription Price: n/a

Discount Subscription Price: n/a

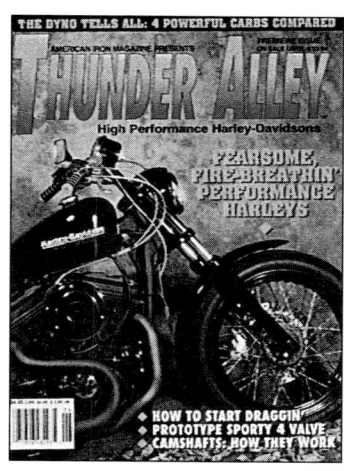

Total Number of Pages: 96

Total Number of Ad Pages: 20

Publisher: Buzz Kanter

Editor: Buzz Kanter

Editorial Concept: Devoted to high-performance, racing Harleys.

Cycle Guide's 1994 Buyer's Guide

Published by:

Hachette Filipacchi Magazines Inc.

1633 Broadway

New York NY 10019

Date: 1994

Frequency: Annually

Cover Price: $4.95

Subscription Price: n/a

Discount Subscription Price: n/a

Total Number of Pages: 124

Total Number of Ad Pages: 23

Publisher: Larry Little

Editor: Robyn Davis

Editorial Concept: Photos and specification on 189 motorcycles for 1994.

Dream Bike Posters

Published by:

n/a

Date: 1994

Frequency: Special

Cover Price: $4.95

Subscription Price: n/a

Discount Subscription Price: n/a

Total Number of Pages: 36

Total Number of Ad Pages: 2

Publisher: n/a

Editor: Mike Chase

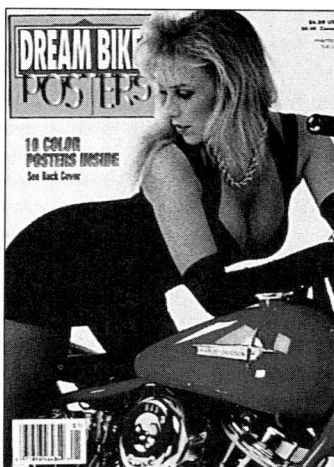

Editorial Concept: "Nine posters of hot Harleys and hotter women."

Hot Rod Harleys Pictorial

Published by:

Petersen Publishing Company

6420 Wilshire Blvd.

Los Angeles CA 90048

Date: 1994

Frequency: Special

Cover Price: $3.95

Subscription Price: n/a

Discount Subscription Price: n/a

Total Number of Pages: 100

Total Number of Ad Pages: 10

Publisher: John Dianna

Editor: Frank Kaisler

Editorial Concept: "Pictorials of customized Harley motorcycles and biker babes."

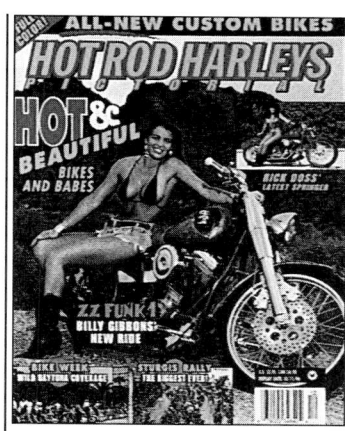

Outlaw Biker Laughlin Nevada River Run

Published by:

Outlaw Biker Enterprises Inc.

450 Seventh Ave., Suite 2305

New York NY 10123-2305

Date: 1994

Frequency: Special

Cover Price: $4.99

Subscription Price: n/a

Discount Subscription Price: n/a

Total Number of Pages: 86

Total Number of Ad Pages: 12

Publisher: Casey Exton

Editor: Eric Wolf

Editorial Concept: Pictures and memories of the Harley-riders rally.

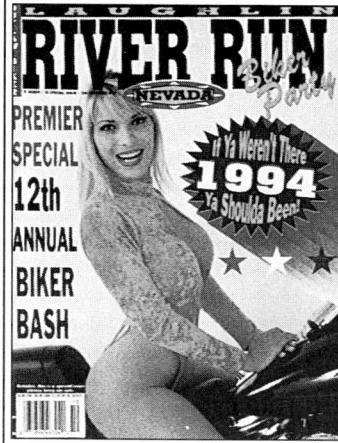

Beat USA

Published by:

Beat Magazine Inc.

3246 Cathedral Drive

Tallahassee FL 32310

Date: June/July 1994

Frequency: Bimonthly

Cover Price: $2.25

Subscription Price: $10.00

Discount Subscription Price: n/a

Total Number of Pages: 32

Total Number of Ad Pages: 11

Publisher: Mario A. Petaccia

Editor: Mario A. Petaccia

Editorial Concept: Profiles in a wide range of musical artists, from country to pop to thrash.

CMJ New Music Monthly

Published by:

College Media Inc.

---

11 Middle Neck Road, Suite 400

Great Neck NY 11021-2301

Date: September 1994 (*first newsstand issue.*)

Frequency: Monthly

Cover Price: $4.99

Subscription Price: $29.95

Discount Subscription Price: n/a

Total Number of Pages: 64

Total Number of Ad Pages: 19

Publisher: Robert K. Haber

Editor: Scott Frampton

Editorial Concept: "The complete guide to new music"

Country Weekly

Published by:

Country Weekly Inc.

600 SE Coast Avenue

Lantana FL 33462

Date: April 12, 1994

Frequency: Weekly

Cover Price: $1.49

Subscription Price: $46.50

Discount Subscription Price: n/a

Total Number of Pages: 60

Total Number of Ad Pages: 8

Publisher: Country Weekly Inc.

Editor: Roger Capettini

Editorial Concept: "An inside look into the lives and lifestyles of…hundreds of… artists that country music fans love."

Fiddler Magazine

Published by:

Fiddler Magazine

P.O. Box 125

Los Altos CA 94022

Date: Spring 1994

Frequency: Quarterly

Cover Price: $4.00

Subscription Price: $14.00

Discount Subscription Price: n/a

Total Number of Pages: 52

Total Number of Ad Pages: 8

Publisher: Mary Larsen

Editor: Mary Larsen

Editorial Concept: "Written for fiddlers of all styles of fiddle music, as well as

---

accompanists and appreciative listeners."

Fizz

Published by:

Fizz

1509 Queen Anne Avenue N. #276

Seattle WA 98109

Date: 1994

Frequency: Bimonthly

Cover Price: $2.50

Subscription Price: $15.00

Discount Subscription Price: n/a

Total Number of Pages: 116

Total Number of Ad Pages: 22

Publisher: Fizz

Editor: Cathy Rundell

Editorial Concept: A very underground look at . . . rock bands and popular culture for Generation X.

Fond Affexxions

Published by:

Necronomicon Graphics

6312 East Santa Ana Canyon Road

Suite 112

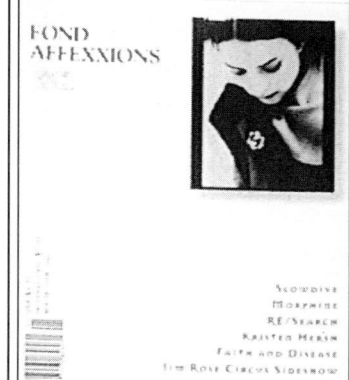

Anaheim Hills CA 92807

Date: Winter Thaw 1994

Frequency: Quarterly

Cover Price: $4.95

Subscription Price: $20.00

Discount Subscription Price: $18.00

Total Number of Pages: 72

Total Number of Ad Pages: 0

Publisher: Necronomicon Graphics

Editor: Jon Gonzaks

Editorial Concept: A highly literary and artistic look at the world of alternative music and culture.

Guitar Shop

Published by:

Cherry Lane Magazines Inc.

10 Midland Avenue

Port Chester NY 10573-1490

Date: Spring 1994

Frequency: Quarterly

Cover Price: $3.95

Subscription Price: n/a

Discount Subscription Price: n/a

Total Number of Pages: 92

Total Number of Ad Pages: 16

Publisher: Howard Cleff

Editor: Pete Brown

Editorial Concept: "The first American music magazine solely dedicated to the world of guitar equipment."

Hypno Magazine

Published by:

Hypno Industries

624 Broadway, 3rd Floor

San Diego CA 92101

Date: February 1994

(*first with new name*)

Frequency: Monthly

Cover Price: $3.50

Subscription Price: $28.00

Discount Subscription Price: n/a

Total Number of Pages: 84

Total Number of Ad Pages: 26

Publisher: Hypno Industries

Editor: Rex Edhlund

Editorial Concept: Super-hip underground culture mag for Generation X.

Industrial Nation

Published by:

Moon Mystique

614 West Belmont

Chicago IL 60657-4529

Date: Summer 1994

(*first national newsstand*)

Frequency: Semi-annually

Cover Price: $2.95

Subscription Price: $10.00/4 issues

Discount Subscription Price: n/a

Total Number of Pages: 100

Total Number of Ad Pages: 25

Publisher: Moon Mystique

Editor: Rev. Paul A. Vaalerio

Editorial Concept: Music and culture fanzine for the seriously underground post-modern youth.

Mobile Beat: The DJ Magazine

Published by:

LA Communications, Inc.

P.O. Box 309

533 West Commercial Street

East Rochester NY 14445

Date: February/March 1994 (*first issue distributed nationally.*)

Frequency: Bimonthly

Cover Price: $2.95

Subscription Price: $19.95

Discount Subscription Price: $34.95

Total Number of Pages: 84

Total Number of Ad Pages: 48

Publisher: LA Communications Inc.

Editor: Robert A. Lindquist

Editorial Concept: Information on music and technology for disc jockeys.

The New Review of Records

Published by:

The New Review of Records

438 West 37th Street

New York NY 10018

Date: Summer 1994 (*first national news-stand issue*)

Frequency: Bimonthly

Cover Price: $2.95

Subscription Price: $20.00

Discount Subscription Price: n/a

Total Number of Pages: 52

Total Number of Ad Pages: 18

Publisher: Brad Balfour

Editor: Steve Holtje

Editorial Concept: Music reviews feature Primal Scream!, Spin Doctors, and Phish.

On the One

Published by:

Modern World Messengers Inc.

23 Lapidge Street

San Francisco CA 94110

Date: Summer 1994

Frequency: Quarterly

Cover Price: $3.00

Subscription Price: $10.00

Discount Subscription Price: n/a

Total Number of Pages: 44

Total Number of Ad Pages: 3

Publisher: Paul Craven, Paul Martinez

Editor: Andrew Jervis

Editorial Concept: "An independent jazz magazine [reaching]. . . across the U.S.A. to cover the continuing return of jazz to the masses."

Plaid

Published by:

Martyr Press

P.O. Box 3006

Peabody MA 01960

Date: May/June 1994

Frequency: Bimonthly

Cover Price: $3.95

Subscription Price: n/a

Discount Subscription Price: n/a

Total Number of Pages: 52

Total Number of Ad Pages: 5

Publisher: John J. Costa

Editor: John J. Costa

Editorial Concept: "The perfect patchwork of modern music and comics."

Q-ME

Published by:

Proper Press Communications Group

8820 S. Sepulveda Boulevard

Suite 203

Los Angeles CA 90045

Date: 1994

Frequency: Bimonthly

Cover Price: $2.50

Subscription Price: $12.95

Discount Subscription Price: $18.95

Total Number of Pages: 48

Total Number of Ad Pages: 10

Publisher: Lorrin C. Bates

Editor: Alfred A.P. Warren

Editorial Concept: Quality music and entertainment articles and interviews.

Renegade One Report

Published by:

Renegade One

678 Main Street

Buffalo NY 14202

Date: 1994

Frequency: Monthly

Cover Price: $4.50

Subscription Price: $36.00

Discount Subscription Price: n/a

Total Number of Pages: 100

Total Number of Ad Pages: 21

Publisher: Renegade One

Editor: Scottpatrick J. Sellitto

Editorial Concept: A look at the merging of music and technology and the cyber-punk lifestyle.

The ROC

Published by:

Rock Out Censorship

P.O. Box 147

Jewett OH 43986

Date: April/May 1994

Frequency: Bimonthly

Cover Price: $2.00

Subscription Price: $15.00

Discount Subscription Price: n/a

Total Number of Pages: 24

Total Number of Ad Pages: 4

Publisher: Rock Out Censorship

Editor: John G. Woods

Editorial Concept: News and editorials on how to fight music censorship.

Unbroken Chain

Published by:

Unbroken Chain, Inc.

P.O. Box 49019

Austin TX 78765

Date: September/October/November 1994 (*first issue with new staff*)

Frequency: Quarterly

Cover Price: $2.50

Subscription Price: $12.00

Discount Subscription Price: n/a

Total Number of Pages: 36

Total Number of Ad Pages: 6

Publisher: Dave Serrins

Editor: Dave Serrins

Editorial Concept: "The best Dead 'zine around!"

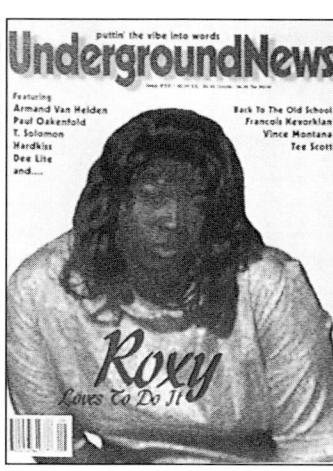

Underground News

Published by:

Pasquale, Inc.

915 Broadway #1005

New York NY 10010

Date: 1994 (*first national newsstand issue.*)

Frequency: Monthly

Cover Price: $2.95

Subscription Price: $36.00

Discount Subscription Price: n/a

Total Number of Pages: 48

Total Number of Ad Pages: 12

Publisher: Tim Richardson

Editor: Andy Shih

Editorial Concept: "Puttin' the vibe into words"

Urb Magazine

Published by:

Urb Magazine

1680 North Vine, Suite 1012

Los Angeles CA 90028

Date: Summer 1994 (*first newsstand issue*)

Frequency: Monthly

Cover Price: $2.50

Subscription Price: $17.50

Discount Subscription Price: n/a

Total Number of Pages: 72

Total Number of Ad Pages: 28

Publisher: Raymond Leon Roker

Editor: Raymond Leon Roker

Editorial Concept: "Hip hop and dance music culture"

Annual, Special or Frequency Unknown

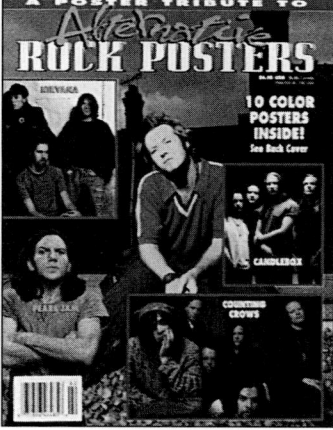

Alternative Rock Posters

Published by:

n/a

Date: 1994

Frequency: Special

Cover Price: $4.95

Subscription Price: n/a

Discount Subscription Price: n/a

Total Number of Pages: 44

Total Number of Ad Pages: 2

Publisher: n/a

Editor: n/a

Editorial Concept: Ten color posters of bands such as Pearl Jam, Nirvana, and Counting Crows.

Best of Guitar Player - The Rolling Stones

Published by:

The GPI Group

411 Borel Avenue #100
San Mateo CA 94402

Date: 1994

Frequency: Special

Cover Price: $4.95

Subscription Price: n/a

Discount Subscription Price: n/a

Total Number of Pages: 84

Total Number of Ad Pages: 12

Publisher: The GPI Group

Editor: n/a

Editorial Concept: "Exclusive new interviews inside the Voodoo Lounge . . . with Mick, Keith, Charlie and Woody."

Best of Guitar Player - Van Halen

Published by:

Miller Freeman Inc.

600 Harrison Street

San Francisco CA 94107

Date: 1994

Frequency: Special

Cover Price: $4.95

Subscription Price: n/a

Discount Subscription Price: n/a

Total Number of Pages: 106

Total Number of Ad Pages: 14

Publisher: Pat Cameron

Editor: Jim Aiken

Editorial Concept: A tribute to the legendary hard-rock guitarist Eddie Van Halen.

Conway Twitty - A Tribute to the Artist

Published by:

Creative Radio Network and Ergo Communications

P.O. Box 3373

Thousand Oaks CA 91359

Date: 1994

Frequency: Special

Cover Price: $5.95

Subscription Price: n/a

Discount Subscription Price: n/a

Total Number of Pages: 68

Total Number of Ad Pages: 0

Publisher: Creative Radio Network and Ergo Communications

Editor: Darwin Lamm

Editorial Concept: "A special edition of *Country Profiles*."

Country Christmas Spectacular

Published by:

Starlog Group, Inc.

475 Park Avenue South

New York NY 10016

Date: 1994

Frequency: Annually

Cover Price: $4.95

Subscription Price: n/a

Discount Subscription Price: n/a

Total Number of Pages: 68

Total Number of Ad Pages: 4

Publisher: Norman Jacobs

Editor: Benjamin Howard Smith

Editorial Concept: "Today's stars on their favorite Christmases."

Country Fever Presents Country's Hottest Hunks

Published by:

L.F.P. Inc.

9171 Wilshire Boulevard, Suite 300

Beverly Hills CA 90210

Date: 1994

Frequency: Special

Cover Price: $3.95

Subscription Price: n/a

Discount Subscription Price: n/a

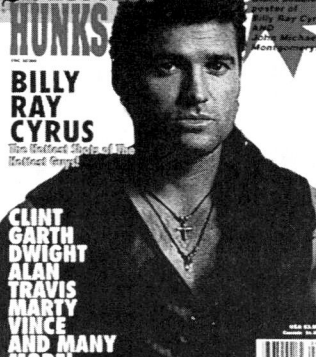

Total Number of Pages: 80

Total Number of Ad Pages: 1

Publisher: Larry Flynt

Editor: Linda F. Cauthen

Editorial Concept: "The hottest shots of the hottest guys."

Country Song Roundup Presents 100 Years of Country Music

Published by:

Country Song Roundup, Inc.

40 Violet Avenue

Poughkeepsie NY 12601

Date: 1994

Frequency: Special

Cover Price: $3.50

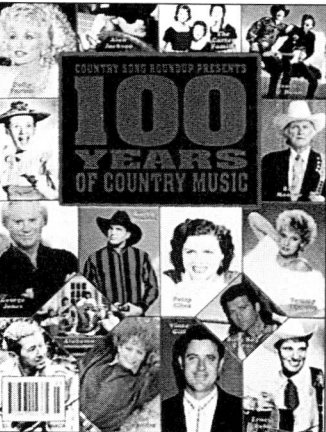

Subscription Price: n/a

Discount Subscription Price: n/a

Total Number of Pages: 68

Total Number of Ad Pages: 3

Publisher: Country Song Roundup, Inc.

Editor: Celeste R. Gomes

Editorial Concept: "From yesterday's legends to today's superstars."

A Definitive Tribute to Frank Zappa

Published by:

Miller Freeman Inc.

600 Harrison Street

San Francisco CA 94107

Date: 1994

Frequency: Special

Cover Price: $4.95

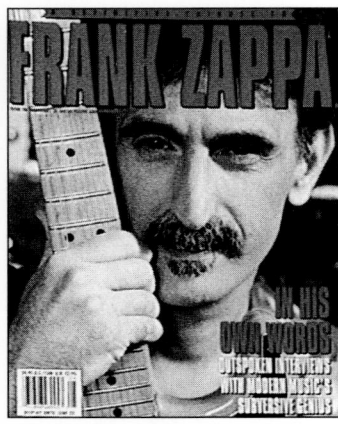

Subscription Price: n/a

Discount Subscription Price: n/a

Total Number of Pages: 92

Total Number of Ad Pages: 7

Publisher: Pat Cameron

Editor: Jim Aikin and Greg Rule

Editorial Concept: A collection of interviews with the late musical genius.

Elvis 60th Birthday Celebration

Published by:

Sterling/Mcfadden Partnership

233 Park Avenue South

New York NY 10003

Date: 1994

Frequency: Special

Cover Price: $3.95

Subscription Price: n/a

Discount Subscription Price: n/a

Total Number of Pages: 108

Total Number of Ad Pages: 12

Publisher: Sterling/Mcfadden Partnership

Editor: Mike Greenblatt

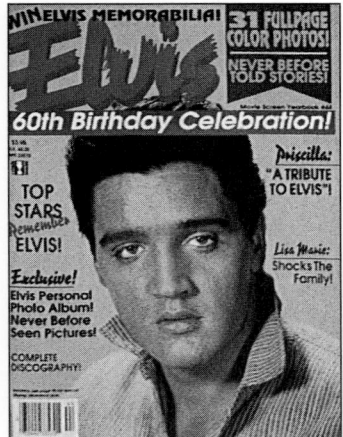

Editorial Concept: A fan's look at the king's music and movies.

Guitar Presents Metal Monsters

Published by:

Cherry Lane Magazines Inc.

10 Midland Avenue

Port Chester NY 10573

Date: 1994

Frequency: Special

Cover Price: $4.95

Subscription Price: n/a

Discount Subscription Price: n/a

Total Number of Pages: 112

Total Number of Ad Pages: 12

Publisher: Howard Cleff

Editor: John Stix

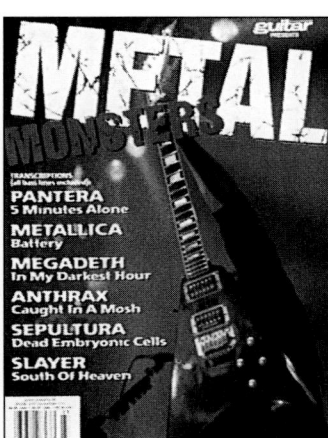

Editorial Concept: Stories about top metal bands and transcriptions of their songs.

Guitar World Presents Alternative Guitar

Published by:

Harris Publications Inc.

1115 Broadway

New York NY 10010

Date: 1994

Frequency: Special

Cover Price: $4.95

Subscription Price: n/a

Discount Subscription Price: n/a

Total Number of Pages: 110

Total Number of Ad Pages: 8

Publisher: Stanley R. Harris

Editor: Daniel B. Levine

Editorial Concept: Profiles of famous guitar players of the alternative scene.

Hard Rock International Special - Metallica, the 10 Commandments

Published by:

E/K/S Group Inc.

740 Front Street

Santa Cruz CA 95060

Date: 1994

Frequency: Special

Cover Price: $6.95

Subscription Price: n/a

Discount Subscription Price: n/a

Total Number of Pages: 72

Total Number of Ad Pages: 0

Publisher: Roland Dreyfus

Editor: Evelyn Putti

Editorial Concept: A poster-heavy love letter to the monster hard-rock band.

How to Play Rock Guitar

Published by:

Miller Freeman Inc.

600 Harrison Street

San Francisco CA 94107

Date: 1994

Frequency: Special

Cover Price: $4.95

Subscription Price: n/a

Discount Subscription Price: n/a

Total Number of Pages: 92

Total Number of Ad Pages: 18

Publisher: Pat Cameron

Editor: Ernie Rideout

Editorial Concept: "Lethal licks and lessons from the *Guitar Player* chop shop."

Ill Literature

Published by:

Ill Literature

1626 N. Poinsettia Place #208

Los Angeles CA 90048

Date: n/a

Frequency: n/a

Cover Price: $3.95

Subscription Price: n/a

Discount Subscription Price: n/a

Total Number of Pages: 108

Total Number of Ad Pages: 17

Publisher: Marco Barbieri

Editor: Marco Barbieri

Editorial Concept: Hard-core metal music - *formerly "No Glam Fags."*

Metal Muscle - Metals New Breed

Published by:

Faces Magazine Inc.

63 Grand Avenue, Suite #220

River Edge NJ 07661

Date: January 1994

Frequency: Special

Cover Price: $3.50

Subscription Price: n/a

Discount Subscription Price: n/a

Total Number of Pages: 68

Total Number of Ad Pages: 5

Publisher: Scott Mitchell Figman

Editor: Andy Secher

Editorial Concept: Stories and posters of hard rock and grunge stars.

Michael Jackson: A Tribute to the Performer

Published by:

E/K/S Group Inc.

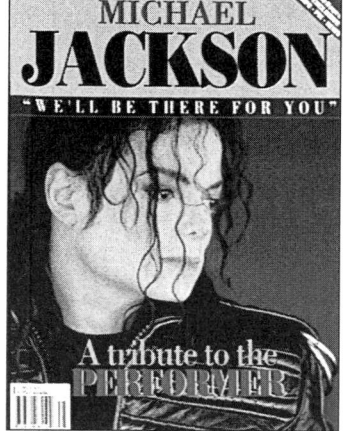

740 Front Street, Suite 380A

Santa Cruz CA 95060

Date: September 1994

Frequency: Special

Cover Price: $5.95

Subscription Price: n/a

Discount Subscription Price: n/a

Total Number of Pages: 84

Total Number of Ad Pages: 0

Publisher: E/K/S Group Inc.

Editor: Roy Zinsenheim

Editorial Concept: "A tribute to the world's most successful and talented performer."

Modern Rock

Published by:

Ashley Communications, Inc.

P.O. Box 91876

Los Angeles CA 90009

Date: August 1994

Frequency: Special

Cover Price: $4.95

Subscription Price: n/a

Discount Subscription Price: n/a

Total Number of Pages: 48

Total Number of Ad Pages: 2

Publisher: Ashley Communications, Inc.

Editor: n/a

Editorial Concept: "Special photo tribute. . . 28 color portraits inside."

Monsters of Hard Rock

Published by:

E/K/S Group Inc.

740 Front Street, Suite 380A

Santa Cruz CA 95060

Date: September 1994

Frequency: Special

Cover Price: $4.95

Subscription Price: n/a

Discount Subscription Price: n/a

Total Number of Pages: 76

Total Number of Ad Pages: 1

Publisher: E/K/S Group Inc.

Editor: Roy Zinsenheim

Editorial Concept: "Supplement to Hard! Monsters N#1."

Nirvana Tribute

Published by:

n/a

Date: 1994

Frequency: Special

Cover Price: $4.95

Subscription Price: n/a

Discount Subscription Price: n/a

Total Number of Pages: 48

Total Number of Ad Pages: 0

Publisher: n/a

Editor: n/a

Editorial Concept: A quicky tribute in words and pinup photos to the dead grunge rocker.

Spice Presents The Love Doctors

Published by:

Starlog Telecommunications Inc.

475 Park Avenue South

New York NY 10016

Date: 1994

Frequency: Special

Cover Price: $3.95

Subscription Price: n/a

Discount Subscription Price: n/a

Total Number of Pages: 60

Total Number of Ad Pages: 5

Publisher: Robert Tate

Editor: Dianne Herly

Editorial Concept: Posters and bios about the sexiest male soul singers, from Boys II Men to James Ingrem.

A Tribute to Nirvana's Kurt Cobain

Published by:

n/a

Date: 1994

Frequency: Special

Cover Price: $4.95

Subscription Price: n/a

Discount Subscription Price: n/a

Total Number of Pages: 36

Total Number of Ad Pages: 0

Publisher: n/a

Editor: n/a

Editorial Concept: Eight fold-out color posters of the dead rock star at various stages of his career.

Whole Guitar Book

Published by:

BPI Communications, Inc.

1515 Broadway

New York NY 10036

Date: 1994

Frequency: Special

Cover Price: $3.95

Subscription Price: n/a

Discount Subscription Price: n/a

Total Number of Pages: 84

Total Number of Ad Pages: 24

Publisher: Gary Krasner

Editor: Ted Greenwald

Editorial Concept: *Musician* magazine's special edition features interviews with Eric Clapton, Dave Navarro and other guitarists.

Woodstock '94

Published by:

Welsh Publishing Group Inc.

300 Madison Avenue

New York NY 10017

Date: 1994

Frequency: Special

Cover Price: $15.00

Subscription Price: n/a

Discount Subscription Price: n/a

Total Number of Pages: 68

Total Number of Ad Pages: 17

Publisher: Donald E. Welsh

Editor: Katy Dobbs

Editorial Concept: The official program book to the massive music festival in New York.

Word Up! Special Tribute to Jodeci

Published by:

Word Up! Publications, Inc.

63 Grand Avenue, Suite 230

River Edge NJ 07661

Date: April 1994

Frequency: Special

Cover Price: $2.95

Subscription Price: n/a

Discount Subscription Price: n/a

Total Number of Pages: 80

Total Number of Ad Pages: 14

Publisher: Scott Mitchell Figman

Editor: Kate Ferguson

Editorial Concept: A fan's look at the popular R & B group, plus other top rap and hip hop acts.

The Year in Black Music

Published by:

Word Up! Publications, Inc.

63 Grand Avenue, Suite 230

River Edge NJ 07661

Date: January 1994

Frequency: Special

Cover Price: $3.50

Subscription Price: n/a

Discount Subscription Price: n/a

Total Number of Pages: 80

Total Number of Ad Pages: 14

Publisher: Scott Mitchell Figman

Editor: Kate Ferguson

Editorial Concept: Features color pin-ups and top ten lists for black music in 1993.

Fate

Published by:

Llewellyn Worldwide Ltd.

84 S. Wabasha

St. Paul MN 55107

Date: June 1994 *(first in new format)*

Frequency: Monthly

Cover Price: $2.95

Subscription Price: $29.95

Discount Subscription Price: $21.50

Total Number of Pages: 84

Total Number of Ad Pages: 27

Publisher: Carl Llewellyn Weschcke

Editor: Phyliss Glade

Editorial Concept: "True reports of the strange and unknown."

Into the Darkness

Published by:

Necro Publications

P.O. Box 677205

Orlando FL 32867-7205

Date: 1994

Frequency: Quarterly

Cover Price: $5.00

Subscription Price: $18.00

Discount Subscription Price: n/a

Total Number of Pages: 60

Total Number of Ad Pages: 4

Publisher: Necro Publications

Editor: David G. Barnett

Editorial Concept: "The magazine of extreme horror."

Justice USA

Published by:

Spectrum Magazines Inc.

Spectrum Building

4901 NW 17th Way, Suite 600

Fort Lauderdale FL 33309

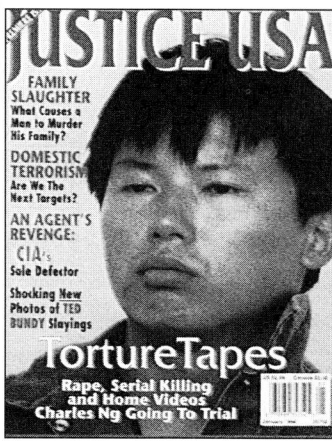

Date: January 1994

Frequency: Bimonthly

Cover Price: $2.95

Subscription Price: $8.95

Discount Subscription Price: n/a

Total Number of Pages: 84

Total Number of Ad Pages: 1

Publisher: David Harvard

Editor: Brenda K. Hutson

Editorial Concept: "Up-close accounts of the crimes, criminals, and victims that affect us all."

Llewellyn's New Worlds of Mind and Spirit

Published by:

Llewellyn Publications

P.O. Box 64383

St. Paul MN 55164-0383

Date: February/March 1994

(first newsstand issue)

Frequency: Bimonthly

Cover Price: $2.95

Subscription Price: $10.00

Discount Subscription Price: n/a

Total Number of Pages: 132

Total Number of Ad Pages: 69

Publisher: Carl Llewellyn Weschcke

Editor: Jana Branch

Editorial Concept: "New age and magickal" community resource.

Mystery Forum Magazine

Published by:

Bob Myers Productions

16503 Third St. North

Independence MO 64056

Date: 1994

Frequency: Bimonthly

(first newsstand issue)

Cover Price: $4.50

Subscription Price: $18.00

Discount Subscription Price: n/a

Total Number of Pages: 52

Total Number of Ad Pages: 14

Publisher: Bob Myers Productions

Editor: Bob Myers

Editorial Concept: "Short mystery fiction, great interviews, and hot tips on getting rid of cold bodies."

Predictions

Published by:

Spectrum Magazines Inc.

Spectrum Building

4901 NW 17th Way, Suite 660

Fort Lauderdale FL 33309

Date: June/July 1994

Frequency: Bimonthly

Cover Price: $3.95

Subscription Price: $27.95

Discount Subscription Price: n/a

Total Number of Pages: 84

Total Number of Ad Pages: 7

Publisher: David Harvard

Editor: Marc Serota

Editorial Concept: "An incredible journey of the imagination into the world of the unknown, dreams, ideas, and the future."

Realms of Fantasy

Published by:

Sovereign Media Company Inc.

457 Carlisle Drive

Herndon VA 22070

Date: October 1994

Frequency: Bimonthly

Cover Price: $3.50

Subscription Price: $14.95

Discount Subscription Price: n/a

Total Number of Pages: 92

Total Number of Ad Pages: 27

Publisher: Mark Hintz

Editor: Shawna McCarthy

Editorial Concept: Short fiction about dragons, fairies, magic kingdoms, etc.

Rescue

Published by:

Jems Communications

1947 Camiro Vida Roble, Suite 200

Carlsbad CA 92008

Date: July/August 1994 *(first newsstand issue)*

Frequency: Bimonthly

Cover Price: $2.95

Subscription Price: $14.95

Discount Subscription Price: $12.97

Total Number of Pages: 84

Total Number of Ad Pages: 36

Publisher: James Page

Editor: Jeffrey Berend

Editorial Concept: "For every member of the rescue team."

UFO's Alien Encounters

Published by:

GCR Publishing Group Inc.

1700 Broadway

New York NY 10019

Date: 1994

Frequency: Quarterly

Cover Price: $4.95

Subscription Price: n/a

Discount Subscription Price: n/a

Total Number of Pages: 68

Total Number of Ad Pages: 8

Publisher: Charles Goodman

Editor: Timothy Green Beckley

Editorial Concept: Stories of UFO sightings and other close encounters of the alien kind.

Wanted by the Law

Published by:

Wanted by the Law Magazine

10400 #396 Overland Road

Boise ID 83709

Date: October 1994

Frequency: Monthly

Cover Price: $1.95

Subscription Price: $15.60

Discount Subscription Price: n/a

Total Number of Pages: 44

Total Number of Ad Pages: 2

Publisher: Wanted by the Law Magazine

Editor: n/a

Editorial Concept: "America's monthly crime report."

Annual, Special or Frequency Unknown

1994 Science Fiction Annual

Published by:

Warrior Publications

1920 Highland Ave., Suite 222

Lombard IL 60148

Date: June 1994

Frequency: Special

Cover Price: $3.95

Subscription Price: n/a

Discount Subscription Price: n/a

Total Number of Pages: 100

Total Number of Ad Pages: 9

Publisher: Steve Harris

Editor: Mike Stokes

Editorial Concept: TV, movies, comics, toys, games.

Bizarre Murders

Published by:

RGH Publishing Group

460 W. 34th St.

New York NY 10001

Date: 1994

Frequency: Special

Cover Price: $2.50

Subscription Price: n/a

Discount Subscription Price: n/a

Total Number of Pages: 78

Total Number of Ad Pages: 20

Publisher: RGH Publishing Group

Editor: Rose Mandelsberg

Editorial Concept: "Gruesome accounts of sensationalized murder, usually of a sexual nature committed against women."

Official Detective Yearbook - Unsolved Murders

Published by:

RGH Publishing Corporation

460 W. 34th St.

New York NY 10001

Date: 1994

Frequency: Special

Cover Price: $2.50

Subscription Price: n/a

Discount Subscription Price: n/a

Total Number of Pages: 78

Total Number of Ad Pages: 25

Publisher: RGH Publishing Corporation

Editor: Christofer Pierson

Editorial Concept: Grisly tales of unsolved murder cases.

Pirates Then & Now

Published by:

Challenge Publications Inc.

7950 Deering Ave.

Canoga Park CA 91304

Date: 1994

Frequency: Special

Cover Price: $5.95

Subscription Price: n/a

Discount Subscription Price: n/a

Total Number of Pages: 96

Total Number of Ad Pages: 6

Publisher: Edwin A. Schnepf

Editor: Edwin A. Schnepf

Editorial Concept: "A gripping review of 300 years of piracy."

Scientific American Ancient Cities

Published by:

Scientific American Inc.

415 Madison Ave.

New York NY 10017-1111

Date: 1994

Frequency: Special

Cover Price: $3.95

Subscription Price: n/a

Discount Subscription Price: n/a

Total Number of Pages: 164

Total Number of Ad Pages: 14

Publisher: John J. Moeling, Jr.

Editor: Jonathan Piel

Editorial Concept: A study of the past as a tool for present and future urban life.

Zoom

Published by:

CTM Associates

21 E. 40th St.

New York NY 10016

Date: 1994

Frequency: n/a

Cover Price: $9.95

Subscription Price: $49.90

Discount Subscription Price: n/a

Total Number of Pages: 100

Total Number of Ad Pages: 0

Publisher: CTM Associates

Editor: Rosanna Checchi

Editorial Concept: International contemporary photography.

Art & Politics

Published by:

Art & Politics

P.O. Box 195

Gardiner NY 12525

Date: August 1994

Frequency: Bimonthly

Cover Price: $3.00

Subscription Price: $18.00

Discount Subscription Price: n/a

Total Number of Pages: 20

Total Number of Ad Pages: 1

Publisher: Diana Campanella

Editor: James Kwiecinski

Editorial Concept: A look at how politics can affect the life of the artist, from street vending laws to freedom of expression.

idq - Issues & Decisions Quarterly

Published by:

Issues & Decisions Quarterly Inc.

90 Park Ave., 16th Floor

New York NY 10016

Date: Winter 1993 - 94

Frequency: Quarterly

Cover Price: $5.00

Subscription Price: $17.00/4 issues

Discount Subscription Price:

$19.95/5 issues

Total Number of Pages: 24

Total Number of Ad Pages: 0

Publisher: Ron Kfoury

Editor: Ron Kfoury

Editorial Concept: "To investigate how great decisions are made, and how great opportunities are squandered."

National Times

Published by:

Krebs Media Corporation

318 E. 84th St.

New York NY 10028

Date: January 1994

Frequency: Bimonthly

Cover Price: $3.95

Subscription Price: $18.00

Discount Subscription Price: n/a

Total Number of Pages: 100

Total Number of Ad Pages: 8

Publisher: David Krebs

Editor: David Krebs

Editorial Concept: "A review of essential news and comment."

North-South, Magazine of the Americas

Published by:

North-South Center

University of Miami

Coral Gables FL 33146-3027

Date: July/August 1994

(first newsstand issue)

Frequency: Bimonthly

Cover Price: $5.95

Subscription Price: $30.00

Discount Subscription Price: n/a

Total Number of Pages: 72

Total Number of Ad Pages: 6

Publisher: North-South Center

Editor: Jaime Suchlicki

Editorial Concept: "Analysis and information [about] countries of our hemisphere."

The People's Warrior

Published by:

The People's Warrior

P.O. Box 488

Rockwall TX 75087

Date: October 1994

Frequency: Monthly

Cover Price: $3.75

Subscription Price: $45.00

Discount Subscription Price: $35.00

Total Number of Pages: 40

Total Number of Ad Pages: 0

Publisher: David Parker

Editor: David Parker

Editorial Concept: "To investigate and report corruption in the political and legal communties."

State Legislatures

Published by:

National Conference of State Legislatures

1560 Broadway, Suite 700

Denver CO 80202

Date: July 1994 *(first newsstand issue)*

Frequency: Monthly

Cover Price: $3.95

Subscription Price: $49.00

Discount Subscription Price: n/a

Total Number of Pages: 60

Total Number of Ad Pages: 18

Publisher: National Conference of State Legislatures

Editor: Karen Hansen

Editorial Concept: Government and policy in America.

Annual, Special or Frequency Unknown

Whitewater Confidential

Published by:

Emery Dalton Communications

P.O. Box 1710

Valley Center, CA 92082

Date: 1994

Frequency: Special

Cover Price: $3.95

Subscription Price: n/a

Discount Subscription Price: n/a

Total Number of Pages: 48

Total Number of Ad Pages: 2

Publisher: Emery Dalton Communications

Editor: Mark Fleming

Editorial Concept: "An insider's report on the scandal that's threatening the Clinton presidency."

5 Minute Crossword Puzzles

Published by:

Official Publication Inc.

7002 W. Butler Pike #100

Ambler PA 19002

Date: September 1994

Frequency: Bimonthly

Cover Price: $1.50

Subscription Price: $7.60

Discount Subscription Price: n/a

Total Number of Pages: 100

Total Number of Ad Pages: 4

Publisher: Official Publications Inc.

Editor: Janis Weiner

Editorial Concept: "Quick-solving crosswords for active people."

Circle-A-Word Collection

Published by:

Ebb Publishing Company

7002 W. Butler Pike

Ambler PA 19002

Date: 1994

Frequency: Quarterly

Cover Price: $2.95

Subscription Price: $10.00

Discount Subscription Price: n/a

Total Number of Pages: 196

Total Number of Ad Pages: 4

Publisher: Ebb Publishing Company

Editor: n/a

Editorial Concept: "Contains 160 puzzles for hours and hours and hours of 100% solving fun."

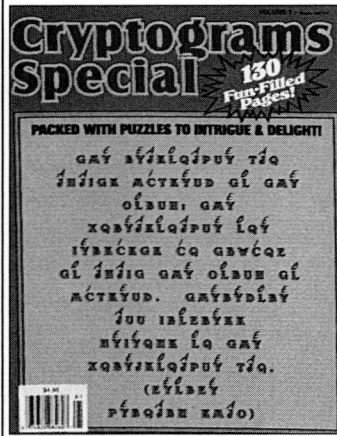

Cryptograms Special

Published by:

Ebb Publications Inc.

7002 W. Butler Pike

Amber PA 19002

Date: 1994

Frequency: Quarterly

Cover Price: $4.95

Subscription Price: $17.50

Discount Subscription Price: n/a

Total Number of Pages: 132

Total Number of Ad Pages: 6

Publisher: Ebb Publications Inc.

Editor: Judy Weightman

Editorial Concept: " Hours and hours of code-breaking pleasure."

Dell 100 Easy Crosswords

Published by:

Bantam Doubleday Dell Magazines

1540 Broadway

New York NY 10036

Date: October 1994

Frequency: Monthly

Cover Price: $1.29

Subscription Price: n/a

Discount Subscription Price: n/a

Total Number of Pages: 68

Total Number of Ad Pages: 9

Publisher: Christopher Haas-Heye

Editor: J.J. Schmalzbach

Editorial Concept: "Our puzzles are easy on the mind, easy on the nerves, easygoing, fun and easy."

Dell Tanglewords

Published by:

Bantam Doubleday Dell Magazines

1540 Broadway

New York NY 10036

Date: 1994

Frequency: Semi-annually

Cover Price: $0.99

Subscription Price: n/a

Discount Subscription Price: n/a

Total Number of Pages: 68

Total Number of Ad Pages: 8

Publisher: Christoph Haas-Heye

Editor: Nancy Schuster

Editorial Concept: "Your favorite kind of word search."

Favorite Fill-In Puzzles

Published by:

Penny Press Inc.

6 Prowitt St.

Norwalk CT 06855

Date: August 1994

Frequency: Bimonthly

Cover Price: $0.99

Subscription Price: $5.88

Discount Subscription Price: n/a

Total Number of Pages: 84

Total Number of Ad Pages: 3

Publisher: Penny Press Inc.

Editor: Dom Loiacano

Editorial Concept: 64 fill-in puzzles.

Games World of Puzzles

Published by:

B. & P. Publishing Company Inc.

575 Boylston St.

Boston MA 02116

Date: May 1994

Frequency: Bimonthly

Cover Price: $2.95

Subscription Price: $17.95

Discount Subscription Price: n/a

Total Number of Pages: 76

Total Number of Ad Pages: 4

Publisher: Alan Segal

Editor: Mike Shenk

Editorial Concept: "Crosswords, word searches, picture puzzles, cryptograms, trivia, logic, double crostics, cryptics, and other pencil puzzles."

The Joy of Crosswords

Published by:

Penny Press Inc.

6 Prowitt St.

Norwalk CT 06855

Date: August 1994

Frequency: Bimonthly

Cover Price: $1.25

Subscription Price: $7.37

Discount Subscription Price: n/a

Total Number of Pages: 84

Total Number of Ad Pages: 5

Publisher: Penny Press Inc.

Editor: Fran Danon

Editorial Concept: Crosswords about movies and television, the Bible, and many other topics.

Official's Variety Puzzles

Published by:

Official Publications Inc.

7002 W. Butler Pike

Ambler PA 19002

Date: Holiday 1994

Frequency: Quarterly

Cover Price: $3.95

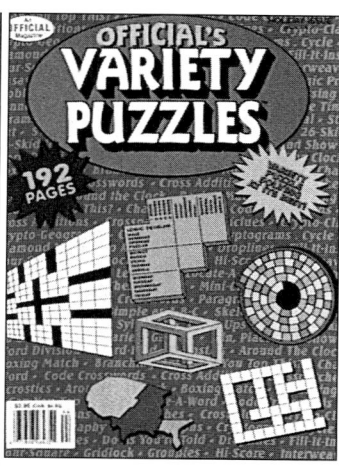

Subscription Price: $14.00

Discount Subscription Price: n/a

Total Number of Pages: 196

Total Number of Ad Pages: 5

Publisher: Official Publications Inc.

Editor: Judy Weightman

Editorial Concept: "192 pages [of] variety puzzle solving at its best."

Penny's Famous Crossword Puzzles Plus

Published by:

Penny Press Inc.

6 Prowitt St.

Norwalk CT 06855-1220

Date: September 1994

Frequency: Bimonthly

Cover Price: $1.25

Subscription Price: $7.37

Discount Subscription Price: n/a

Total Number of Pages: 84

Total Number of Ad Pages: 5

Publisher: Penny Press Inc.

Editor: Fran Danon

Editorial Concept: "65 great puzzles!"

Solver's Choice Crosswords

Published by:

Bantam Doubleday Dell Magazines

1540 Broadway

New York NY 10036

Date: 1994

Frequency: Quarterly

Cover Price: $1.99

Subscription Price: n/a

Discount Subscription Price: n/a

Total Number of Pages: 68

Total Number of Ad Pages: 9

Publisher: Christoph Haas-Heye

Editor: Nancy Schuster

Editorial Concept: "Crosswords only, and plenty of them."

Star Crosswords

Published by:

Hachette Filipacchi Magazines Inc.

1633 Broadway

New York NY 10019

Date: Spring 1994

Frequency: Quarterly

Cover Price: $1.49

Subscription Price: n/a

Discount Subscription Price: n/a

Total Number of Pages: 68

Total Number of Ad Pages: 2

Publisher: Patrice Listfiel

Editor: Linda Montera Saltzman

Editorial Concept: Crossword puzzles that focus on celebrities.

Super Fill-Ins Digest

Published by:

Harle Publications Inc.

7002 W. Butler Pike #100

Ambler PA 19002

Date: September 1994 (*formerly entitled All-Star Fill-Ins*)

Frequency: 17/year

Cover Price: $0.99

Subscription Price: $16.25

Discount Subscription Price: $11.75

Total Number of Pages: 100

Total Number of Ad Pages: 7

Publisher: Harle Publications Inc.

Editor: Janis Weiner

Editorial Concept: Easy puzzles.

World's Best Crosswords

Published by:

Penny Press Inc.

6 Prowitt St.

Norwalk CT 06855-1220

Date: 1994

Frequency: Bimonthly

Cover Price: $1.25

Subscription Price: $7.37

Discount Subscription Price: n/a

Total Number of Pages: 84

Total Number of Ad Pages: 3

Publisher: Penny Press Inc.

Editor: Fran Danon

Editorial Concept: "All crosswords easy to solve."

Angel Times

Published by:

Angelic Realms Unlimited Inc.

4360 Chamblee-Dunwoody Rd.

Suite 400

Atlanta GA 30341

Date: November/December 1994

Frequency: Bimonthly

Cover Price: $5.00

Subscription Price: $24.00

Discount Subscription Price: n/a

Total Number of Pages: 68

Total Number of Ad Pages: 11

Publisher: Linda Vephula

Editor: n/a

Editorial Concept: Articles and art about angels and angelic encounters.

Aspire

Published by:

Royal Magazine Group

404 BNA Dr., Suite 600,

Bld. 200

Nashville TN 37217

Date: August/September 1994 *(formerly Today's Better Life)*

Frequency: Bimonthly

Cover Price: $3.50

Subscription Price: $21.00

Discount Subscription Price: $17.95

Total Number of Pages: 84

Total Number of Ad Pages: 15

Publisher: Timothy L. Gilmour

Editor: Mary Hopkins

Editorial Concept: "To aspire to a healthier body, a stronger self-image, and a closer relationship with God."

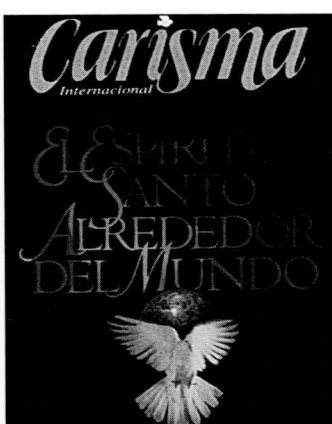

Carisma Internacional

Published by:

Strang Communications

600 Rinehart Rd.

Lake Mary FL 32746

Date: 1994

Frequency: Monthly

Cover Price: $2.95

Subscription Price: n/a

Discount Subscription Price: $16.97

Total Number of Pages: 52

Total Number of Ad Pages: 15

Publisher: Steve Strang

Editor: Steve Strang

Editorial Concept: A religious magazine for the Hispanic community.

Clarity

Published by:

The Navigators/NavPress

7899 Lexington

Colorado Springs CO 80920

Date: March/April 1994

Frequency: Bimonthlly

Cover Price: $3.50

Subscription Price: $18.97

Discount Subscription Price: n/a

Total Number of Pages: 84

Total Number of Ad Pages: 15

Publisher: The Navigators/NavPress

Editor: Judith Couchman

Editorial Concept: "A personal, healthy mind and body magazine for Christian women."

Creation Spirituality

Published by:

Friends of Creation Spirituality Inc.

4185 Park Blvd.

Oakland CA 94602

Date: Spring 1994

Frequency: Quarterly

Cover Price: $6.00

Subscription Price: $24.00

Discount Subscription Price: n/a

Total Number of Pages: 68

Total Number of Ad Pages: 13

Publisher: Friends of Creation Spirituality Inc.

Editor: Dan Turner

Editorial Concept: "The voice of the creation spirituality movement."

One Light Out of Jerusalem

Published by:

One Light Publications

3944 Murphy Canyon Rd.

Suite C-207

San Diego CA 92123-9554

Date: Autumn 1994

Frequency: Quarterly

Cover Price: $2.95

Subscription Price: $10.00

Discount Subscription Price: n/a

Total Number of Pages: 32

Total Number of Ad Pages: 7

Publisher: Daphna Kau-Venaki

Editor: Daphna Kau-Venaki

Editorial Concept: "Promoting universal spiritual growth."

Annual, Special or Frequency Unknown

Inspiration!

Published by:

House of White Birches

306 East Parr Rd.

Berne IN 46711

Date: 1994

Frequency: Special

Cover Price: $1.95

Subscription Price: n/a

Discount Subscription Price: n/a

Total Number of Pages: 48

Total Number of Ad Pages: 1

Publisher: Carl H. and Arthur K. Muselman

Editor: Vivian Rothe

Editorial Concept: "Stories of faith, hope, love, and courage."

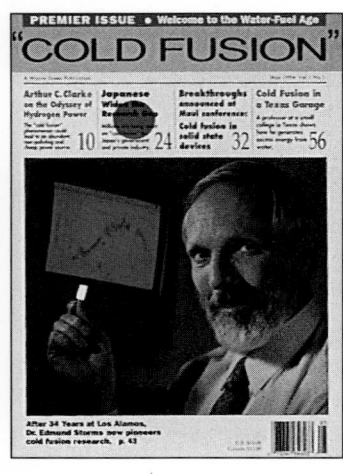

Cold Fusion

Published by:

Wayne Green Inc.

70 Route 202 N.

Peterborough NH 03458

Date: May 1994

Frequency: Monthly

Cover Price: $10.00

Subscription Price: $98.00

Discount Subscription Price: n/a

Total Number of Pages: 100

Total Number of Ad Pages: 12

Publisher: Wayne Green

Editor: Eugene F. Mallove, Sc.D.

Editorial Concept: "Detailed reports about the ongoing science, technology, and business of cold fusion."

Enterprise Communications

Published by:

Advanstar Communications

201 E. Sandpointe Ave.

Suite 600

Date: October 1994 *(formerly Voice Processing Magazine)*

Frequency: Monthly

Cover Price: $4.95

Subscription Price: $39.00

Discount Subscription Price: n/a

Total Number of Pages: 90

Total Number of Ad Pages: 32

Publisher: Kurt Induik

Editor: Laura Dalton

Editorial Concept: A technical look at computer networking and information technology.

Extraordinary Science

Published by:

International Tesla Society Inc.

P.O. Box 5636

Colorado Springs CO 80931

Date: April/May/June 1994 *(first newsstand issue)*

Frequency: Quarterly

Cover Price: $8.95

Subscription Price: n/a

Discount Subscription Price: n/a

Total Number of Pages: 52

Total Number of Ad Pages: 6

Publisher: International Tesla Society Inc.

Editor: Steven Elswick

Editorial Concept: "The official magazine of the International Tesla Society."

Gadgetworld

Published by:

Gadget World Inc.

Spectrum Building

4901 N.W. 17th Way, Suite 600

Fort Lauderdale FL 33309

Date: January 1994

Frequency: Bimonthly

Cover Price: $2.95

Subscription Price: $8.85

Discount Subscription Price: n/a

Total Number of Pages: 84

Total Number of Ad Pages: 1

Publisher: David Harvard

Editor: Bill Lovell

Editorial Concept: Product reviews on virtual reality equipment, wrist phones, and more.

Geo Info Systems

Published by:

Advanstar Communications

859 Willamette St.

Eugene OR 97401

Date: September 1994

(first newsstand issue)

Frequency: Monthly

Cover Price: $4.00

Subscription Price: $12.00

Discount Subscription Price: n/a

Total Number of Pages: 60

Total Number of Ad Pages: 10

Publisher: Advanstar Communications

Editor: Guy Maynard

Editorial Concept: Applications of GIS.

Managing Technology Today

Published by:

The Quality Observer Corporation

P.O. Box 1111

Fairfax VA 22030

Date: Winter 1994 *(first newsstand issue)*

Frequency: Quarterly

Cover Price: $4.95

Subscription Price: $69.00

Discount Subscription Price: n/a

Total Number of Pages: 24

Total Number of Ad Pages: 7

Publisher: The Quality Observer Corporation

Editor: Kay Moore

Editorial Concept: Technical advice on how companies can make use of the technology advances of the day.

Mathematica in Education

Published by:

TELOS/Springer Verlag

3600 Prunaridge Ave., Suite 200

Santa Clara CA 95051

Date: Spring 1994 *(first newsstand issue)*

Frequency: Quarterly

Cover Price: $8.95

Subscription Price: $30.00

Discount Subscription Price: n/a

Total Number of Pages: 56

Total Number of Ad Pages: 4

Publisher: Alan Wylde

Editor: Paul R. Wellin

Editorial Concept: Articles on advanced math principles of the academic community.

PCVR

Published by:

PCVR Magazine

P.O. Box 475

Stoughton WI 53589

Date: January/February 1994

Frequency: Bimonthly

Cover Price: $4.50

Subscription Price: $26.00

Discount Subscription Price: n/a

Total Number of Pages: 68

Total Number of Ad Pages: 3

Publisher: Joseph D. Gradecki

Editor: Joseph D. Gradecki

Editorial Concept: "The magazine dedicated to low-end virtual reality."

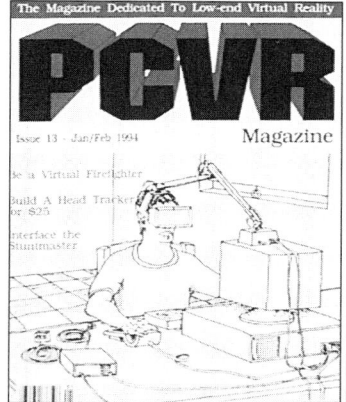

Solar Today

Published by:

American Solar Energy Society Inc.

2400 Central, Unit G-1

Boulder CO 80301

Date: January/February 1994 *(first news-stand issue)*

Frequency: Bimonthly

Cover Price: $3.75

Subscription Price: $29.00

Discount Subscription Price: n/a

Total Number of Pages: 40

Total Number of Ad Pages: 13

Publisher: American Solar Energy Society Inc.

Editor: Maureen McIntyre

Editorial Concept: "The application of energy efficient and solar energy technologies in buildings."

Virtual Reality Special Report

Published by:

Miller Freeman Inc.

600 Harrison St.

San Francisco CA 94107

Date: 1994

Frequency: Quarterly

Cover Price: $9.95

Subscription Price: $32.00

Discount Subscription Price: n/a

Total Number of Pages: 84

Total Number of Ad Pages: 20

Publisher: Regina Starr Ridley

Editor: Kay Keppler

Editorial Concept: Articles about advances and applications in virtual reality technology.

Bedroom Games

Published by:

Vanity Publishing Company

475 Park Ave. South, Suite 2201

New York NY 10016

Date: April 1994

Frequency: Bimonthly

Cover Price: $3.50

Subscription Price: n/a

Discount Subscription Price: n/a

Total Number of Pages: 292

Total Number of Ad Pages: 9

Publisher: Vanity Publishing Company

Editor: Sally Wright

Editorial Concept: "First-hand stories of hot, raunchy sex, illustrated with explicit photos."

Bedroom Kicks

Published by:

Value Publishing Company

P.O. Box 20147

Greeley Square Station

New York NY 10001

Date: January 1994

Frequency: Bimonthly

Cover Price: $3.50

Subscription Price: n/a

Discount Subscription Price: n/a

Total Number of Pages: 100

Total Number of Ad Pages: 14

Publisher: John Pelory

Editor: Sam Bettay

Editorial Concept: "First-hand stories of raunchy sex with photos."

The Best of Hawk

Published by:

Killer Joe Productions Inc.

801 Second Ave.

New York NY 10017

Date: 1994

Frequency: Quarterly

Cover Price: $5.99

Subscription Price: n/a

Discount Subscription Price: n/a

Total Number of Pages: 130

Total Number of Ad Pages: 49

Publisher: Killer Joe Production Inc.

Editor: n/a

Editorial Concept: "A collection of hot, explicit pictorials from the pages of *Hawk*."

Black Beauties

Published by:

TUX Magazine Inc.

462 Broadway, 4th Floor

New York NY 10013

Date: 1994

Frequency: Quarterly

Cover Price: $4.99

Subscription Price: $17.95

Discount Subscription Price: n/a

Total Number of Pages: 100

Total Number of Ad Pages: 15

Publisher: Jay Epstein

Editor: Patti B. Goode

Editorial Concept: "Explicit pictorials of nude black women, with a couple of urban contemporary music articles thrown in."

Black Pleasure

Published by:

Black Pleasure Inc.

P.O. Box 90, Radio City Station

New York NY 10019

Date: 1994

Frequency: Bimonthly

Cover Price: $4.95

Subscription Price: n/a

Discount Subscription Price: n/a

Total Number of Pages: 76

Total Number of Ad Pages: 0

Publisher: Black Pleasure Inc.

Editor: n/a

Editorial Concept: Explicit nude photos of black women.

Black Satin

Published by:

Galaxy Publications Inc.

462 Broadway, 4th Floor

New York NY 10013

Date: 1994

Frequency: Bimonthly

Cover Price: $4.99

Subscription Price: $26.00

Discount Subscription Price: n/a

Total Number of Pages: 100

Total Number of Ad Pages: 26

Publisher: Jay Epstein

Editor: Jessie Smith

Editorial Concept: Explicit pictorials of black women.

Candy

Published by:

Candy Publications Inc.

310 Cedar Lane

Teaneck NJ 07666

Date: November 1994

Frequency: 9/Year

Cover Price: $3.99

Subscription Price: n/a

Discount Subscription Price: n/a

Total Number of Pages: 100

Total Number of Ad Pages: 24

Publisher: Candy Publications Inc.

Editor: Lisa Roven

Editorial Concept: "First-person tales of erotic sexual encounters."

Hard

Published by:

Second Wind Publications Inc.

310 Cedar Lane

Teaneck NJ 07666

Date: October 1994

Frequency: 9/Year

Cover Price: $3.99

Subscription Price: $25.97

Discount Subscription Price: n/a

Total Number of Pages: 100

Total Number of Ad Pages: 22

Publisher: Second Wind Publications

Editor: Lisa Rosen

Editorial Concept: "First-hand tales of wild sexual exploits, with illustrations."

Homegirls

Published by:

Onyx Publishing

55 Avenue of the Americas

New York NY 10013

Date: 1994

Frequency: Bimonthly

Cover Price: $4.99

Subscription Price: $27.00

Discount Subscription Price: n/a

Total Number of Pages: 100

Total Number of Ad Pages: 12

Publisher: n/a

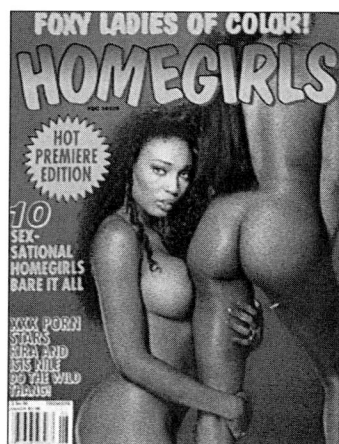

Hot 2-Somes

Published by:

Eton Publishing Company Inc.

475 Park Ave. South

New York NY 10016

Date: May 1994

Frequency: Special

Cover Price: $4.99

Subscription Price: n/a

Discount Subscription Price: n/a

Editor: n/a

Editorial Concept: "Dedicated to beautiful black women and the men who appreciate them."

Horny Partners

Published by:

Value Publishing Company

P.O. Box 20147

Greeley Square Station

New York NY 10001

Date: July 1994

Frequency: Bimonthly

Cover Price: $3.50

Subscription Price: n/a

Discount Subscription Price: n/a

Total Number of Pages: 138

Total Number of Ad Pages: 30

Publisher: John Pelory

Editor: Sam Bettay

Editorial Concept: "First-person tales of hot sex, illustrated with explicit black-and-white photos.

Total Number of Pages: 76

Total Number of Ad Pages: 24

Publisher: Eton Publishing Company Inc.

Editor: William T. Wood

Editorial Concept: Explicit pictorials of heterosexual and lesbian couples.

Hot Salsa!

Published by:

Heartland Publications Inc.

462 Broadway, 4th Floor

New York NY 10013

Date: November 1994

Frequency: Monthly

Cover Price: $6.95

Subscription Price: $44.95

Discount Subscription Price: n/a

Total Number of Pages: 100

Total Number of Ad Pages: 25

Publisher: Jay Epstein

Editor: Savannah Allende

Editorial Concept: Explicit pictorials of sexy Latino women.

Leg Tease

Published by:

Rem-Mer Ltd.

P.O. Box 700, Canal St. Station

New York NY 10013

Date: December 1994

Frequency: Monthly

Cover Price: $5.95

Subscription Price: $75.00

Discount Subscription Price: n/a

Total Number of Pages: 116

Total Number of Ad Pages: 24

Publisher: Richard Shore

Editor: Victoria Reeves

Editorial Concept: "To bring erotic pleasure to men who are turned on by a shapely leg, a trim ankle, and a pretty foot."

Lovers Handbook

Published by:

Value Publishing Company

P.O. Box 20147

Greeley Square Station

New York NY 10007

Date: January 1994

Frequency: Bimonthly

Cover Price: $3.50

Subscription Price: n/a

Discount Subscription Price: n/a

Total Number of Pages: 148

Total Number of Ad Pages: 25

Publisher: John Pelory

Editor: Sam Bettay

Editorial Concept: First-hand tales of erotica, illustrated with explicit photos.

Mid-Night

Published by:

Second Wind Publications Inc.

310 Cedar Lane

Teaneck NJ 07666

Date: October 1994

Frequency: Monthly

Cover Price: $3.99

Subscription Price: n/a

Discount Subscription Price: n/a

Total Number of Pages: 132

Total Number of Ad Pages: 24

Publisher: Second Wind Publications

Editor: Lisa Rosen

Editorial Concept: "Better-written than usual stories of erotic sex, illustrated with explicit drawings."

Naughty Nights

Published by:

Vanity Publishing Company

475 Park Ave. S., Suite 2201

New York NY 10016

Date: April 1994

Frequency: Bimonthly

Cover Price: $3.50

Subscription Price: n/a

Discount Subscription Price: n/a

Total Number of Pages: 292

Total Number of Ad Pages: 13

Publisher: H.N. Smith

Editor: J.H. Hartley

Editorial Concept: "First-hand tales of hot and raunchy sex, illustrated with explicit photos."

Oui Women in Prison Letters

Published by:

Laurant Publishing Ltd.

28 W. 25th St.

New York NY 10010

Date: Spring 1994

Frequency: Quarterly

Cover Price: $3.50

Subscription Price: n/a

Discount Subscription Price: n/a

Total Number of Pages: 136

Total Number of Ad Pages: 10

Publisher: Steve Blesen

Editor: Pat Reynolds

Editorial Concept: Alleged letters from women behind bars.

Paradise

Published by:

Paradise Entertainment

P.O. Box 2116

New York NY 10116-2116

Date: June 1994

Frequency: Monthly

Cover Price: $4.95

Subscription Price: n/a

Discount Subscription Price: n/a

Total Number of Pages: 100

Total Number of Ad Pages: 47

Publisher: Thomas Barris

Editor: Cindy Grecco

Editorial Concept: Explicit pics and stories centered around adult phone line services.

Pure

Published by:

HG Publications

9171 Wilshire Blvd., Suite 300

Beverly Hills CA 90210

Date: August 1994

Frequency: Bimonthly

Cover Price: $4.99

Subscription Price: $19.95

Discount Subscription Price: $14.95

Total Number of Pages: 100

Total Number of Ad Pages: 31

Publisher: Larry Flynt

Editor: S. Mallory

Editorial Concept: "Explicit pictorials of sexy women and articles on sexual techniques."

Small Tops

Published by:

Magcorp

P.O. Box 801434

Santa Clara CA 91380

Date: May 1994

Frequency: Bimonthly

Cover Price: $4.95

Subscription Price: $30.00

Discount Subscription Price: n/a

Total Number of Pages: 100

Total Number of Ad Pages: 20

Publisher: Magcorp

Editor: Arturo C. Moss

Editorial Concept: "Page after page of erotica and delicious photo layouts."

Sugah

Published by:

Dugent Publishing Corporation

2600 Douglas Rd., Suite 600

Coral Gables FL 33134

Date: June 1994

Frequency: Bimonthly

Cover Price: $4.95

Subscription Price: n/a

Discount Subscription Price: n/a

Total Number of Pages: 84

Total Number of Ad Pages: 14

Publisher: Dugent Publishing Corporation

Editor: Al Noland

Editorial Concept: "Explicit photos and fiction devoted to the appreciation of black women."

Tease

Published by:

Candy Publications Inc.

310 Cedar Lane

Teaneck NJ 07666

Date: November 1994

Frequency: 9/Year

Cover Price: $3.99

Subscription Price: $25.97

Discount Subscription Price: n/a

Total Number of Pages: 100

Total Number of Ad Pages: 17

Publisher: Candy Publications Inc.

Editor: Lisa Rosen

Editorial Concept: Erotic stories illustrated with explicit drawings.

Voluptuous

Published by:

Quad International Inc.

112 Temple Ave.

Hackensack NJ 07601

Date: Spring 1994

Frequency: Quarterly

Cover Price: $5.95

Subscription Price: $20.00

Discount Subscription Price: n/a

Total Number of Pages: 100

Total Number of Ad Pages: 13

Publisher: Sam Lessner

Editor: Bruce Arthur

Editorial Concept: "The new magazine for men who love big women."

XXX TV

Published by:

Eton Publishing Company

475 Park Ave. South

New York NY 10016

Date: May 1994

Frequency: Bimontly

Cover Price: $4.99

Subscription Price: n/a

Discount Subscription Price: n/a

Total Number of Pages: 84

Total Number of Ad Pages: 31

Publisher: Eton Publishing Company

Editor: Marc Verlaire

Editorial Concept: Previews of upcoming X-rated films

Annual, Special or Frequency Unknown

Adam Film World Black Video Illustrated

Published by:

Knight Publishing Corporation

8060 Melrose Ave.

Los Angeles CA 90046-7082

Date: December 1994

Frequency: Special

Cover Price: $5.95

Subscription Price: n/a

Discount Subscription Price: n/a

Total Number of Pages: 100

Total Number of Ad Pages: 8

Publisher: Knight Publishing Corporation

Editor: John Slade

Editorial Concept: "Reviews of X-rated films featuring women of color and pictorials of the top stars in the field."

Bizarre X-Films

Published by:

Eton Publishing Company

475 Park Ave. South

New York NY 10016

Date: September 1994

Frequency: Special

Cover Price: $4.99

Subscription Price: n/a

Discount Subscription Price: n/a

Total Number of Pages: 84

Total Number of Ad Pages: 29

Publisher: Eton Publishing Company

Editor: Bob Jones

Editorial Concept: Explicit scenes from X-rated films.

BJ

Published by:

Men's World Publications Inc.

801 Second Ave.

New York NY 10017

Date: 1994

Frequency: n/a

Cover Price: $5.99

Subscription Price: n/a

Discount Subscription Price: n/a

Total Number of Pages: 100

Total Number of Ad Pages: 27

Publisher: Men's World Publications Inc.

Editor: Emil Ihasz Jr.

Editorial Concept: "Explicit pictorials devoted to the art of fellatio."

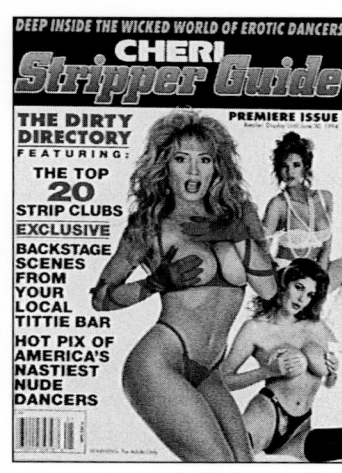

Cheri Stripper Guide

Published by:

Cheri Magazine Inc.

801 Second Ave.

New York NY 10017

Date: 1994

Frequency: Annually

Cover Price: $5.99

Subscription Price: n/a

Discount Subscription Price: n/a

Total Number of Pages: 130

Total Number of Ad Pages: 31

Publisher: Cheri Magazine Inc.

Editor: n/a

Editorial Concept: A directory of top strip clubs, with photos.

Exotic Blondes of Scandinavia

Published by:

The Crescent Publishing Group

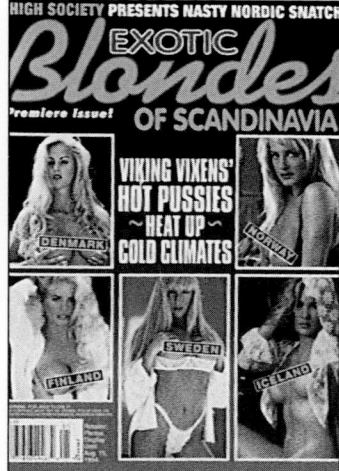

Gent's Girls with Girls

Published by:

Dugent Publishing Corporation

2600 Douglas Rd.

---

801 Second Ave.

New York NY 10017

Date: 1994

Frequency: n/a

Cover Price: $5.99

Subscription Price: n/a

Discount Subscription Price: n/a

Total Number of Pages: 100

Total Number of Ad Pages: 28

Publisher: The Crescent Publishing Group

Editor: n/a

Editorial Concept: "Explicit pictorials of Viking vixens."

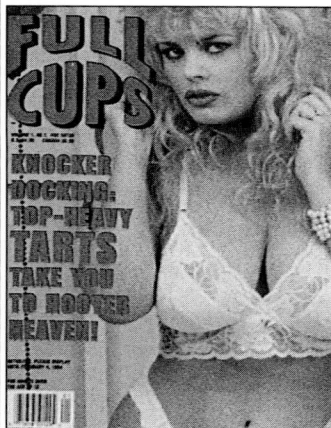

Full Cups

Published by:

Leisure Plus Publications Inc.

462 Broadway, 4th Floor

New York NY 10013

Date: 1994

Frequency: Annually

Cover Price: $4.99

Subscription Price: n/a

Discount Subscription Price: n/a

Total Number of Pages: 100

Total Number of Ad Pages: 13

Publisher: Jay Epstein

Editor: Joe Morgan

Editorial Concept: "Top-heavy tarts take you to hooter heaven."

Coral Gable FL 33134

Date: 1994

Frequency: Special

Cover Price: $4.95

Subscription Price: n/a

Discount Subscription Price: n/a

Total Number of Pages: 100

Total Number of Ad Pages: 27

Publisher: Dugent Publishing Corporation

Editor: n/a

Editorial Concept: "Giant-breasted women go one-on-one—or two-on-two, more accurately."

Gent's Natural D-Cups

Published by:

Dugent Publishing Corporation

2600 Douglas Rd.

Coral Gables FL 33134

Date: 1994

Frequency: Special

Cover Price: $4.95

Subscription Price: n/a

Discount Subscription Price: n/a

Total Number of Pages: 100

Total Number of Ad Pages: 19

Publisher: Dugent Publishing Corporation

Editor: n/a

Editorial Concept: "A collection of nude photos of women with super-huge breasts—no silicone allowed."

Horny Babes

Published by:

Paragon Publishing Inc.

P.O. Box 380

Sandy Hook CT 06482

Date: 1994

Frequency: Special

Cover Price: $5.99

Subscription Price: n/a

Discount Subscription Price: n/a

Total Number of Pages: 136

Total Number of Ad Pages: 20

Publisher: Simon Belter

Editor: Lee Lewis

Editorial Concept: "A collection of steamy pictorials from the pages of *Club International*."

Hot Sex!

Published by:

Paragon Publishing Inc.

P.O. Box 380

Sandy Hook CT 06482

Date: April/May 1994

Frequency: Special

Cover Price: $5.95

Subscription Price: n/a

Discount Subscription Price: n/a

Total Number of Pages: 134

Total Number of Ad Pages: 20

Publisher: Paragon Publishing Inc.

Editor: n/a

Editorial Concept: "Explicit pictorials of beautiful nude women, hot couples, and threesomes."

Hottest Adult Stars

Published by:

Eton Publishing Company Inc.

475 Park Ave. South, Suite 2201

New York NY 10016

Date: July 1994

Frequency: Special

Cover Price: $4.99

Subscription Price: n/a

Discount Subscription Price: n/a

Total Number of Pages: 84

Total Number of Ad Pages: 25

Publisher: Eton Publishing Company Inc.

Editor: n/a

Editorial Concept: "Shocking, uncensored photos of your favorite porn stars in action."

Hustler X-Rated Movie Guide 1994

Published by:

H-G Publications Inc.

9171 Wilshire Blvd., Suite 300

Beverly Hills CA 90210

Date: 1994

Frequency: Special

Cover Price: $5.95

Subscription Price: n/a

Discount Subscription Price: n/a

Total Number of Pages: 100

Total Number of Ad Pages: 16

Publisher: Larry Flynt

Editor: Tim Conaway

Editorial Concept: Reviews of and scenes from recently released X-rated movies.

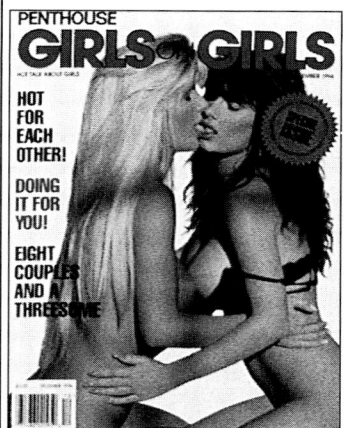

Penthouse Girls on Girls

Published by:

Hot Talk Publications Ltd.

1965 Broadway

New York NY 10023-5965

Date: December 1994

Frequency: Special

Cover Price: $5.00

Subscription Price: n/a

Discount Subscription Price: n/a

Total Number of Pages: 116

Total Number of Ad Pages: 22

Publisher: Bob Guccione

Editor: Carmen Ficarra

Editorial Concept: "Glamorous nude photos of women in sexual situations with each other."

Playgirl Fantasies

Published by:

Playgirl Inc.

801 Second Ave.

New York NY 10017

Date: 1994

Frequency: Special

Cover Price: $4.95

Subscription Price: n/a

Discount Subscription Price: n/a

Total Number of Pages: 108

Total Number of Ad Pages: 14

Publisher: Playgirl Inc.

Editor: Charmain Carl

Editorial Concept: "A sensual collection of erotic encounters."

Plump and Pink

Published by:

Swank Publications

210 Route 4 E., Suite 401

Paramus NJ 07652

Date: July 1994

Frequency: Special

Cover Price: $5.95

Subscription Price: n/a

Discount Subscription Price: n/a

Total Number of Pages: 100

Total Number of Ad Pages: 30

Publisher: Swank Publications

Editor: Bobby Paradise

Editorial Concept: "Wide-body babes in XXX action!"

Private Desires

Published by:

Eton Publishing Company

475 Park Ave. South

New York NY 10016

Date: April 1994

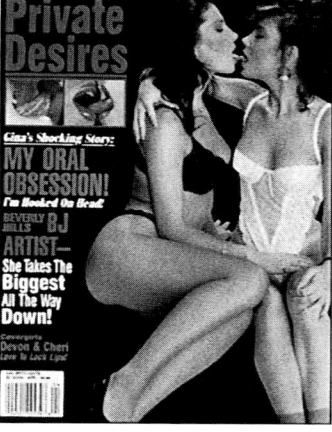

Frequency: Special

Cover Price: $4.99

Subscription Price: n/a

Discount Subscription Price: n/a

Total Number of Pages: 84

Total Number of Ad Pages: 24

Publisher: Eton Publishing Company

Editor: Soames Porter

Editorial Concept: "Explicit pictorials devoted heavily to the theme of oral sex."

Racquel Darrian Uncensored

Published by:

Stag Publications Inc.

63 Grand Ave.

River Edge NJ 07661

Date: June 1994

Frequency: Special

Cover Price: $5.99

Subscription Price: $

Discount Subscription Price: n/a

Total Number of Pages: 116

Total Number of Ad Pages: 48

Publisher: Stag Publications Inc.

Editor: n/a

Editorial Concept: "Pom's hottest star in a variety of explicit pictorials."

Steamy Letters

Published by:

AJA Publishing Corp.

P.O. Box 470

Port Chester NY 10573

Date: December 1994

Frequency: Special

Cover Price: $3.50

Subscription Price: n/a

Discount Subscription Price: n/a

Total Number of Pages: 116

Total Number of Ad Pages: 13

Publisher: Jack Dean

Editor: Josh Piano

Editorial Concept: "First-person tales of kinky sex, illustrated with vintage '70s photos."

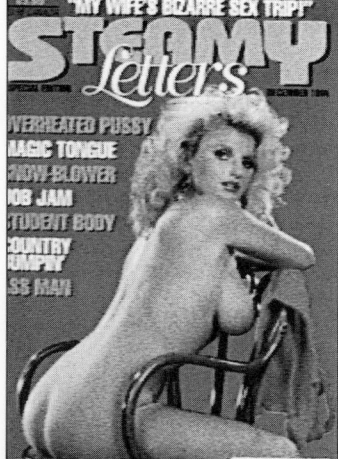

Swank's Peep Show

Published by:

Swank Publications Inc.

210 Route 4 E., Suite 401

Paramus NJ 07652

Date: August 1994

Frequency: Special

Cover Price: $5.99

Subscription Price: n/a

Discount Subscription Price: n/a

Total Number of Pages: 84

Total Number of Ad Pages: 25

Publisher: Swank Publications Inc.

Editor: Ross Williams

Editorial Concept: "Erotic pictorials from a voyeuristic, anonymous viewpoint."

True Lust Letters

Published by:

Dojo Publications

28 W. 25th St.

New York NY 10010

Date: Spring 1994

Frequency: Special

Cover Price: $3.50

Subscription Price: n/a

Discount Subscription Price: n/a

Total Number of Pages: 136

Total Number of Ad Pages: 8

Publisher: Steve Nelson

Editor: Dawn Kirwin

Editorial Concept: "First-person tales of hot sexual escapades, illustrated with explicit photos."

Beckett Racing Monthly

Published by:

Statabase Inc.

15850 Dallas Parkway

Dallas TX 75248

Date: September 1994

Frequency: Monthly

Cover Price: $3.95

Subscription Price: n/a

Discount Subscription Price: n/a

Total Number of Pages: 84

Total Number of Ad Pages: 10

Publisher: Dr. James Beckett

Editor: Dr. James Beckett

Editorial Concept: "Your new entertainment and information source for motorsports and motorsports collectibles."

Bike Magazine

Published by:

Surfer Publications Inc.

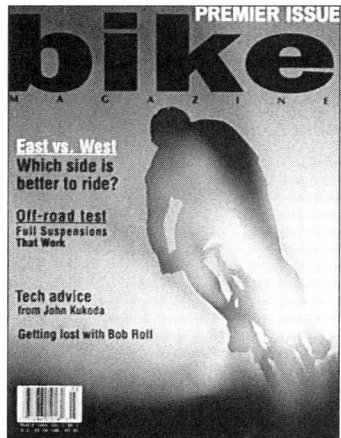

33046 Calle Aviador

San Juan Capistrano CA 92675

Date: March 1994

Frequency: 6/Year

Cover Price: $3.50

Subscription Price: $12.95

Discount Subscription Price: n/a

Total Number of Pages: 116

Total Number of Ad Pages: 24

Publisher: Brent Diamond

Editor: Rob Story

Editorial Concept: "Compelling words and mindblowing photos " for the dedicated mountain bike rider.

Chop Talk

Published by:

Atcomm Publishing

1801 Peachtree St. Northeast

Atlanta GA 30309

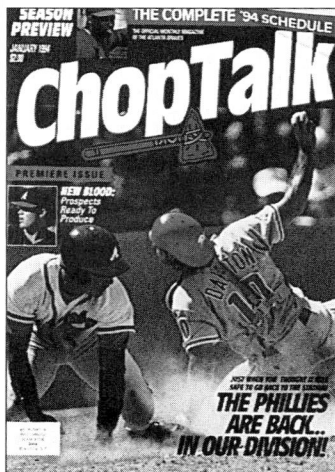

Date: January 1994

Frequency: Monthly

Cover Price: $2.00

Subscription Price: $19.95

Discount Subscription Price: n/a

Total Number of Pages: 36

Total Number of Ad Pages: 13

Publisher: Ed Baker

Editor: Carol Carter

Editorial Concept: "The official monthly magazine of the Atlanta Braves."

Cross Trainer

Published by:

Cross Trainer Publications Inc.

40 Violet Ave.

Poughkeepsie NY 12601

Date: January 1994

Frequency: Monthly

Cover Price: $3.95

Subscription Price: $39.50

Discount Subscription Price: n/a

Total Number of Pages: 132

Total Number of Ad Pages: 19

Publisher: Cross Trainer Publications Inc.

Editor: A.J. Paul

Editorial Concept: "The journal of total body fitness."

Dojang

Published by:

Pacific Rim Publishing

P.O. Box 4657

Santa Clara CA 95056

Date: Spring 1994

Frequency: Quarterly

Cover Price: $4.95

Subscription Price: $19.80

Discount Subscription Price: n/a

Total Number of Pages: 92

Total Number of Ad Pages: 22

Publisher: Gigi C. Oh

Editor: Marian K. Castinado

Editorial Concept: "All Korean martial arts."

Fighting Females

Published by:

Opal Inc.

P.O. Box 386

New York NY 10013

Date: 1994

Frequency: Quarterly

Cover Price: $3.95

Subscription Price: n/a

Discount Subscription Price: n/a

Total Number of Pages: 84

Total Number of Ad Pages: 19

Publisher: Opal Inc.

Editor: CeeDee

Editorial Concept: Pictures of bikiniclad women in various competitions across the country.

Full Contact

Published by:

LFP Inc.

9171 Wilshire Blvd., Suite 300

Beverly Hills CA 90210

Date: April 1994

Frequency: Bimonthly

Cover Price: $3.95

Subscription Price: $14.95

Discount Subscription Price: $11.95

Total Number of Pages: 80

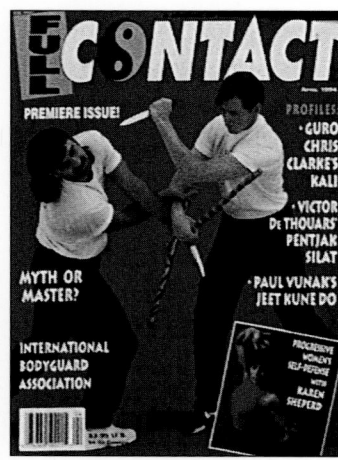

Total Number of Ad Pages: 11

Publisher: Larry Flynt

Editor: Greg Walker

Editorial Concept: Articles on the sometimes lethal application of the martial arts and profiles of the masters.

The Golfer

Published by:

Briar-Wood Inc.

42 W. 38th St.

New York NY 10018

Date: 1994

Frequency: Bimonthly

Cover Price: $4.00

Subscription Price: $24.00

Discount Subscription Price: $18.00

Total Number of Pages: 148

Total Number of Ad Pages: 39

Publisher: H.K. Pickens

Editor: H.K. Pickens

Editorial Concept: "Capturing the essence of golf in words and pictures."

International Figure Skating

Published by:

Paragraph Communications, L.P.

55 Ideal Road

Worcester MA 01604

Date: August/September 1994

Frequency: 8/Year

Cover Price: $2.50

Subscription Price: $25.00

Discount Subscription Price: n/a

Total Number of Pages: 32

Total Number of Ad Pages: 5

Publisher: Mark A. Lund

Editor: Gerard J. Waggett

Editorial Concept: Articles about the

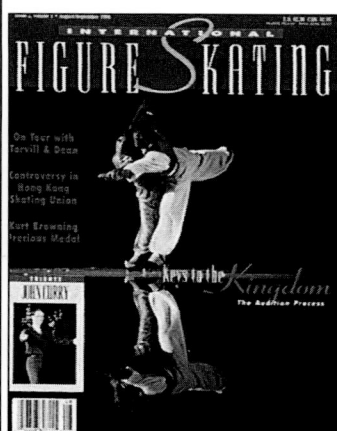

events and competitors of the world-class figure skating world.

Men's Sports

Published by:

One Look Publishing Inc.

10340 Camino Santa Fe, Suite A

San Diego CA 92121

Date: 1994

Frequency: Quarterly

Cover Price: $3.95

Subscription Price: $14.95

Discount Subscription Price: $9.97

Total Number of Pages: 100

Total Number of Ad Pages: 6

Publisher: Gary R. Dubie

Editor: Gary R. Dubie

Editorial Concept: "A superficial sports magazine that shows barely-clothed women."

MTB

Published by:

Petersen Publishing Company

6420 Wilshire Blvd.-5th Floor

Los Angeles CA 90048-5515

Date: October 1994

Frequency: Monthly

Cover Price: $2.95

Subscription Price: $11.97

Discount Subscription Price: n/a

Total Number of Pages: 116

Total Number of Ad Pages: 46

Publisher: Joe Kensil

Editor: Ari Cheren

Editorial Concept: "The ultimate mountain bike magazine."

Official Karate

Published by:

GCR Publishing Group Inc.

1770 Broadway

New York NY 10019

Date: January/February 1994

Frequency: Quarterly

Cover Price: $3.95

Subscription Price: n/a

Discount Subscription Price: n/a

Total Number of Pages: 84

Total Number of Ad Pages: 7

Publisher: Charles Goodman

Editor: Alan Paul

Editorial Concept: Techniques, moves, and personality profiles for karate enthusiasts.

Over The Edge

Published by:

HG Publications Inc.

9171 Wilshire Blvd., Suite 300

Beverly Hills CA 90210

Date: July 1994

Frequency: Bimonthly

Cover Price: $3.99

Subscription Price: $19.95

Discount Subscription Price: $11.95

Total Number of Pages: 96

Total Number of Ad Pages: 10

Publisher: Larry Flynt

Editor: Michael Bane

Editorial Concept: Features adventure sports, adventure travel, how-tos, training tips, and gear.

Petersen's Golfing

Published by:

Petersen Publishing Company

6420 Wilshire Blvd.

Los Angeles CA 90048-5515

Date: March 1994

Frequency: Monthly

Cover Price: $2.95

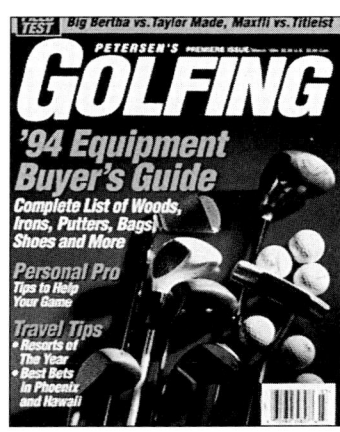

Subscription Price: $19.94

Discount Subscription Price: $12.97

Total Number of Pages: 124

Total Number of Ad Pages: 24

Publisher: Lee Kelley

Editor: Mike Corcoran

Editorial Concept: "A golf products review magazine that gives you all the truth and substance you can handle when it comes to your game and your money."

Powerhouse

Published by:

Snyder Productions

5770 W. Irlo Bronson Memorial Hwy.,

Suite #324 Upper

Kissimmee FL 34746

Date: January 1994 (first newsstand issue)

Frequency: Quarterly

Cover Price: $2.95

Subscription Price: $10.00

Discount Subscription Price: n/a

Total Number of Pages: 100

Total Number of Ad Pages: 43

Publisher: Will, Norm, and Krystal Dabish

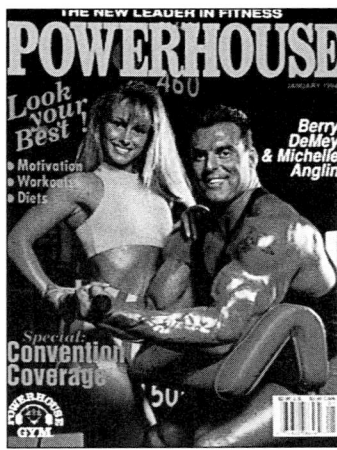

Editor: Norm Dabish

Editorial Concept: "Pumping iron for that competitive physique."

ProAction Magazine

Published by:

Marvel Entertainment Group

387 Park Ave. S.

New York NY 10016

Date: 1994

Frequency: 4/year

Cover Price: $2.95

Subscription Price: $11.80

Discount Subscription Price: n/a

Total Number of Pages: 52

Total Number of Ad Pages: 19

Publisher: Stan Lee

Editor: Chuck Garrity Sr.

Editorial Concept: "Where football, comics, and pop culture collide—a magazine for young fans of super-heroes and pro football."

Pro/Am Volleyball

Published by:

Pro/Am Volleyball Inc.

3079 Crossing Park, Suite 4

Norcross GA 30071

Date: May 1994

Frequency: Monthly

Cover Price: $2.50

Subscription Price: $17.95

Discount Subscription Price: $14.95

Total Number of Pages: 48

Total Number of Ad Pages: 16

Publisher: Pro/Am Volleyball Inc.

Editor: Jack J. Camarda Jr.

Editorial Concept: Coverage and information about grassroots tournaments.

Replay! Magazine

Published by:

International Sports Replay Association

Dept. C,

2679 State Highway 70

Manasquan NJ 08739

Date: March 1994

Frequency: Monthly

Cover Price: $2.95

Subscription Price: $19.95

Discount Subscription Price: n/a

Total Number of Pages: 64

Total Number of Ad Pages: 6

Publisher: Ron Henley

Editor: Paul "Doc" Hodges

Editorial Concept: "Latest sports news

and game playing theory."

SF Sports

Published by:

Big City Sports Publications Inc.

160 NW 176 St., Suite 302

Miami FL 33169

Date: June/July 1994

Frequency: Monthly

Cover Price: $2.50

Subscription Price: $30.00

Discount Subscription Price: $11.97

Total Number of Pages: 68

Total Number of Ad Pages: 20

Publisher: Oscar Linares

Editor: Jason Molinet

Editorial Concept: "The voice of the South Florida sports fan."

Slam

Published by:

Harris Publications Inc.

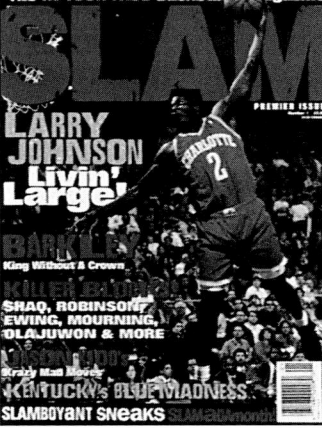

1115 Broadway

New York NY 10010

Date: 1994

Frequency: Quarterly

Cover Price: $3.95

Subscription Price: $9.97

Discount Subscription Price: n/a

Total Number of Pages: 100

Total Number of Ad Pages: 28

Publisher: Dennis S. Page

Editor: Cory Johnson

Editorial Concept: "The larger-than-life players who have made the NBA so popular."

Snap BMX Magazine

Published by:

Ride BMX

5225 Canyon Crest Dr. #71-352

Riverside CA 92507

Date: September 1994

Frequency: Bimonthly

Cover Price: $2.95

Subscription Price: $12.00

Discount Subscription Price: n/a

Total Number of Pages: 56

Total Number of Ad Pages: 21

Publisher: Brad McDonald

Editor: Steve Buddendeck

Editorial Concept: "The only complete BMX racing magazine."

Soccer Action

Published by:

Southwestern News Syndicate

5380 Clairemont Mesa Blvd., Suite 206

San Diego CA 92117

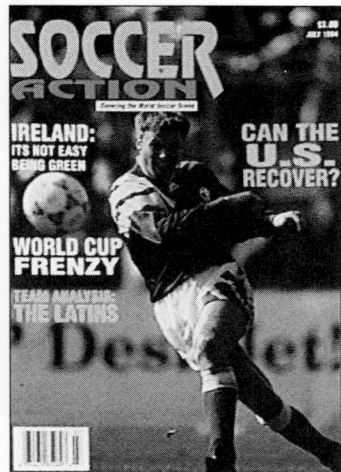

Soccer News Magazine

Published by:

Peter Romero Companies Inc.

591 Camino de la Reina, Suite 329

San Diego CA 92108

Date: July 1994

Frequency: Monthly

Cover Price: $3.00

Subscription Price: $24.90

Discount Subscription Price: $19.94

Total Number of Pages: 64

Total Number of Ad Pages: 9

Publisher: Chris Martinez

Editor: Paul C. Martinez

Editorial Concept: Covering the world soccer scene.

Soccer Illustrated

Published by:

Soccer Illustrated

P.O. Box 99050

Collingswood NJ 08108

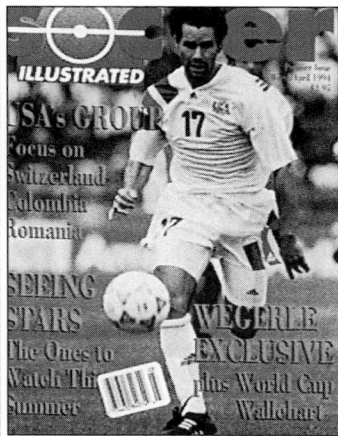

Date: March/April 1994

Frequency: Bimonthly

Cover Price: $2.95

Subscription Price: $14.95

Discount Subscription Price: n/a

Total Number of Pages: 68

Total Number of Ad Pages: 17

Publisher: Soccer Illustrated

Editor: Phil Walder

Editorial Concept: Features, news, and photographs about soccer in the U.S. and around the world.

Sports Review Wrestling

Published by:

London Publishing Company

7002 W. Butler Pike

Amber PA 19002

Date: March 1994

Frequency: Bimonthly

Cover Price: $2.50

Subscription Price: $15.00

Discount Subscription Price: n/a

Total Number of Pages: 72

Date: 1994

Frequency: Monthly

Cover Price: $3.00

Subscription Price: $21.60

Discount Subscription Price: n/a

Total Number of Pages: 64

Total Number of Ad Pages: 29

Publisher: Peter Romero

Editor: Paul C. Martinez

Editorial Concept: A look at the international world of professional soccer.

Total Number of Ad Pages: 10

Publisher: Stuart M. Saks

Editor: Bill Apter

Editorial Concept: "Profiles and grisly photos from the world of professional wrestling."

The Sportspage

Published by:

Haithcock Communications

3340 Poplar Ave., Suite 22G

Memphis TN 38111

Date: September 1994

Frequency: Monthly

Cover Price: Free

Subscription Price: $15.00

Discount Subscription Price: n/a

Total Number of Pages: 16

Total Number of Ad Pages: 3

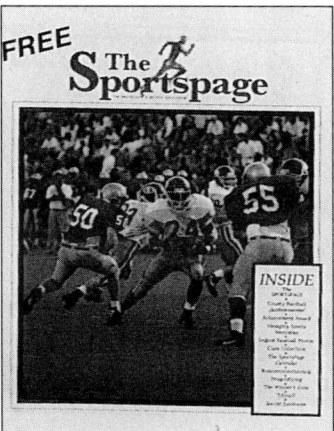

Publisher: Roy Haithcock

Editor: David Tankerlsey

Editorial Concept: Covering high-school and amateur athletics in the Memphis area.

Street and Smith's Sports Weekly - SEC Edition

Published by:

Advance Publications

304 Government St.

Mobile AL 36602

Date: August 31, 1994

Frequency: Weekly

Cover Price: $2.00

Subscription Price: $22.50

Discount Subscription Price: $21.00

Total Number of Pages: 48

Total Number of Ad Pages: 0

Publisher: Howard Bronson

Editor: Stan Tiner

Editorial Concept: "Complete coverage of college football's toughest conference."

The Surfer's Journal

Published by:

Steve and Debbee Pezman

1050 Calle Cordillera, Suite 106

San Clemente CA

Date: Summer 1994

(first newsstand issue)

Frequency: Quarterly

Cover Price: $12.95

Subscription Price: $35.00

Discount Subscription Price: n/a

Total Number of Pages: 132

Total Number of Ad Pages: 4

Publisher: Steve and Debbee Pezman

Editor: Steve Pezman

Editorial Concept: "Brain food and surf stoke for serious thinking readers."

Wrestling Bad Guys

Published by:

London Publishing Company

7002 W. Butler Pike

Ambler PA 19002

Date: Winter 1994

Frequency: Quarterly

Cover Price: $3.95

Subscription Price: n/a

Discount Subscription Price: n/a

Total Number of Pages: 92

Total Number of Ad Pages: 14

Publisher: Stuart M. Saks

Editor: David Lenker

Editorial Concept: *"Pro Wrestling Illustrated's* evil sister publication."

Annual, Special or Frequency Unknown

1994 Angels Yearbook

Published by:

Woodford Publishing Inc.

660 Market St.

San Francisco CA 94104

Date: 1994

Frequency: Annually

Cover Price: $4.00

Subscription Price: n/a

Discount Subscription Price: n/a

Total Number of Pages: 52

Total Number of Ad Pages: 10

Publisher: Laurence J. Hyman

Editor: Jon Rochmis

Editorial Concept: Features the base-

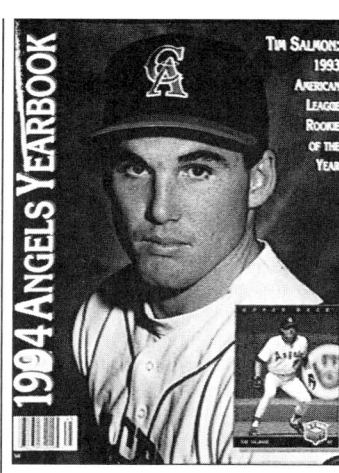

ball players, coaches, staff, and more.

1994 Buyer's Guide: Bike, Run, Swim

Published by:

Winning International Inc.

744 Roble Road, Suite 190

Allentown PA 18103-9100

Date: 1994

Frequency: Special

Cover Price: $4.95

Subscription Price: n/a

Discount Subscription Price: n/a

Total Number of Pages: 180

Total Number of Ad Pages: 32

Publisher: Jean Claude Garot

Editor: Roy M. Wallack

Editorial Concept: "800 new products - the ultimate product guide."

1994 Soccer World Cup Preview

Published by:

H & S Media Inc.

3400 Dundee Road

Northbrook II 60062

Date: 1994

Frequency: Special

Cover Price: $4.95

Subscription Price: n/a

Discount Subscription Price: n/a

Total Number of Pages: 152

Total Number of Ad Pages: 4

Publisher: H & S Media Inc.

Editor: Eduardo Beltramini

Editorial Concept: "Complete information on all World Cup teams."

Athlon College Basketball 1994-95

Published by:

Athlon Sports Communications Inc.

220 25th Ave. North

Nashville TN 37203

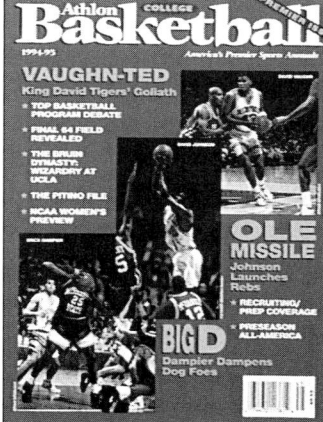

Date: 1994

Frequency: Annually

Cover Price: $4.99

Subscription Price: n/a

Discount Subscription Price: n/a

Total Number of Pages: 228

Total Number of Ad Pages: 38

Publisher: Athlon Sports Communications Inc.

Editor: George Leonard

Editorial Concept: Team and player profiles for the upcoming college basketball season.

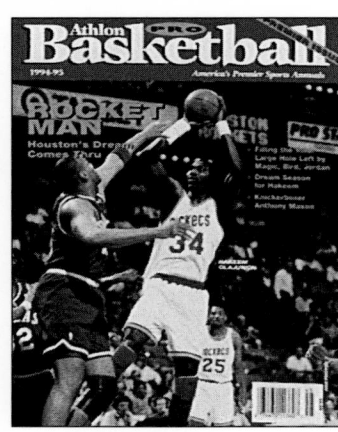

Athlon Pro Basketball 1994-95

Published by:

Athlon Sports Communications Inc.

220 25th Ave. North

Nashville TN 37203

Date: 1994

Frequency: Annually

Cover Price: $4.99

Subscription Price: n/a

Discount Subscription Price: n/a

Total Number of Pages: 196

Total Number of Ad Pages: 40

Publisher: Athlon Sports Communications Inc.

Editor: George Leonard

Editorial Concept: Team and player profiles for the NBA season.

Autoweek's Official Indycar Fan Guide

Published by:

Crain Communications Inc.

1400 Woodbridge

Detroit MI 48207-3187

Date: 1994

Frequency: Special

Cover Price: $2.95

Subscription Price: n/a

Discount Subscription Price: n/a

Total Number of Pages: 116

Total Number of Ad Pages: 23

Publisher: Leon Mandel

Editor: Leon Mandel

Editorial Concept: "A preseason guide to Indycar racing."

Blades on Ice Presents Skating Stars '95

Published by:

H & S Media Inc.

3400 N. Dundee Road

Northbrook IL 60062

Date: 1994

Frequency: Special

Cover Price: $4.95

Subscription Price: n/a

Discount Subscription Price: n/a

Total Number of Pages: 52

Total Number of Ad Pages: 7

Publisher: H & S Media Inc.

Editor: Gerri Walbert

Editorial Concept: "Over 60 photos of the world's greatest stars on ice!"

Drop The Puck Yearbook

Published by:

Blueline Publishing

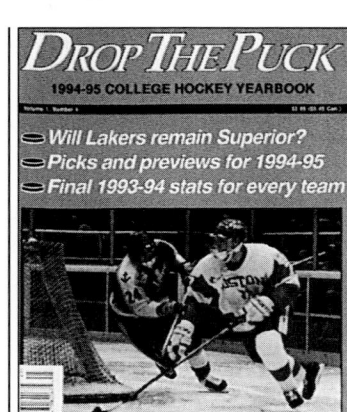

P.O. Box 8686

Minneapolis MN 55408-0686

Date: 1994-95

Frequency: Annually

Cover Price: $3.95

Subscription Price: n/a

Discount Subscription Price: n/a

Total Number of Pages: 76

Total Number of Ad Pages: 5

Publisher: Kerby W. Meyers

Editor: Kerby W. Meyers

Editorial Concept: "1994-95 college hockey yearbook."

Fantasy Baseball Index

Published by:

DFL Publishing

18247 66th Ave. NE

Seattle WA 98155

Date: 1994

Frequency: Annually

Cover Price: $4.95

Subscription Price: n/a

Discount Subscription Price: n/a

Total Number of Pages: 132

Total Number of Ad Pages: 21

Publisher: Ian Allan

Editor: Bruce Taylor

Editorial Concept: Statistics for players of fantasy baseball.

Fantasy Season 1994 Game Kit

Published by:

Fantasy Season

P.O. Box 29041

Columbus OH 43229

Date: Fall 1994

Frequency: Annual

Cover Price: $5.95

Subscription Price: n/a

Discount Subscription Price: n/a

Total Number of Pages: 24

Total Number of Ad Pages: 2

Publisher: Fantasy Season

Editor: n/a

Editorial Concept: "Everything you need to organize and play fantasy football."

Golf Courses of Arizona

Published by:

America Publishing Inc.

4545 Post Oak Place, Suite 333

Houston TX 77027

Date: 1994

Frequency: Annually

Cover Price: $4.95

Subscription Price: n/a

Discount Subscription Price: n/a

Total Number of Pages: 84

Total Number of Ad Pages: 16

Publisher: Michael A. Haines and Brenda Jackson

Editor: Wil Barnes

Editorial Concept: A look at the prestigious golf courses of Arizona.

Golf Courses of California

Published by:

Jackson-Haines Media

4615 Post Oak Place, Suite 140

Houston TX 77027

Date: 1994

Frequency: Annually

Cover Price: $5.95

Subscription Price: $5.95

Discount Subscription Price: n/a

Total Number of Pages: 116

Total Number of Ad Pages: 21

Publisher: Michael A. Haines and Brenda Jackson

Editor: Chuck Garrison

Editorial Concept: Photos and features of California's "golf treasures."

Golf Guide Special: Power Golf

Published by:

Werner Publishing Corporation

12121 Wilshire Blvd.

Suite 1220

Los Angeles CA 90025-1175

Date: 1994

Frequency: Annually

Cover Price: $3.95

Subscription Price: n/a

Discount Subscription Price: n/a

Total Number of Pages: 108

Total Number of Ad Pages: 5

Publisher: Steven D. Werner

Editor: Joe Curtis

Editorial Concept: "Your guide to power, distance and control."

Hawes Fantasy Football Guide

Published by:

Ultimate Sports Publishing Inc.

P.O. Box 75299

Seattle WA 98125

Date: 1994

Frequency: Special

Cover Price: $4.95

Subscription Price: n/a

Discount Subscription Price: n/a

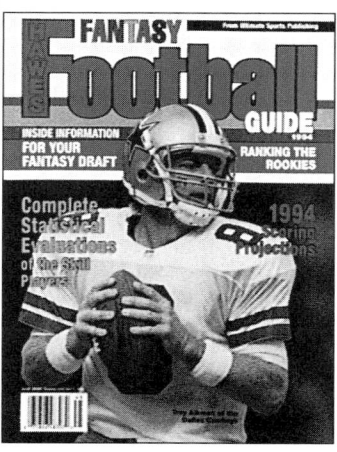

Total Number of Pages: 132

Total Number of Ad Pages: 18

Publisher: Shane O'Neill

Editor: Bob Keisser

Editorial Concept: Stats and projections for players of NFL fantasy football.

IKF Presents Martial Arts Around the World

Published by:

CFW Enterprises Inc.

4201 Vanowen Place

Burbank CA 91505

Date: February 1994

Frequency: Special

Cover Price: $3.00

Subscription Price: n/a

Discount Subscription Price: n/a

Total Number of Pages: 80

Total Number of Ad Pages: 22

Publisher: Mark Komuro

Editor: John Corcoran

Editorial Concept: Experts "demonstrate practical techniques against six types of modern attacks."

Inside Baseball

Published by:

London Publishing Company

7002 W. Butler Pike

Amber PA 19002

Date: Spring 1994

Frequency: Annually

Cover Price: $2.95

Subscription Price: n/a

Discount Subscription Price: n/a

Total Number of Pages: 80

Total Number of Ad Pages: 0

Publisher: Stuart M. Saks

Editor: n/a

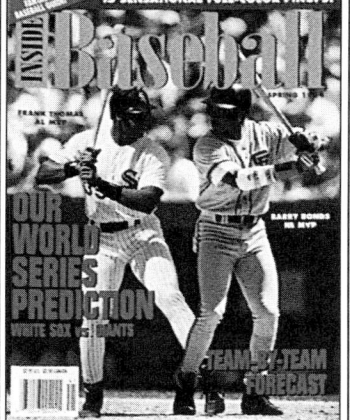

Editorial Concept: A team-by-team look at the 1994 baseball season.

Inside Martial Arts

Published by:

CFW Enterprises Inc.

4201 W. Vanowen Place

Burbank CA 91505

Date: Summer 1994

Frequency: n/a

Cover Price: $3.00

Subscription Price: n/a

Discount Subscription Price: n/a

Total Number of Pages: 84

Total Number of Ad Pages: 34

Publisher: Mark Komuro

Editor: John Steven Soet

Editorial Concept: "Features on technique, history, personality, martial arts movies, commentary, fitness, self-defense, etc."

Inside Sports 1994 Baseball Yearbook

Published by:

Inside Sports

990 Grove St.

Evanston IL 60201-4370

Date: 1994

Frequency: Annual

Cover Price: $4.95

Subscription Price: n/a

Discount Subscription Price: n/a

Total Number of Pages: 148

Total Number of Ad Pages: 19

Publisher: Inside Sports

Editor: Vince Aversano

Editorial Concept: Rankings, rosters,

and schedules for the 1994 baseball season.

Jeff Allen's College Football Preview

Published by:

Allen Communications

5025 S. Eastern #19

Las Vegas NV 89119

Date: 1994

Frequency: Annually

Cover Price: $5.95

Subscription Price: n/a

Discount Subscription Price: n/a

Total Number of Pages: 148

Total Number of Ad Pages: 34

Publisher: Jeff Allen

Editor: Jeff Allen

Editorial Concept: "Preview and betting guide, more! Stats, info and winners, schedules and predictions."

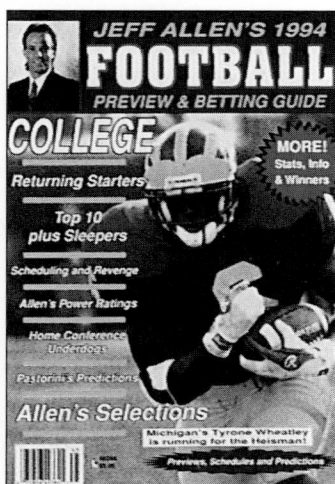

Lindy's College Basketball '94-'95 Annual - Southwestern

Published by:

D.M.D. Publications Inc.

2700 Highway 280, Suite 108

Birmingham AL 35223-2472

Date: 1994-95

Frequency: Annually

Cover Price: $4.95

Subscription Price: n/a

Discount Subscription Price: n/a

Total Number of Pages: 196

Total Number of Ad Pages: 27

Publisher: J. Lindy Davis Jr.

Editor: Mike Douchant

Editorial Concept: "Solid information in one package."

Lindy's College Basketball '94-'95 Annual - Big East

Published by:

D.M.D. Publications Inc.

2700 Highway 280, Suite 108

Birmingham AL 35223-2472

Date: 1994-95

Frequency: Annually

Cover Price: $4.95

Subscription Price: n/a

Discount Subscription Price: n/a

Total Number of Pages: 184

Total Number of Ad Pages: 24

Publisher: J. Lindy Davis Jr.

Editor: Mike Douchant

Editorial Concept: "Solid information in one package."

Lindy's Pro Basketball '94-'95 Annual

Published by:

D.M.D. Publications Inc.

2700 Highway 280, Suite 108

Birmingham AL 35223-2472

Date: 1994

Frequency: Annually

Cover Price: $4.95

Subscription Price: n/a

Discount Subscription Price: n/a

Total Number of Pages: 180

Total Number of Ad Pages: 19

Publisher: J. Lindy Davis

Editor: Roland Lazenby

Editorial Concept: Team previews and predictions for the season.

Lynx Golf

Published by:

Aqua-Field Publishing Company

66 W. Gilbert St.

Shrewsbury NJ 07702

Date: 1994

Frequency: n/a

Cover Price: $2.95

Subscription Price: n/a

Discount Subscription Price: n/a

Total Number of Pages: 64

Total Number of Ad Pages: 17

Publisher: Stephen Ferber

Editor: Edward Montague, Catherine

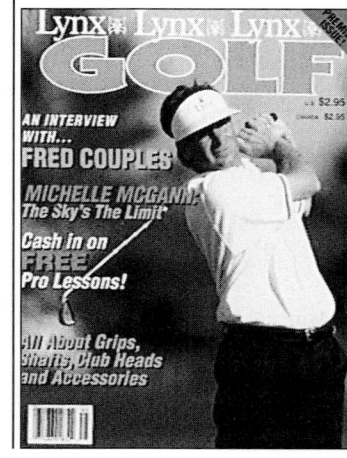

San Filippo

Editorial Concept: Pro lessons, golf technology, and interviews with golfers.

Martial Arts Legends

Published by:

C.F.W. Enterprises Inc.

4201 W. Vanowen Pl.

Burbank CA 91505

Date: 1994

Frequency: n/a

Cover Price: $4.95

Subscription Price: n/a

Discount Subscription Price: n/a

Total Number of Pages: 164

Total Number of Ad Pages: 31

Publisher: Mark Komuro

Editor: Dave Carter

Editorial Concept: "A tribute to the life, films, and unparalleled martial artistry of the late Bruce Lee."

Michael! Baseball Photo Album Magazine

Published by:

Hollywood Collectibles

3400 Dundee Rd.

Northbrook IL 60062

Date: 1994

Frequency: Special

Cover Price: $4.95

Subscription Price: n/a

Discount Subscription Price: n/a

Total Number of Pages: 56

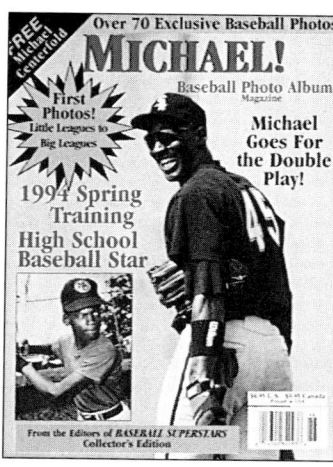

Total Number of Ad Pages: 0

Publisher: Harvey Wasselman

Editor: n/a

Editorial Concept: A collection of photos of Michael Jordan trying his hand at baseball.

Mountain Biking Special-Schwinn '95

Published by:

Challenge Publications Inc.

7950 Deering Ave.

Canoga Park CA 91304

Date: 1994

Frequency: Special

Cover Price: $4.95

Subscription Price: n/a

Discount Subscription Price: n/a

Total Number of Pages: 124

Total Number of Ad Pages: 20

Publisher: Edwin A. Schnepf

Editor: Brian Hemsworth

Editorial Concept: Photos and specs plus buying tips, riding tips, and more.

Nancy Kerrigan Photo Album

Published by:

H & S Media Inc.

3400 Dundee Rd.

Northbrook IL 60062

Date: 1994

Frequency: Special

Cover Price: $4.95

Subscription Price: n/a

Discount Subscription Price: n/a

Total Number of Pages: 58

Total Number of Ad Pages: 1

Publisher: Hollywood Collectibles Magazine

Editor: n/a

Editorial Concept: Photos and poster of Olympic skater Nancy Kerrigan.

NFL Football '94

Published by:

London Publishing Company

7002 W. Butler Pike

Ambler PA 19002

Date: Fall 1994

Frequency: Annually

Cover Price: $3.95

Subscription Price: n/a

Discount Subscription Price: n/a

Total Number of Pages: 112

Total Number of Ad Pages: 1

Publisher: Stuart M. Saks

Editor: Eric A. Karabell

Editorial Concept: Answers the question 'Where's everybody going?' and offers insight on just how these changes will affect each team.''

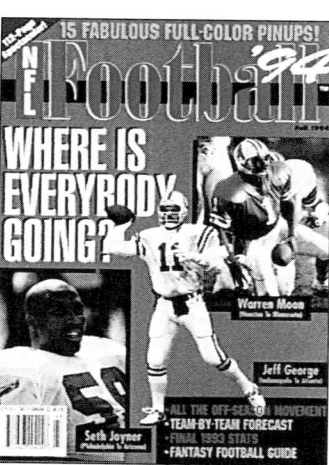

Cover Price: $6.95

Subscription Price: n/a

Discount Subscription Price: n/a

Total Number of Pages: 116

Total Number of Ad Pages: 40

Publisher: Atlas Sports

Editor: Brent Barnett, Glen Evans

Editorial Concept: ''An in-depth look at the 1994 World Cup of Soccer.''

Ski Racing Annual Competition Guide

Published by:

Ski Racing International

Route 100, Box 1125

Waitsfield VT 05673

Date: 1994-95

Frequency: Annually

Cover Price: $3.50

Subscription Price: n/a

Discount Subscription Price: n/a

Total Number of Pages: 140

Total Number of Ad Pages: 38

Publisher: Gary Black Jr.

Editor: Andy Bigford

Editorial Concept: Features an Olympic retrospective, biographies and scoreboard.

The Soccer Almanac

Published by:

Atlas Sports

Date: 1994

Frequency: Special

Soccer World Cup '94: The Complete Preview

Published by:

E/K/S Group Inc.

P.O. Box 66

Boulder Creek CA 95006

Date: May/June 1994

Frequency: Special

Cover Price: $5.95

Subscription Price: n/a

Discount Subscription Price: n/a

Total Number of Pages: 116

Total Number of Ad Pages: 2

Publisher: E/K/S Group Inc.

Editor: Jean-Pierre Frimbois

Editorial Concept: ''This collector's edition features World Cup match schedules, player profiles, and more.''

Sports Mirror Basketball

Published by:

Sports Mirror Publications Inc.

805 Third Ave.

New York NY 10022

Date: July 1994

Frequency: Special

Cover Price: $4.95

Subscription Price: n/a

Discount Subscription Price: n/a

Total Number of Pages: 100

Total Number of Ad Pages: 3

Publisher: Gerald Rothberg

Editor: Gerald Rothberg

Editorial Concept: "A basketball magazine primed for the playoffs."

Sports Mirror Golf

Published by:

Sports Mirror Publications Inc.

805 Third Ave.

New York NY 10022

Date: October 1994

Frequency: Special

Cover Price: $4.95

Subscription Price: n/a

Discount Subscription Price: n/a

Total Number of Pages: 100

Total Number of Ad Pages: 0

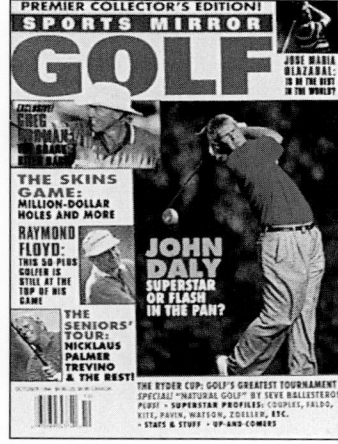

Publisher: Gerald Rothberg

Editor: Gerald Rothberg

Editorial Concept: "An up-close-and-personal look at the top names in pro golf."

Tuff Stuff Magazine Presents: 125 Years of Baseball Collectibles

Published by:

Tuff Stuff Publications Inc.

1934 E. Parham Rd.

Richmond VA 23228

Date: Fall 1994

Frequency: Special

Cover Price: $4.95

Subscription Price: n/a

Discount Subscription Price: n/a

Total Number of Pages: 100

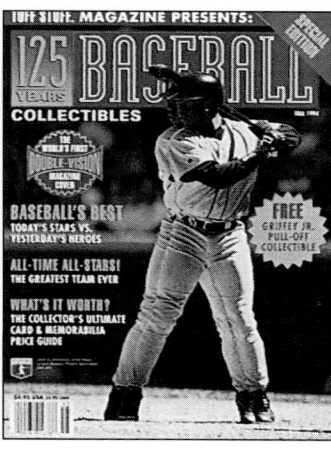

Total Number of Ad Pages: 29

Publisher: Tuff Stuff Publications

Editor: Larry Canale

Editorial Concept: "The players we admire and, especially, the memorabilia we collect."

The Ultimate Fighting Championship

Published by:

CFW Enterprises Inc.

4201 Vanowen Pl.

Burbank CA 91505

Date: 1994

Frequency: Special

Cover Price: $4.95

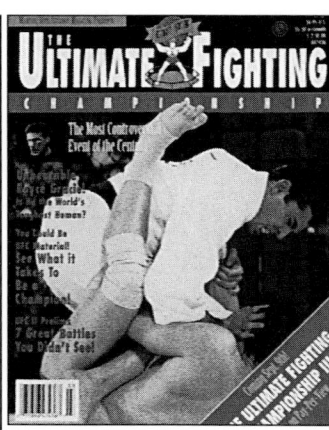

Subscription Price: n/a

Discount Subscription Price: n/a

Total Number of Pages: 116

Total Number of Ad Pages: 34

Publisher: CFW Enterprises Inc.

Editor: Dave Carter and Kathy Kidd

Editorial Concept: Full-contact martial arts tournaments.

Ultimate Sports Baseball 1994

Published by:

Ultimate Sports Publishing Inc.

P.O. Box 75299

Seattle WA 98125

Date: 1994

Frequency: Special

Cover Price: $5.95

Subscription Price: n/a

Discount Subscription Price: n/a

Total Number of Pages: 180

Total Number of Ad Pages: 12

Publisher: Shane O'Neill

Editor: Shane O'Neill

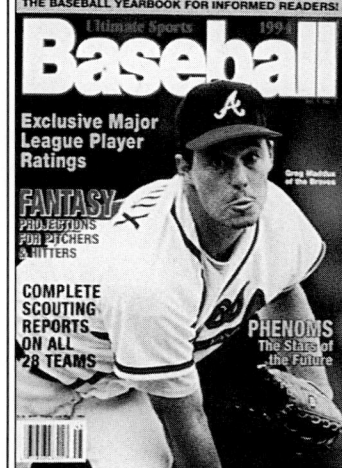

Editorial Concept: Previews of the baseball season.

Ultimate Sports Pro Football '94

Published by:

Ultimate Sports Publishing Inc.

P.O. Box 75299

Seattle WA 98125

Date: 1994

Frequency: Annually

Cover Price: $5.95

Subscription Price: n/a

Discount Subscription Price: n/a

Total Number of Pages: 180

Total Number of Ad Pages: 17

Publisher: Shane O'Neill

Editor: Shane O'Neill

Editorial Concept: "The pro football yearbook for informed readers!"

Weekend Outdoors

Published by:

Aqua-Field Publishing Company Inc.

66 W. Gilbert St.

Shrewsbury NJ 07702

Date: 1994

Frequency: Special

Cover Price: $2.95

Subscription Price: n/a

Discount Subscription Price: n/a

Total Number of Pages: 84

Total Number of Ad Pages: 18

Publisher: Stephen Ferber

Editor: Stephen Ferber

Editorial Concept: "An 84-page advertisement for Columbia Sportswear disguised as an outdoor sports and activities magazine."

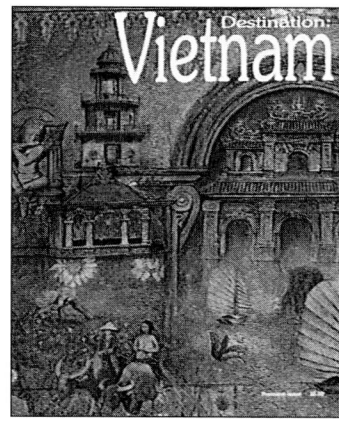

Destination: Vietnam

Published by:
Global Directions Inc.
58 Genebern Way
San Francisco CA 94112
Date: September 1994
Frequency: Bimonthly
Cover Price: $5.00
Subscription Price: $20.00
Discount Subscription Price: n/a
Total Number of Pages: 52
Total Number of Ad Pages: 10
Publisher: Lisa Spivey, Albert Wen
Editor: n/a
Editorial Concept: "Up-to-date information about Vietnam for the American market."

Eco Traveler

Published by:
Skies American Publishing Company
2230 S.W. Mohawk St.
Tualatin OR 97062
Date: March/April 1994

Frequency: Bimonthly
Cover Price: $3.95
Subscription Price: $36.00
Discount Subscription Price: $19.95
Total Number of Pages: 84
Total Number of Ad Pages: 20
Publisher: Lisa Tabb
Editor: Suzanne Eggleston
Editorial Concept: "For people who want to see the world and protect its environmental integrity."

Escape: The Global Guide for the Adventurous Traveler

Published by:
Escape Magazine Inc.
P.O. Box 5159, 2720 Neilson Way
Santa Monica CA 90409-5159
Date: Winter 1994
Frequency: Quarterly

Cover Price: $3.95
Subscription Price: $18.00
Discount Subscription Price: n/a
Total Number of Pages: 100
Total Number of Ad Pages: 15
Publisher: Joe Robinson
Editor: Steve Ginsberg
Editorial Concept: "A travel magazine that chronicles the spirit of the road."

Forty West

Published by:
Infinite Loop Graphics
P.O. Box 438
Chloride AZ 86431

Date: January 1994
Frequency: Quarterly
Cover Price: $2.50
Subscription Price: $12.50
Discount Subscription Price: n/a
Total Number of Pages: 44
Total Number of Ad Pages: 14
Publisher: Maggie Minton
Editor: Maggie Minton
Editorial Concept: The people, places, and history along Highway 40 in the western states.

Historic Traveler

Published by:
Cowles History Group
602 S. King St., Suite 300
Leesburg VA 22075
Date: Autumn 1994
Frequency: Quarterly
Cover Price: $3.95
Subscription Price: $14.95
Discount Subscription Price: n/a
Total Number of Pages: 92
Total Number of Ad Pages: 34

Publisher: Thomas G. O'Keefe
Editor: John E. Stanchak
Editorial Concept: "The guide to great American destinations—the places where our history was made."

The List Magazine

Published by:
The Gay & Lesbian Visitors
Center of NY Inc.
135 W. 20th St.
New York NY 10011
Date: Fall 1994
Frequency: Bimonthly
Cover Price: $3.95
Subscription Price: $35.00

Discount Subscription Price: n/a
Total Number of Pages: 48
Total Number of Ad Pages: 18
Publisher: Mark A. Gilbert
Editor: Mark A. Gilbert
Editorial Concept: A travel guide for gays and lesbians.

Outdoor Traveler - Mid-Atlantic

Published by:
WMS Publications Inc.
1 Morton Dr., Suite 102
Charlottesville VA 22903
Date: Autumn 1994
Frequency: Quarterly
Cover Price: $3.00
Subscription Price: $12.00
Discount Subscription Price: n/a
Total Number of Pages: 68

Total Number of Ad Pages: 13

Publisher: Marianne Marks

Editor: Marianne Marks

Editorial Concept: "Outdoor sports, destinations, and nature. With this issue, the mid-Atlantic's magazine adds New York state to its coverage."

Vacation World

Published by:

JPB Inc.

P.O. Box 1320

Issaquah WA 98027

Date: February/March 1994

Frequency: Bimonthly

Cover Price: $2.95

Subscription Price: $19.97

Discount Subscription Price: n/a

Total Number of Pages: 72

Total Number of Ad Pages: 14

Publisher: JPB Inc.

Editor: Cliff Creager

Editorial Concept: Destination suggestions for travel, recreation, and leisure.

Country Living Country Travels

Published by:

The Hearst Corporation

224 W. 57th St.

New York NY 10019

Date: Spring/Summer 1994

Frequency: Annually

Cover Price: $2.95

Subscription Price: n/a

Discount Subscription Price: n/a

Total Number of Pages: 134

Total Number of Ad Pages: 24

Publisher: Jay McGill

Editor: Carol Cooper Garey

Editorial Concept: "Brings familiar places into fresh focus, with an emphasis on the out-of-the-way and laid-back excursions."

National Geographic Traveler National Parks

Published by:

National Geographic Society

1145 17th St. N.W.

Washington DC 20036

Date: 1994

Frequency: Special

Cover Price: $5.95

Subscription Price: n/a

Discount Subscription Price: n/a

Total Number of Pages: 134

Total Number of Ad Pages: 20

Publisher: National Geographic Society

Editor: Richard Busch

Editorial Concept: "Profiles seven of North America's favorite national parks."

New England Travel Guide

Published by:

Boston Magazine's Contract Publishing Division

300 Massachusetts Ave.

Boston MA 02115

Date: 1994

Frequency: Special

Cover Price: $3.95

Subscription Price: n/a

Discount Subscription Price: n/a

Total Number of Pages: 148

Total Number of Ad Pages: 50

Publisher: Alan J. Klein

Editor: Art Jahnke

Editorial Concept: "Features the best of New England."

Snow Country Action Vacations

Published by:

NYT Sports/Leisure Magazines

5520 Park Ave.

Trumball CT 06611-0395

Date: May/June 1994

Frequency: Special

Cover Price: $2.50

Subscription Price: n/a

Discount Subscription Price: n/a

Total Number of Pages: 108

Total Number of Ad Pages: 53

Publisher: Tom Brown

Editor: John Fry

Editorial Concept: Summer fun in the mountains.

Southern Living Family Vacations

Published by:

Southern Living Inc.

2100 Lakeshore Dr.

Birmingham AL 35209

Date: February-March 1994

Frequency: Special

Cover Price: $3.95

Subscription Price: n/a

Discount Subscription Price: n/a

Total Number of Pages: 126

Total Number of Ad Pages: 52

Publisher: Scott Sheppard

Editor: Karen Lingo

Editorial Concept: Ideas for planning vacations in the South.

Southern Living Weekend Vacations

Published by:

Southern Living Inc.

2100 Lakeshore Dr.

Birmingham AL 35209

Date: September-October 1994

Frequency: Special

Cover Price: $3.95

Subscription Price: n/a

Discount Subscription Price: n/a

Total Number of Pages: 180

Total Number of Ad Pages: 91

Publisher: Scott Sheppard

Editor: Karen Lingo

Editorial Concept: Trips, shopping, and entertainment for the weekend traveler.

Alternative Cinema

Published by:

Tempa Press

P.O. Box 6573

Akron OH

Date: Spring 1994

Frequency: Quarterly

Cover Price: $3.95

Subscription Price: $15.00

Discount Subscription Price: n/a

Total Number of Pages: 60

Total Number of Ad Pages: 11

Publisher: J.R. Bookwalter

Editor: J.R. Bookwalter

Editorial Concept: Trashy B-movies.

American Interactive Video Magazine

Published by:

Charles Rau III

2900 Bristol St., Suite G-206

Costa Mesa CA 92626

Date: Summer 1994

Frequency: Monthly

Cover Price: $2.50

Subscription Price: $19.94

Discount Subscription Price: n/a

Total Number of Pages: 84

Total Number of Ad Pages: 30

Publisher: Charles Rau III

Editor: KRISTAN

Editorial Concept: "To help people in general understand the interactive industry."

Cinescape

Published by:

Sendai Publishing Group Inc.

1920 Highland Ave., Suite 222

Lombard IL 60148

Date: 1994

Frequency: Monthly

Cover Price: $4.99

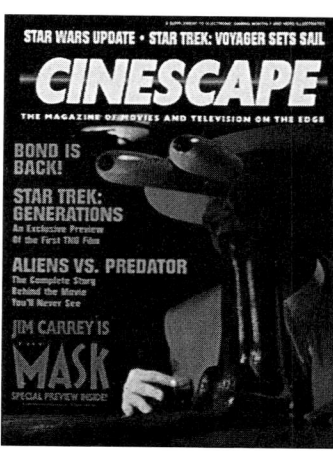

Subscription Price: $29.95

Discount Subscription Price: $19.95

Total Number of Pages: 84

Total Number of Ad Pages: 10

Publisher: Steve Harris

Editor: Edward Gross

Editorial Concept: "The magazine of movies and television on the edge."

Hollywood Horror Classics

Published by:

Hollywood Horror Classics

P.O. Box 510492

Salt Lake City UT 84151

Date: 1994

Frequency: Quarterly

Cover Price: $3.50

Subscription Price: n/a

Discount Subscription Price: n/a

Total Number of Pages: 36

Total Number of Ad Pages: 5

Publisher: Hollywood Horror Classics

Editor: Mike Gelino, David Harlan

Editorial Concept: "Dedicated to the preservation of a unique American art form."

Home Theater Technology

Published by:

CurtCo Publishing

20700 Ventura Blvd., Suite 100

Woodland Hills CA 91364

Date: October 1994

Frequency: Monthly

Cover Price: $3.95

Subscription Price: $23.95

Discount Subscription Price: n/a

Total Number of Pages: 164

Total Number of Ad Pages: 52

Publisher: Megean Roberts

Editor: Lawrence E. Ullman

Editorial Concept: Equipment and technical tips to set up your own home theater.

Movie Club

Published by:

Movie Club Inc.

12 Moray Court

Baltimore MD 21236

Date: March 1994

Frequency: Bimonthly

Cover Price: $3.50

Subscription Price: $21.00

Discount Subscription Price: $15.75

Total Number of Pages: 44

Total Number of Ad Pages: 8

Publisher: Don Dohler

Editor: Don Dohler

Editorial Concept: Articles and photographs about movies.

Movie Maker Magazine

Published by:

Rice Entertainment

229 Broadway East, Suite 21

Seattle WA 98102

Date: August 1994

Frequency: 10/Year

Cover Price: $2.50

Subscription Price: $18.00

Discount Subscription Price: n/a

Total Number of Pages: 48

Total Number of Ad Pages: 12

Publisher: Tim Rice

Editor: Tim Rice

Editorial Concept: "For serious film fans."

Oriental Cinema

Published by:

Draculina Publishing

P.O. Box 969

Centralia IL 62801

Date: August 1994 (first newsstand issue)

Frequency: Quarterly

Cover Price: $3.25

Subscription Price: $15.00

Discount Subscription Price: n/a

Total Number of Pages: 36

Total Number of Ad Pages: 1

Publisher: Hugh Gallagher

Editor: Damon Foster

Editorial Concept: "Concerned with Asian filmdom as a whole"

Producer

Published by:

Producers Quarterly Publishing Inc.

25 Willowdale Ave.

Port Washington NY 11050

Date: August 1994 (first newsstand issue)

Frequency: Bimonthly

Cover Price: $4.00

Subscription Price: $15.00

Discount Subscription Price: n/a

Total Number of Pages: 82

Total Number of Ad Pages: 21

Publisher: Vincent P. Testa

Editor: Randi Altman

Editorial Concept: "For creative image and sound professionals."

Satellite Choice

Published by:

Fortuna Communications Corporation

140 S. Fortuna Blvd.

Fortuna CA 95540

Date: September 1994

Frequency: Monthly

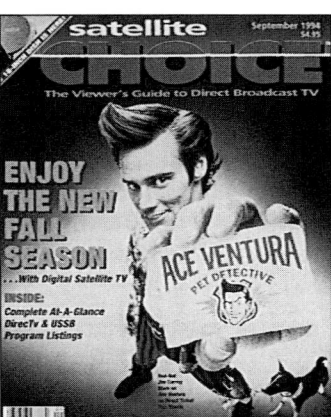

Cover Price: $4.95

Subscription Price: $52.00

Discount Subscription Price: n/a

Total Number of Pages: 248

Total Number of Ad Pages: 9

Publisher: Patrick O'Dell

Editor: James E. Scott

Editorial Concept: "The viewers guide to direct broadcast TV."

Satellite Direct

Published by:

Orbit Publishing

8330 Boone Blvd., Suite 600

Vienna VA 22182

Date: April 1994

Frequency: Monthly

Cover Price: $4.95

Subscription Price: $52.00

Discount Subscription Price: n/a

Total Number of Pages: 252

Total Number of Ad Pages: 7

Publisher: Orbit Publishing

Editor: Phillip Swan

Editorial Concept: "Dedicated solely to serving [the] needs of Digital Satellite System owners."

Sci-Fi Entertainment

Published by:

Sovereign Media Company Inc.

457 Carlisle Drive

Herndon VA 22070

Date: June 1994

Frequency: Bimonthly

Cover Price: $3.50

Subscription Price: $14.95

Discount Subscription Price: n/a

Total Number of Pages: 76

Total Number of Ad Pages: 23

Publisher: Mark Hinz

Editor: Ted Klein

Editorial Concept: The official magazine of the Sci-Fi channel.

Star Trek Communicator

Published by:

The Official Fan Club Inc.

537 Olathe St., Suite C

Aurora CO 80011

Date: December/January 1994-95 (first newsstand issue)

Frequency: Bimonthly

Cover Price: $3.50

Subscription Price: $14.95

Discount Subscription Price: n/a

Total Number of Pages: 88

Total Number of Ad Pages: 44

Publisher: Dan Madsen

Editor: Dan Madsen

Editorial Concept: The magazine of Star Trek: The Official Fan Club.

Star Wars Galaxy Magazine

Published by:

The Topps Company Inc.

1 Whitehall St.

New York NY 10004

Date: Fall 1994

Frequency: Quarterly

Cover Price: $3.50

Subscription Price: $13.97

Discount Subscription Price: n/a

Total Number of Pages: 68

Total Number of Ad Pages: 11

Publisher: Ira Friedman

Editor: Bob Woods

Editorial Concept: "Explores the ways the *Star Wars* movies are still alive today."

Video Guide

Published by:

Vision Enterprises

Date: August 1994

Frequency: Bimonthly

Cover Price: $1.50

Subscription Price: n/a

Discount Subscription Price: n/a

Total Number of Pages: 36

Total Number of Ad Pages: 0

Publisher: Jerry Austin

Editor: Karen Austin

Editorial Concept: "Showcases the most popular releases of the last 18 months."

Entertainment Weekly Academy Awards Extra

Published by:

Time Inc.

1675 Broadway

New York NY 10019

Date: March 1994

Frequency: Special

Cover Price: $3.95

Subscription Price: Newsstand only

Discount Subscription Price: Newsstand only

Total Number of Pages: 132

Total Number of Ad Pages: 43

Publisher: Michael J. Klingensmith

Editor: James W. Seymore Jr.

Editorial Concept: "The complete viewer's guide, the year's best, worst, and wackiest movie movements!" and more.

Entertainment Weekly Special Star Trek Issue

Published by:

Entertainment Weekly Inc.

1675 Broadway

New York NY 10019

Date: Fall 1994

Frequency: Special

Cover Price: $3.95

Subscription Price: Newsstand only

Discount Subscription Price:

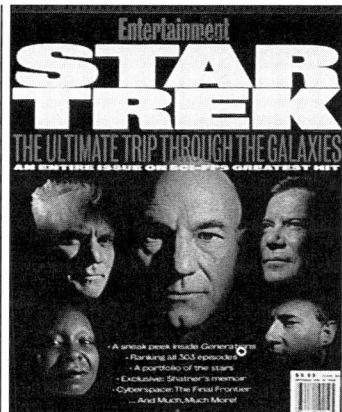

Newsstand only

Total Number of Pages: 108

Total Number of Ad Pages: 32

Publisher: Michael J. Klingensmith

Editor: James W. Seymore Jr.

Editorial Concept: "Special obsessive-compulsive collector's edition."

Gorezone Special - Frankenstein

Published by:

Starlog Communications Inc.

475 Park Ave. South

New York NY 10016

Date: 1994

Frequency: Special

Cover Price: $5.95

Subscription Price: n/a

Discount Subscription Price: n/a

Total Number of Pages: 68

Total Number of Ad Pages: 13

Publisher: Norman Jacobs

Editor: Anthony Timpone

Editorial Concept: Facts, pictures, and interviews.

The Mask Collector's Magazine

Published by:

Cinescape Group Inc.

1920 Highland Ave., Suite 222

Lombard IL 60148

Date: July 1994

Frequency: Special

Cover Price: $4.95

Subscription Price: n/a

Discount Subscription Price: n/a

Total Number of Pages: 68

Total Number of Ad Pages: 9

Publisher: Steve Harris

Editor: Mike Stokes

Editorial Concept: "The complete authorized guide to the blockbuster movie."

The Official Stargate Movie Magazine

Published by:

Starlog Communications International

475 Park Ave. South, 8th Floor

New York NY 10016

Date: 1994

Frequency: Special

Cover Price: $4.95

Subscription Price: n/a

Discount Subscription Price: n/a

Total Number of Pages: 68

Total Number of Ad Pages: 13

Publisher: Norman Jacobs

Editor: David McDonnell

Editorial Concept: "Inside the science-fiction spectacular."

Premiere Special

Published by:
K-III Magazine Corporation
2 Park Ave.
New York NY 10016
Date: 1994
Frequency: Special
Cover Price: $3.95
Subscription Price: n/a
Discount Subscription Price: n/a
Total Number of Pages: 130
Total Number of Ad Pages: 30
Publisher: K-III Magazine Corporation
Editor: Cyndi Stivers
Editorial Concept: "New York and the Movies."

The Shadow

Published by:
Starlog Communications
475 Park Ave. South, 8th Floor
New York NY 10016
Date: 1994
Frequency: Special
Cover Price: $4.95

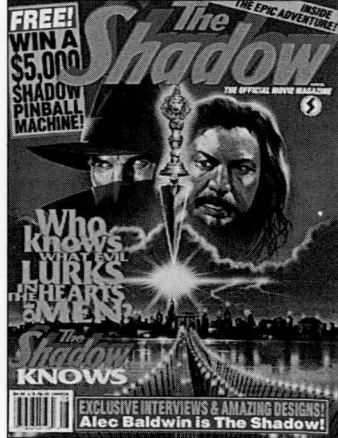

Subscription Price: n/a
Discount Subscription Price: n/a
Total Number of Pages: 68
Total Number of Ad Pages: 13
Publisher: Norman Jacobs
Editor: David McDonnell
Editorial Concept: Stories on the making of the super-hero movie and the history of the character.

Star Trek Generations

Published by:
Starlog Communications International
475 Park Ave. South, 8th Floor
New York NY 10016
Date: 1994
Frequency: Special
Cover Price: $9.95

Subscription Price: n/a
Discount Subscription Price: n/a
Total Number of Pages: 84
Total Number of Ad Pages: 23
Publisher: Norman Jacobs
Editor: David McDonnell
Editorial Concept: The official movie magazine.

Steven Spielberg Dreaming the Movies

Published by:
E/K/S Group Inc.
740 Front St., Suite 380A
Santa Cruz CA 95060

Date: September 1994
Frequency: Special
Cover Price: $5.95
Subscription Price: n/a
Discount Subscription Price: n/a
Total Number of Pages: 84
Total Number of Ad Pages: 0
Publisher: E/K/S Group Inc.
Editor: Roy Zinsenheim
Editorial Concept: "Tool for anyone interested in getting to know better Steven Spielberg's universe."

Street Fighter

Published by:
Starlog Group Inc.
475 Park Ave. South, 8th Floor
New York NY 10016
Date: 1994
Frequency: Special
Cover Price: $4.95
Subscription Price: n/a
Discount Subscription Price: n/a
Total Number of Pages: 56

Total Number of Ad Pages: 10
Publisher: Norman Jacobs
Editor: David McDonnell
Editorial Concept: The making of the action movie starring Jean-Claude Van Damme.

Video Watchdog Special Edition

Published by:
Tim and Donna Lucas
P.O. Box 5283
Cincinnati OH 45205-0283
Date: 1994
Frequency: Annually
Cover Price: $7.95
Subscription Price: n/a
Discount Subscription Price: n/a
Total Number of Pages: 180
Total Number of Ad Pages: 30
Publisher: Tim and Donna Lucas
Editor: n/a
Editorial Concept: "To tackle film-and-video-related subjects with book-length indulgence."

Aurora Rising

Published by:

Aurora Concepts Inc.

2992 N. Kimberly Court

Atlanta GA 30340

Date: n/a *(formerly Aurora)*

Frequency: Quarterly

Cover Price: $4.50

Subscription Price: $15.00

Discount Subscription Price: n/a

Total Number of Pages: 100

Total Number of Ad Pages: 20

Publisher: Aurora Concept Inc.

Editor: Karen Willis

Editorial Concept: "A new-age magazine of consciousness, creativity, and spiritual growth."

Married Woman

Published by:

News America Publishing Incorporated

1211 Avenue of the Americas

New York NY 10036

Date: February/March 1994

Frequency: Bimonthly

Cover Price: $2.50

Subscription Price: $19.98

Discount Subscription Price: n/a

Total Number of Pages: 124

Total Number of Ad Pages: 22

Publisher: Elaine Shindler

Editor: Kelly Good McGhee

Editorial Concept: "The lifestyle for after the wedding."

Pageantry

Published by:

Pageantry Talent and Entertainments Services Inc.

P.O. Box 160307

Altamonte Springs FL 32716

Date: Fall 1994 *(first newsstand issue)*

Frequency: Quarterly

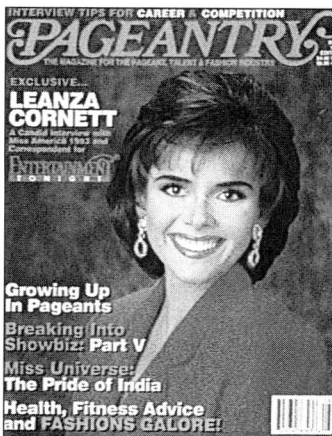

Cover Price: $4.95

Subscription Price: $19.80

Discount Subscription Price: $16.00

Total Number of Pages: 108

Total Number of Ad Pages: 65

Publisher: Charles Dunn

Editor: Brian Chambers

Editorial Concept: "For the pageant, talent and fashion industries."

Playgirl International

Published by:

Playgirl Inc.

801 Second Ave.

New York NY 10017

Date: 1994

Frequency: Semi-annually

Cover Price: $4.95

Subscription Price: n/a

Discount Subscription Price: n/a

Total Number of Pages: 108

Total Number of Ad Pages: 18

Publisher: n/a

Editor: n/a

Editorial Concept: "Presenting the World's Most Exotic Men."

Que Linda!

Published by:

PRP Publishing

1342 Maxella Ave., Suite 296

Marina Del Ray CA 90292-5671

Date: Spring 1994

Frequency: Quarterly

Cover Price: $2.95

Subscription Price: $5.99

Discount Subscription Price: n/a

Total Number of Pages: 48

Total Number of Ad Pages: 9

Publisher: PRP Publishing

Editor: Linda Peebles

Editorial Concept: "Beauty, fashion,

community issues, and exclusive star interviews "for today's Latina."

Women's Self Defense

Published by:

Creative Arts Inc.

Spectrum Building

4901 Northwest 17th Way, Suite 600

Fort Lauderdale FL 33309

Date: June 1994

Frequency: 9/Year

Cover Price: $3.95

Subscription Price: $24.00

Discount Subscription Price: n/a

Total Number of Pages: 84

Total Number of Ad Pages: 5

Publisher: David Harvard

Editor: Kathy S. Bentley

Editorial Concept: "How women can protect themselves not only physically, but in other areas, such as law and medicine."

Women Vs. Men

Published by:

Creative Arts Inc.

Spectrum Building

4901 Northwest 17th Way, Suite 600

Fort Lauderdale FL 33309

Date: October 1994

Frequency: Bimonthly

Cover Price: $3.95

Subscription Price: $24.00/2 Years

Discount Subscription Price: n/a

Total Number of Pages: 84

Total Number of Ad Pages: 1

Publisher: David Harvard

Editor: Kathy Bentley

Editorial Concept: Observes and celebrates the differences between women and men.

Annual, Special or Frequency Unknown

Know-How

Published by:

Hachette Filipacchi Magazines Inc.

1633 Broadway

New York NY 10019

Date: Spring 1994

Frequency: n/a

Cover Price: $2.95

Subscription Price: n/a

Discount Subscription Price: n/a

Total Number of Pages: 114

Total Number of Ad Pages: 39

Publisher: Daniel Filipacchi

Editor: Margot Gilman

Editorial Concept: "A magazine that recognizes that a woman's interests

extend beyond the three Fs—food, fat, and fashion!"

Sisters In Style

Published by:

The Sterling/Macfadden Partnership

233 Park Ave. South

New York NY 10003

Date: September 1994

Frequency: Special

Cover Price: $2.95

Subscription Price: n/a

Discount Subscription Price: n/a

Total Number of Pages: 92

Total Number of Ad Pages: 20

Publisher: The Sterling/Macfadden Partnership

Editor: Cynthia Horner

Editorial Concept: "A

beauty/fashion/service oriented publication for today's young black woman."

Black Hair Styles

Published by:

GCR Publishing Group Inc.

1700 Broadway

New York NY 10019

Date: April 1994

Frequency: Quarterly

Cover Price: $3.75

Subscription Price: n/a

Discount Subscription Price: n/a

Total Number of Pages: 84

Total Number of Ad Pages: 12

Publisher: Charles Goodman

Editor: Shelly Dawson-Davies

Editorial Concept: "Hundreds of red-hot new hairdos for black women, inspired by their favorite celebrities."

Cut & Style

Published by:

Harris Publications Inc.

1115 Broadway

New York NY 10010

Date: 1994

Frequency: Bimonthly

Cover Price: $3.95

Subscription Price: n/a

Discount Subscription Price: n/a

Total Number of Pages: 84

Total Number of Ad Pages: 17

Publisher: Stanley R. Harris

Editor: Mary Greenberg

Editorial Concept: "One hundred of the hottest styles and latest cuts."

Extra Woman

Published by:

Michele Durant

P.O. Box 57194

Sherman Oaks CA 91413

Date: October/November 1994

(formerly called Extra!)

Frequency: Bimonthly

Cover Price: $2.50

Subscription Price: $15.00

Discount Subscription Price: n/a

Total Number of Pages: 48

Total Number of Ad Pages: 8

Publisher: Michele Durant

Editor: Michele Durant

Editorial Concept: "To change the way large people feel about themselves."

Fashion Catalogs of America

Published by:

L.F.P. Inc.

9171 Wilshire Blvd., Suite 300

Beverly Hills CA 90210

Date: 1994

Frequency: Quarterly

Cover Price: $2.99

Subscription Price: $11.80

Discount Subscription Price: n/a

Total Number of Pages: 80

Total Number of Ad Pages: 3

Publisher: Larry Flynt

Editor: Paul Verhelst

Editorial Concept: A magazine of shopping catalogues.

Finished Looks

Published by:

MacRon Publications Inc.

P.O. Box 22649

Beachwood OH 44122

Date: Summer/Fall 1994

Frequency: Quarterly

Cover Price: $3.95

Subscription Price: $14.00

Discount Subscription Price: n/a

Total Number of Pages: 100

Total Number of Ad Pages: 11

Publisher: Ronn Hale

Editor: Bernice Moore

Editorial Concept: A fashion and lifestyle magazine for the contemporary black woman.

Flair

Published by:

DRB Publications Inc.

P.O. Box 1053

Malibu CA 90265

Date: February 1994

Frequency: Bimonthly

Cover Price: $3.95

Subscription Price: n/a

Discount Subscription Price: n/a

Total Number of Pages: 80

Total Number of Ad Pages: 0

Publisher: Brian Ashley

Editor: Debi Fee

Editorial Concept: "Black hair Hollywood style."

Marie Claire

Published by:

Hearst Corporation & Comary Inc.

250 W. 55th St., 5th Floor

New York NY 10019

Date: September/October 1994

Frequency: Bimonthly

Cover Price: $2.95

Subscription Price: $14.97

Discount Subscription Price: $7.97

Total Number of Pages: 268

Total Number of Ad Pages: 128

Publisher: Hearst Corp. & Comary Inc.

Editor: Bonnie Fuller

Editorial Concept: Fashion and beauty trend information and advice.

Persuasive Hair

Published by:

Dave Publishing Company

P.O. Box 361319

Date: Fall 1994 *(first newsstand issue)*

Frequency: Quarterly

Cover Price: $2.95

Subscription Price: $9.95

Discount Subscription Price: n/a

Total Number of Pages: 24

Total Number of Ad Pages: 5

Publisher: Reginald N. Parker Jr.

Editor: Carol A. Parker

Editorial Concept: "Irresistible hairdos for African-Americans."

Rebelle

Published by:

Clerlin Inc.

c/o Rebelle

130 Prince St.

New York NY 10012

Date: Summer 1994

Frequency: 10/Year

Cover Price: $2.95

Subscription Price: $15.00

Discount Subscription Price: n/a

Total Number of Pages: 124

Total Number of Ad Pages: 28

Publisher: Clerlin Inc.

Editor: Randall Koral

Editorial Concept: "A reflection and a product of multiculturalism. It shows how this country's ethnic communities drive fashion and popular culture."

Vie

Published by:

Vie Publications

5443 E. La Palma Ave.

Anaheim CA 92807-2022

Date: July/August 1994

Frequency: Quarterly

Cover Price: $3.95

Subscription Price: $18.00/6 Issues

Discount Subscription Price: n/a

Total Number of Pages: 100

Total Number of Ad Pages: 36

Publisher: Vie Publications

Editor: Lorraine Eastman

Editorial Concept: Health, fitness, beauty.

Annual, Special or Frequency Unknown

Braids and Beauty

Published by:

Word Up! Video Productions Inc.

210 Route 4 East, Suite 401

Paramus NJ 07661

Date: Summer 1994

Frequency: Special

Cover Price: $3.50

Subscription Price: n/a

Discount Subscription Price: n/a

Total Number of Pages: 68

Total Number of Ad Pages: 6

Publisher: Word Up! Video Productions Inc.

Editor: Marcia A. Cole

Editorial Concept: "The best natural hair and skincare."

Country Star Hairstyles

Published by:

Harris Publications Inc.

1115 Broadway

New York NY 10010

Date: 1994

Frequency: Annually

Cover Price: $2.95

Subscription Price: n/a

Discount Subscription Price: n/a

Total Number of Pages: 92

Total Number of Ad Pages: 4

Publisher: Stanley R. Harris

Editor: Mary James

Editorial Concept: "Big hairstyle roundup! The 18 most popular country hairstyles and exactly how to style them!"

Extra!

Published by:

Michele Durant

P.O. Box 57194

Sherman Oaks CA 91413

Date: January 1994 *(first newsstand issue)*

Frequency: n/a

Cover Price: $2.50

Subscription Price: $30.00

Discount Subscription Price: n/a

Total Number of Pages: 32

Total Number of Ad Pages: 9

Publisher: Michele Durant

Editor: Michele Durant

Editorial Concept: "The publication for the voluptuous woman."

How To Style Braids

Published by:

Publications International Ltd.

Date: 1994

Frequency: Special

Cover Price: $2.95

Subscription Price: n/a

Discount Subscription Price: n/a

Total Number of Pages: 100

Total Number of Ad Pages: 0

Publisher: Publications International Ltd.

Editor: Carol Eastman

Editorial Concept: An illustrated step-by-step guide.

Makeover

Published by:

Time Inc.

Time and Life Building,

Rockefeller Center

New York NY 10020-1393

Date: Summer 1994

Frequency: Special

Cover Price: $1.99

Subscription Price: n/a

Discount Subscription Price: n/a

Total Number of Pages: 78

Total Number of Ad Pages: 12

Publisher: Time Inc.

Editor: Susan Toepfer

Editorial Concept: "Making the best of what you've got."

Soap Opera Hair

Published by:

Starline Publications Inc.

63 Grand Ave.

River Edge NJ 07661

Date: 1994

Frequency: Special

Cover Price: $2.95

Subscription Price: n/a

Discount Subscription Price: n/a

Total Number of Pages: 68

Total Number of Ad Pages: 0

Publisher: Scott Mitchell Figman

Editor: Anne M. Raso

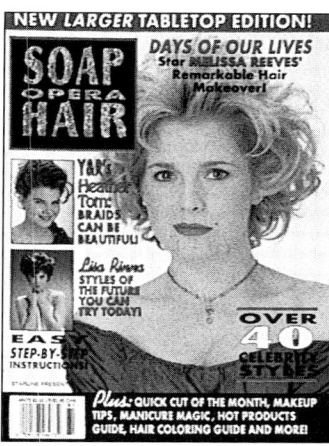

Editorial Concept: "How to achieve the hairdos of your favorite soap opera stars."

Step-By-Step Hairstyling

Published by:

GCR Publishing Group Inc.

1700 Broadway

New York NY 10019

Date: 1994

Frequency: Special

Cover Price: $3.75

Subscription Price: n/a

Discount Subscription Price: n/a

Total Number of Pages: 84

Total Number of Ad Pages: 12

Publisher: Charles Goodman

Editor: Shelly Dawson-Davies

Editorial Concept: "Sassy styling tips that really work."

Esteem

Published by:

CarWel Communications Inc.

5733 Windridge Drive

Cincinnati OH 45243

Date: Fall/Winter 1994

Frequency: Quarterly

Cover Price: $1.95

Subscription Price: $7.80

Discount Subscription Price: n/a

Total Number of Pages: n/a

Total Number of Ad Pages: n/a

Publisher: Carla Welborn

Editor: Carla Welborn

Editorial Concept: "To promote self-esteem among young sisters of all hues, sizes and backgrounds."

Flux

Published by:

Harris Publications Inc.

1115 Broadway

New York NY 10010

Date: 1994

Frequency: Quarterly

Cover Price: $3.95

Subscription Price: $9.97

Discount Subscription Price: n/a

Total Number of Pages: 100

Total Number of Ad Pages: 29

Publisher: Dennis S. Page

Editor: Jeff Kitts

Editorial Concept: Video games, music, comics."

KGB

Published by:

KGB Media Inc.

133 Bowery

New York NY 10002

Date: June/July 1994

Frequency: Monthly

Cover Price: $2.95

Subscription Price: $15.00

Discount Subscription Price: n/a

Total Number of Pages: 64

Total Number of Ad Pages: 10

Publisher: Lukas Barr, Sean Gullette

Editor: Lukas Barr, Sean Gullette

Editorial Concept: "Media, culture, ideas, and style for the twentysomething generation."

Link

Published by:

Creative Media Generations Inc.

188 Sherwood Place

Englewood NJ 07631

Date: 1994

Frequency: 6/Year

Cover Price: $2.95

Subscription Price: $15.00

Discount Subscription Price: n/a

Total Number of Pages: 40

Total Number of Ad Pages: 16

Publisher: Peter Kraft

Editor: Mark Charnock

Editorial Concept: "Provides insight, not just information, for college students."

Might

Published by:

Gigantic Publishing

544 Second St.

San Francisco CA 94107

Date: 1994

Frequency: Bimonthly

Cover Price: $3.50

Subscription Price: $20.00/6 issues

Discount Subscription Price: n/a

Total Number of Pages: 68

Total Number of Ad Pages: 9

Publisher: Gigantic Publishing

Editor: n/a

Editorial Concept: "For young people, but there are no beauty tips, no dating hints or articles about partying."

Mouth 2 Mouth

Published by:

Time Publishing Ventures Inc.

270 N. Canon Drive #2038

Beverly Hill CA 90210

Date: Spring 1994

Frequency: Bimonthly

Cover Price: $2.50

Subscription Price: $15.00

Discount Subscription Price: $12.00

Total Number of Pages: 138

Total Number of Ad Pages: 36

Publisher: Carol A. Smith

Editor: Angela Janklow Harrington

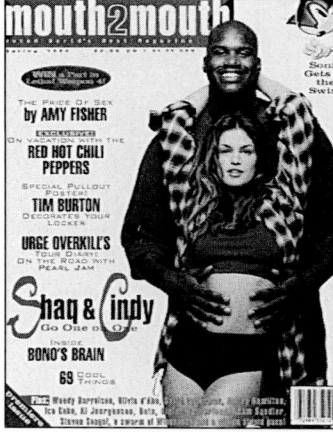

Editorial Concept: "A super-hip look at celebrities, fashion, and trends, targeted at teenagers of both sexes."

Spec

Published by:

24th Street Publishing Inc.

P.O. Box 4028

San Francisco CA 94140

Date: 1994

Frequency: Bimonthly

Cover Price: $4.00

Subscription Price: $19.00

Discount Subscription Price: n/a

Total Number of Pages: 52

Total Number of Ad Pages: 10

Publisher: Matthew Jaffe

Editor: Matthew Jaffe

Editorial Concept: A theme-oriented mix of fanzine and general interest magazine for Generation X.

Swing

Published by:

The Swing Corporation

342 Madison Ave.

New York NY 10017

Date: November 1994

Frequency: 10/Year

Cover Price: $2.00

Subscription Price: $16.00

Discount Subscription Price: n/a

Total Number of Pages: 108

Total Number of Ad Pages: 40

Publisher: David Lauren

Editor: David Lauren

Editorial Concept: "About men and women in their twenties who have ingeniously realized their aspirations in the face of hardships."

Annual, Special or Frequency Unknown

ESPN2 Dirt

Published by:

Lang Communications Inc.

230 Park Ave.

New York NY 10169

Date: 1994

Frequency: n/a

Cover Price: $2.95

Subscription Price: n/a

Discount Subscription Price: n/a

Total Number of Pages: 84

Total Number of Ad Pages: 25

Publisher: Lang Communications Inc.

Editor: Mark Lewman

Editorial Concept: An MTV-styled magazine of action sports, music, style, and culture.

Teen Special All About You

Published by:

Petersen Publishing Company

6420 Wilshire Blvd.

Los Angeles CA 90048-5515

Date: 1994

Frequency: Special

Cover Price: $2.95

Subscription Price: n/a

Discount Subscription Price: n/a

Total Number of Pages: 132

Total Number of Ad Pages: 27

Publisher: Jay W. Cole

Editor: Roxanne Camron

Editorial Concept: "Guys, quizzes, hot trends, celebs."

YM Love Special

Published by:

Gruner & Jahr USA Publishing

685 Third Ave.

New York NY 10017

Date: Summer/Fall 1994

Frequency: Special

Cover Price: $2.95

Subscription Price: n/a

Discount Subscription Price: n/a

Total Number of Pages: 108

Total Number of Ad Pages: 21

Publisher: Victoria Lasdon

Editor: Bonnie Fuller

Editorial Concept: "Your ultimate guide to sex, love, and dating."

YM Prom Special 1994

Published by:

Gruner & Jahr USA Publishing

685 Third Ave.

New York NY 10017

Date: 1994

Frequency: Special

Cover Price: $2.95

Subscription Price: n/a

Discount Subscription Price: n/a

Total Number of Pages: 124

Total Number of Ad Pages: 28

Publisher: Victoria Lasdon

Editor: Bonnie Fuller

Editorial Concept: Fashion, etiquette, and sex tips for girls as they prepare for the big prom.

20th Century Guitar

Published by:

Seventh String Press Inc.

135 Oser Ave.

Hauppauge NY 11788

Date: September/October 1993 *(first newsstand issue)*

Frequency: Bimonthly

Cover Price: $3.95

Subscription Price: $18.00

Discount Subscription Price: n/a

Total Number of Pages: 76

Total Number of Ad Pages: 38

Publisher: James Acunto

Editor: Lawrence Acunto

Editorial Concept: Stories about vintage and collectible guitars.

American Wind Surfer

Published by:

Grapho Inc.

Bayview Business Park

Gilford NH 03246

Date: 1993

Frequency: 5/Year

Cover Price: $5.00

Subscription Price: $20.00

Discount Subscription Price: n/a

Total Number of Pages: 92

Total Number of Ad Pages: 31

Publisher: John Chao

Editor: John Chao

Editorial Concept: "About interesting people and their windsurfing lifestyle [rather] than equipment and techniques."

And ...

Published by:

And Magazine

P.O. Box 590548

San Francisco CA 94159

Date: Winter 1993

Frequency: Quarterly

Cover Price: $3.00

Subscription Price: $12.00

Discount Subscription Price: n/a

Total Number of Pages: 24

Total Number of Ad Pages: 5

Publisher: Lisa Gluskin

Editor: Lisa Gluskin

Editorial Concept: San Francisco arts and culture.

Answers: The Magazine for Adult Children of Aging Parents

Published by:

S.R.K. Publishing Corporation

201 Tamal Vista Blvd.

Corte Madera CA 94925

Date: 1993 *(first newsstand issue)*

Frequency: Bimonthly

Cover Price: $3.50

Subscription Price: $20.00

Discount Subscription Price: $15.00

Total Number of Pages: 36

Total Number of Ad Pages: 10

Publisher: Susan R. Keller

Editor: Susan R. Keller

Editorial Concept: "Covers all aspects of looking after an elderly parent."

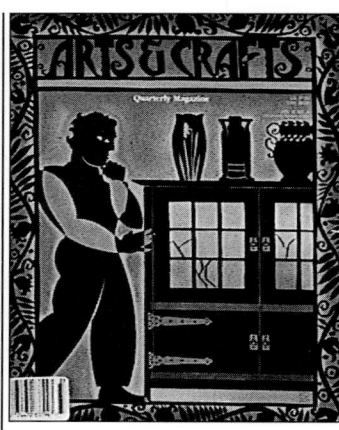

Arts & Crafts Quarterly

Published by:

Arts & Crafts Quarterly

9 S. Main St.

Lambertville NJ 08530

Date: 1993 *(first newsstand issue)*

Frequency: Quarterly

Cover Price: $7.00

Subscription Price: $25.00

Discount Subscription Price: n/a

Total Number of Pages: 52

Total Number of Ad Pages: 19

Publisher: Steven Becker

Editor: David Rago

Editorial Concept: Articles about the arts and crafts design movement.

Bible Resources

Published by:

Strang Communications

600 Rinehart Rd.

Lake Mary FL 32746

Date: Spring 1993

Frequency: Quarterly

Cover Price: n/a

Subscription Price: n/a

Discount Subscription Price: n/a

Total Number of Pages: 36

Total Number of Ad Pages: 12

Publisher: Timothy L. Gilmour

Editor: John Archer

Editorial Concept: "A guide to the best in Bible study."

Birmingham Healthscope 2000

Published by:

R & M Publications Inc.

P.O. Box 20562

Birmingham AL 35216

Date: Spring 1993

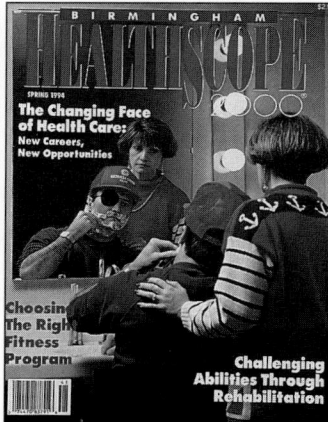

Frequency: Quarterly

Cover Price: $2.95

Subscription Price: $10.00

Discount Subscription Price: n/a

Total Number of Pages: 44

Total Number of Ad Pages: 18

Publisher: Joe and Billie Moan

Editor: Fran Rittenberry

Editorial Concept: "Interesting health care information."

Destiny

Published by:

Destiny Publications Inc.

809 Center St.

Lansing MI 48906

Date: n/a

Frequency: Bimonthly

Cover Price: $2.95

Subscription Price: $19.95

Discount Subscription Price: n/a

Total Number of Pages: 52

Total Number of Ad Pages: 12

Publisher: Destiny Publications Inc.

Editor: Emanuel McLittle

Editorial Concept: Articles about talk radio, politics, education, and medicine.

The Doors Collector's Magazine

Published by:

Three Dimensional Marketing Inc.

P.O. Box 1441

Orem UT 84059-1441

Date: Summer 1993

Frequency: Quarterly

Cover Price: $5.00

Subscription Price: $20.00

Discount Subscription Price: n/a

Total Number of Pages: 44

Total Number of Ad Pages: 6

Publisher: Three Dimensional Marketing Inc.

Editor: Kerry Humphreys

Editorial Concept: The unofficial magazine for Doors collectors and fans.

Handcraft Illustrated

Published by:

Natural Health Limited Partners

17 Station St., Box 509

Brookline MA 02147

Date: November/December 1993

Frequency: Bimonthly

Cover Price: $4.00

Subscription Price: $24.95

Discount Subscription Price: $19.95

Total Number of Pages: 36

Total Number of Ad Pages: 0

Publisher: Christopher Kimball

Editor: Carol Endler Sterbenz

Editorial Concept: "Crafts are reconceptualized and made user-friendly."

Harsh Mistress

Published by:

DNA Publications

P.O. Box 13

Greenfield MA 01302-0013

Date: n/a

Frequency: Quarterly

Cover Price: $4.00

Subscription Price: $14.00

Discount Subscription Price: n/a

Total Number of Pages: 88

Total Number of Ad Pages: 6

Publisher: Tim Ballou

Editor: Warren Lapine

Editorial Concept: "Science fiction adventures. Each issue features fiction and art from established talents."

Hermenaut

Published by:

Shapely Mind Press

3010 Hennepin Ave. S. #165

Minneapolis MN 55408

Date: Pre-1994

Frequency: Quarterly

Cover Price: $2.50

Subscription Price: $10.00/Year

Discount Subscription Price: n/a

Total Number of Pages: 52

Total Number of Ad Pages: 3

Publisher: Shapely Mind Press

Editor: Josh Glenn

Editorial Concept: "The digest of heady philosophy for teens."

Home & Studio Recording

Published by:

Music Maker Publications Inc.

7318 Topanga Canyon Blvd.

Canoga Park CA 91303

Date: December 1993 *(Spanish edition)*

Frequency: Bimonthly

Cover Price: $2.95

Subscription Price: $14.95

Discount Subscription Price: n/a

Total Number of Pages: 52

Total Number of Ad Pages: 10

Publisher: Music Maker Publications Inc.

Editor: Nicholas Batzdorf

Editorial Concept: Recording techniques and equipment.

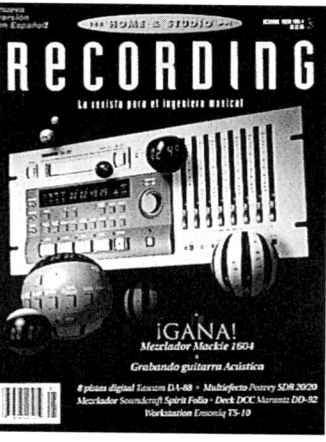

The Illustrated USA Digest

Published by:

The USA Digest

P.O. Box 227

Jackson KY 41339

Date: July 1993

Frequency: Bimonthly

Cover Price: $2.00

Subscription Price: $10.00

Discount Subscription Price: n/a

Total Number of Pages: 96

Total Number of Ad Pages: 1

Publisher: The USA Digest

Editor: Charles Hayes

Editorial Concept: "Featuring things old and new about America."

Informed Consent

Published by:

INRCH

6200 #C Tapia Drive

Malibu CA 90265

Date: November/December 1993

Frequency: Bimonthly

Cover Price: $3.75

Subscription Price: $14.00

Discount Subscription Price: n/a

Total Number of Pages: 60

Total Number of Ad Pages: 12

Publisher: INRCH

Editor: Cindy Duehring

Editorial Concept: "The magazine of health, prevention and environmental news."

International Quarterly

Published by:

International Quarterly Inc.

P.O. Box 10521

Tallahassee FL 32302-0521

Date: Summer 1993

Frequency: Quarterly

Cover Price: $8.00

Subscription Price: $19.00

Discount Subscription Price: n/a

Total Number of Pages: 180

Total Number of Ad Pages: 0

Publisher: International Quarterly

Editor: Van K. Brock

Editorial Concept: Essays, fiction, drama, poetry, and art reviews.

Inside Track

Published by:

Mallicote Printing Inc.

P.O. Box 4

Bristol TN 37620

Date: 1993

Frequency: Monthly

Cover Price: $4.50

Subscription Price: $36.00

Discount Subscription Price: n/a

Total Number of Pages: 58

Total Number of Ad Pages: 4

Publisher: Lional J. Mallicote

Editor: Lional J. Mallicote

Editorial Concept: "The magazine for Winston Cup and Busch Grand National Racing."

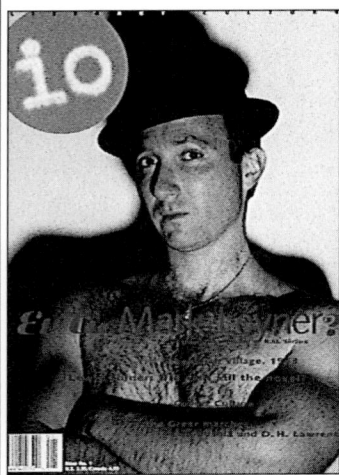

io

Published by:

Io Productions

P.O. Box 164254

Austin TX 78716

Date: 1993

Frequency: Quarterly

Cover Price: $3.95

Subscription Price: $12.95

Discount Subscription Price: n/a

Total Number of Pages: 60

Total Number of Ad Pages: 6

Publisher: Io Productions

Editor: Benjamin Cohen

Editorial Concept: Short fiction, essays, book reviews, and poetry by younger authors, as well as interviews.

Mobilia

Published by:

Hyatt Research Corporation

P.O. Box 575

Middlebury VT 05753

Date: July 1993

Frequency: Monthly

Cover Price: $4.50

Subscription Price: n/a

Discount Subscription Price: n/a

Total Number of Pages: 36

Total Number of Ad Pages: 21

Publisher: Eric H. Killorin

Editor: Eric H. Killorin

Editorial Concept: Collecting auto artifacts, from models to posters.

Nexus Six

Published by:

Parasite Productions

P.O. Box 1394

Hollywood CA 90078

Date: 1993

Frequency: Bimonthly

Cover Price: $2.00

Subscription Price: n/a

Discount Subscription Price: n/a

Total Number of Pages: 36

Total Number of Ad Pages: 7

Publisher: Parasite Productions

Editor: Steven Janas, Brian McNeils

Editorial Concept: Underground culture, with an emphasis on the macabre.

PC Kids

Published by:

Falsoft Inc.

P.O. Box 385

Prospect KY 40059

Date: Pre-1994

Frequency: Monthly

Cover Price: $1.95

Subscription Price: $19.95

Discount Subscription Price: n/a

Total Number of Pages: 36

Total Number of Ad Pages: 8

Publisher: Lawrence C. Falk

Editor: Lawrence C. Falk

Editorial Concept: A computer magazine for kids.

Perceptions

Published by:

Gypsy Spirit

11664 National Blvd. #314

Los Angeles CA 90064

Date: Winter 1993

Frequency: Quarterly

Cover Price: $3.95

Subscription Price: $15.00

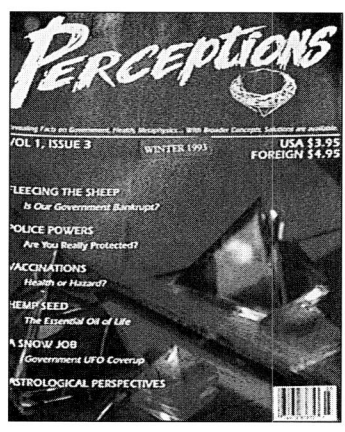

Discount Subscription Price: n/a

Total Number of Pages: 48

Total Number of Ad Pages: 12

Publisher: Gwenn H. Wycoff

Editor: Judi V. Brewer

Editorial Concept: Non-mainstream media information in the areas of government, health, and metaphysics.

Photo Emporium

Published by:

Photo Emporium

2720 Woodhaven Drive

Los Angeles CA 90068

Date: December 1993

Frequency: Monthly

Cover Price: $1.95

Subscription Price: $19.00

Discount Subscription Price: n/a

Total Number of Pages: 32

Total Number of Ad Pages: 16

Publisher: Karynn Wright-Hough

Editor: Joel Schiller

Editorial Concept: A buyer's and seller's guide to antiques, fine art, folk art, and collectibles.

Profit: Information Technology for Entrepreneurs

Published by:

International Business Machines Corporation

Old Orchard Rd.

Armonk NY 10504

Date: November/December 1993

Frequency: Bimonthly

Cover Price: $2.95

Subscription Price: $17.00

Discount Subscription Price: n/a

Total Number of Pages: 68

Total Number of Ad Pages: 20

Publisher: James A. Mitchell

Editor: Timothy Nolan

Editorial Concept: Personalities and cutting-edge ideas that embody the entrepreneurial spirit.

Rising Tide

Published by:

Republican National Committee

310 First St. S.E.

Washington DC 20003

Date: November-December 1993

Frequency: Bimonthly

Cover Price: $2.95

Subscription Price: $12.00

Discount Subscription Price: n/a

Total Number of Pages: 28

Total Number of Ad Pages: 2

Publisher: Haley Barbour

Editor: Lisa McCormack

Editorial Concept: "Sound proposals and new initiatives."

Rosebud

Published by:

Rosebud Inc.

208 E. Adams St.

Cambridge WI 53523

Date: Winter 1993/1994

Frequency: Semi-annually

Cover Price: $5.00

Subscription Price: $12.00/2 Years

Discount Subscription Price: n/a

Total Number of Pages: 120

Total Number of Ad Pages: 6

Publisher: John Lehman

Editor: Roderick Clark

Editorial Concept: "Stimulating reading and a creative outlet for blossoming writers."

Route 66 Magazine

Published by:

Two Guns Publishing Company

P.O. Box 2569

Bullhead City AZ 86430

Date: Winter 1993/1994

Frequency: Quarterly

Cover Price: $3.95

Subscription Price: $20.00

Discount Subscription Price: n/a

Total Number of Pages: 68

Total Number of Ad Pages: 14

Publisher: Howard Armstrong

Editor: Paul Taylor

Editorial Concept: The people, places, and history to be found on the Mother Road - Route 66.

Sidekicks

Published by:

The Southern Media Corporations

9625 W. Sample Rd.

Coral Springs FL 33065

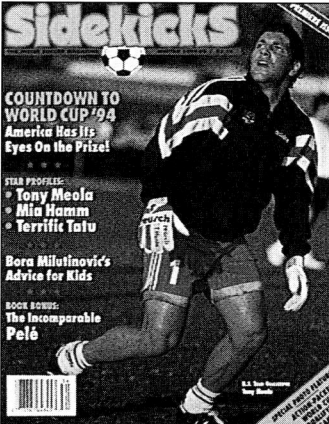

Date: Winter 1993/1994

Frequency: Bimonthly

Cover Price: $2.95

Subscription Price: $17.70

Discount Subscription Price: n/a

Total Number of Pages: 60

Total Number of Ad Pages: 17

Publisher: Frank R. Genouese, Robert B. Kahn

Editor: Stephen Hanks

Editorial Concept: To reflect the passion and excitement of the world's most popular sport.

Toon Magazine

Published by:

Black Bear Press

2828 Cochran St., Suite 152

Simi Valley CA 93065

Date: Fall 1993

Frequency: Quarterly

Cover Price: $7.95

Subscription Price: n/a

Discount Subscription Price: n/a

Total Number of Pages: 84

Total Number of Ad Pages: 5

Publisher: Black Bear Press

Editor: Michael Swanigan

Editorial Concept: An inside look at the animation industry and its most popular characters.

Wood Strokes

Published by:

EGW Publishing Company

1041 Shary Circle

Concord CA 94518

Date: November 1993

Frequency: Bimonthly

Cover Price: $3.95

Subscription Price: $23.70

Discount Subscription Price: $17.97

Total Number of Pages: 48

Total Number of Ad Pages: 3

Publisher: EGW Publishing Company

Editor: Margo M. Lemas

Editorial Concept: Easy paint designs for wood.

Women's Harpoon

Published by:

Women's Free Press

57 S. Triangle Rd.

South Somerville NJ 08876

Date: 1993

Frequency: Bimonthly

Cover Price: $3.95

Subscription Price: $20.00

Discount Subscription Price: n/a

Total Number of Pages: 32

Total Number of Ad Pages: 7

Publisher: Hally Abbott

Editor: Melanie J. Davis

Editorial Concept: "The humor magazine for women, by women."

Worship Today

Published by:

Strang Communications Company

600 Rinehart Rd.

Lake Mary FL 32746

Date: November/December 1993

Frequency: Bimonthly

Cover Price: Free

Subscription Price: n/a

Discount Subscription Price: n/a

Total Number of Pages: 36

Total Number of Ad Pages: 15

Publisher: Timothy L. Gilmour

Editor: Barbie Eslin

Editorial Concept: Christianity and worship in the modern world.

Annual, Special or Frequency Unknown

Beat Down

Published by:

Beat-Down Publications Inc.

P.O. Box 1266

New York NY 10274

Date: December 1993

Frequency: n/a

Cover Price: $2.00

Subscription Price: $15.95

Discount Subscription Price: n/a

Total Number of Pages: 32

Total Number of Ad Pages: 9

Publisher: Haji R. Akhigbade

Editor: Haji R. Akhigbade

Editorial Concept: A fanzine about hip-hop music.

CD Review's 1994 Buyer's Guide

Published by:

Connell Communications Inc.

86 Elm St.

Peterborough NH 03458

Date: Fall/Winter 1993

Frequency: Special

Cover Price: $4.95

Subscription Price: n/a

Discount Subscription Price: n/a

Total Number of Pages: 132

Total Number of Ad Pages: 22

Publisher: Connell Communications Inc.

Editor: Jimmy Guterman

Editorial Concept: "One thousand reviews of the best music of the year."

A Century On Wheels

Published by:

Rocco International Inc.

10225 Ulmerton Rd., Suite 12B

Largo FL 34641

Date: 1993

Frequency: Special

Cover Price: $4.95

Subscription Price: n/a

Discount Subscription Price: n/a

Total Number of Pages: 196

Total Number of Ad Pages: 74

Publisher: Terry Kear

Editor: Bob Yehling

Editorial Concept: A year-by-year history of the automobile's first century.

Christmas Cookies

Published by:

GCR Publishing Group Inc.

1700 Broadway

New York NY 10019

Date: 1993

Frequency: Special

Cover Price: $2.95

Subscription Price: n/a

Discount Subscription Price: n/a

Total Number of Pages: 84

Total Number of Ad Pages: 0

Publisher: Charles Goodman

Editor: Sallie Batson

Editorial Concept: "An exciting assortment of cookies guaranteed to tempt your tastebuds."

The Complete Brand Name Calorie Counter

Published by:

GCR Publishing Group Inc.

1700 Broadway

New York NY 10019

Date: 1993

Frequency: Annually

Cover Price: $2.95

Subscription Price: n/a

Discount Subscription Price: n/a

Total Number of Pages: 68

Total Number of Ad Pages: 0

Publisher: Charles Goodman

Editor: Sandra Kosherick

Editorial Concept: "Precise calorie counts of all your favorite foods."

Computer Telephony

Published by:

Computer Telephony

12 W. 21st Ave.

New York NY 10010

Date: Fall 1993

Frequency: n/a

Cover Price: n/a

Subscription Price: $38.00

Discount Subscription Price: n/a

Total Number of Pages: 132

Total Number of Ad Pages: 45

Publisher: Harry Newton, Gerry Frierson

Editor: Rick Luhmann

Editorial Concept: "The magazine for computer and telephone integration."

Grand Royal

Published by:

Grand Royal Magazine

P.O. Box 26689

Los Angeles CA 90026

Date: Fall/Winter 1993

Frequency: "Whenever we feel like it."

Cover Price: $2.95

Subscription Price: n/a

Discount Subscription Price: n/a

Total Number of Pages: 80

Total Number of Ad Pages: 20

Publisher: Grand Royal Magazine

Editor: Mike Diamon

Editorial Concept: A music and style magazine put out by and reflecting the tastes of the Beastie Boys.

Kidding Around Magazine

Published by:

Kidding Around Magazine

4521 PGA Blvd., Suite 289

Palm Beach FL 33418

Date: 1993

Frequency: n/a

Cover Price: Free

Subscription Price: $14.00

Discount Subscription Price: n/a

Total Number of Pages: 16

Total Number of Ad Pages: 7

Publisher: Mary Murray

Editor: n/a

Editorial Concept: An activities magazine for children in the Palm Beach, Florida area.

tell

Published by:

Hachette Filipacchi USA Inc.

1633 Broadway

New York NY 10019

Date: Fall 1993

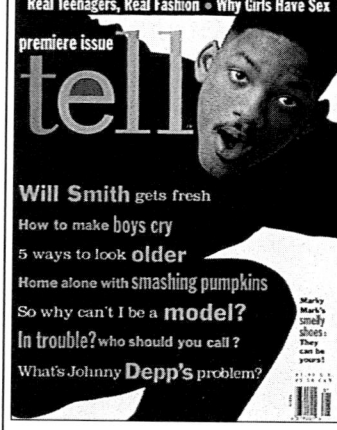

Frequency: n/a

Cover Price: $1.95

Subscription Price: n/a

Discount Subscription Price: n/a

Total Number of Pages: 124

Total Number of Ad Pages: 54

Publisher: Elinore Carmody

Editor: Roberta Anne Myers

Editorial Concept: Fashion, celebrity interviews, music, and articles for teenagers.

C

H

N

O

P

Q

T

U